HOLLYWOOD HEARTBREAK|NEW YORK DREAMS

LEO ♡

SO HAPPY TO BE WORKING
ON THIS FILM WITH YOU.

KEEP DOING EXACTLY WHAT
YOU'RE DOING. YOU ARE
INSPIRING MANY!
SEE YOU AT THE CAKE
SHOP!

Kody Christin

917-886-5515

HOLLYWOOD HEARTBREAK

NEW YORK DREAMS

KODY
CHRISTIANSEN

Official Book Website
www.HeartbreakDreams.com

Twitter/Instagram
KodyKitty

Facebook
www.Facebook.com/HollywoodHeartbreakNewYorkDreams

Email
info@heartbreakdreams.com

First Edition

978-1-941-96988-5

To Everyone.
Everyone who loved me before.
Everyone who loves me now, and in the future.
And Everyone who will learn to love
themselves again after reading this book.
The way I did, after living this story.

FOREWORD

Kody Christiansen came into my life exuding enough energy to light West Hollywood. He was brash, self-confident and more entertaining than a normal person should be. But normal is not in his vocabulary. He enters a party looking for the spotlight, even if he wasn't invited. For all those reasons, I hired him. My business deals with all the Hollywood titans, so having a sparkplug manager made sense.

Kody's life reads like a Hollywood script. The journey he's taken is filled with enough melodrama to make any soap opera pale in comparison. I've seen him at the top of his game, mesmerizing an audience with his talents. I've also seen him curled up at a doorstep, suffering through an alcoholic blackout.

Kody often refers to me as the father he never had. It's a title I wear with both love and concern. So many friends and acquaintances have told me over the years to give up on the boy. They say I'm just an enabler for his transgressions. But I've always seen the latent potential just percolating below his addictive personality.

The story that unfolds in these pages is a testament to both Kody's strengths and weaknesses. But ultimately it's a story of triumph over unbelievable adversity. I am the proud surrogate father to this prodigal son whose journey is still a work in progress.

Thomas Rosa
Cake and Art
West Hollywood, California

CONTENTS

PROLOGUE:
WELCOME TO MY WORLD

"Welcome to my world..." he says, teasing me with his raspy voice, as he opens the sliding metal door to his swanky loft apartment.

This is the way I had pictured us living our life together, in a place just like this. Even though it is dark in the room, I can already tell this is a step up from his previous house. All the hard work we had done together allowed him to spend more money on a new home and this place did not disappoint.

I can barely see as he guides me through the large open space of the entry way towards the bedroom, holding my hand so I won't trip. I love when he holds my hand. He is so open, so free with himself now and it makes our relationship so much better...so much sexier too.

He lights a candle next to his California king-sized bed covered in 300-thread count black Egyptian cotton sheets and points in the direction of the bathroom. We are both still hot and bothered from the event that evening and the sexual tension is palpable.

I lay him down on the bed and head toward the bathroom mirror, still within his view. This is not the first time we will have sex, but it is the first time I will strip 'her' off of me in front of him.

The black trench coat falls effortlessly to the floor, revealing a tied-up men's shirt, blue jean short shorts and boots. I had ended my show that night with the sexy 'country' song "These Boots are made for Walkin'" (the Jessica Simpson version of course). The shirt and shorts come off quite easily, exposing a front-clasp bra and cute underwear (appropriately hiding the goods). I turn around to look at him – my long blonde hair swinging in the air as my crystal blue eyes look longingly into his.

He smiles.

I smile too.

I turn back around toward the lighted rectangular vanity mirror while simultaneously kicking the bathroom door closed behind me. Not being one to break character, or shatter the one in someone's mind, I usually did close the door.

I take off my boots and I can hear his shoes hitting the floor outside. As I unclasp my bra, I can almost feel him unbuttoning his shirt revealing his gorgeous abs and chest. I peel away my underwear and wrap myself in a small towel as he takes off his tight black Armani boxer briefs and slightly covers up with the sheet. As I take off the wig, he tousles his shaggy blonde hair. As I wash the makeup off my face, he wipes a drop of sweat from his forehead.

Looking back into the mirror, there I am, Kaleb, the tight-bodied, dark-haired, light blue-eyed, 5'10", good looking, funny and charming boy he had met at that bar, a little over a year ago. I fix my hair a little and turn around and shut off the light.

I exit the bathroom door to see my Adonis, lying in his bed in his luxurious New York apartment surrounded by candle light. He must have been busy setting all of that up while I was changing. I love this new, whole heartedly open, romantic version of him I had been hoping would come out for a long time.

As I inch closer to him, my heart begins to race. I can almost sense his do the same. Our souls are connected like never before and that night is the hottest sex we ever had – maybe the hottest and most romantic I have ever had in my life. His moans and our multiple orgasms each seem to make me think that Liam is in agreement.

The next morning, the sun rises over the upper west side of Manhattan and I awake in 'the nook' (you know that special place under his arm where you feel so safe and loved).

He wakes around the same time and looks down into my eyes.

"Good morning, beautiful," he says.

"Good morning, handsome," I reply

He kisses me on the forehead. Then we share a passionate kiss on the lips. I could have stayed in this bed, in his arms, in this moment forever. Unfortunately, we both have extremely busy days ahead of us. We have to get out of bed now or we will both miss it all completely.

As we get out of bed and begin looking for our clothes, I put on a pair of his cute boxer briefs and make my way to the window.

"You know I'll probably see her today," he says.

The 'her' he was referring to is Anna Lynn, a fun, flirty blonde, who works for one of those celebrity gossip magazines and just happens to have a mutual friend who lives across the shaft way.

"It is okay if you say 'hi' to her. She was a friend of both of ours before all this," I say, opening the black satin window treatment to let some light in to his rock 'n' roll decorated abode.

"I know but it is weir.... OH MY GOD! Look at those two!" he exclaims.

There in Cheri's window are the two of them, dancing in their underwear, drinks in hand, like the three of us had done many a time in the past. They are still up from the night before and it seems like their partying ways have continued, even after our friendship had ended so dramatically.

"Those two are crazy!" I say, chuckling with a smile, turning back towards him to see his face fixated directly out the window at the fiesta across the way.

I get a little nervous seeing him gawk at the girls like that and hope he isn't having second thoughts about our now official relationship. "You're still going to be my date for the big charity event tonight, right?" I ask, sitting next to him, putting my hand on his tight, muscular thigh.

"Of course babe, I love you," he responds, still staring out the floor-to-ceiling window, fumbling to put on his sock.

"Well it's kind of hard to tell when I can't see it in your

eyes," I reply, still looking directly at his masculine and distractingly handsome face.

He shakes his head like he is coming out of a daydream – refocusing – and turns his head to look deep into my eyes, while dropping his sock and grasping my hand.

"Kaleb, I love you. I love you more than anyone I have ever loved in my life," he says.

His eyes speak the same words as his mouth does, but my mind begins to wander. Did he really love me like no one else he had ever loved or was it because I truly was like no one else he had ever loved? (I was definitely his first 'boyfriend,' if you will, and the first female illusionist he had ever been involved with.) He is finally all mine and I am finally his. I just hope it will last this time around. He gives me a passionate kiss, walks over to the window and forcefully pulls the satin panels closed.

He smiles at me and we continue to get ready. The rest of the morning becomes a blur, but I am so completely happy with the way my life has come together with him that I have to pinch myself to see if it is real.

When I woke up, I kept my eyes closed for a few minutes, trying to soak up the lovely feelings the dream had created. It felt so real and made me miss the life I had before. The vision made me feel emotions I hadn't felt in a long time... since the last time I was with him.

Laying in a twin-size bed, I finally opened my eyes to the sight of bare beige walls and the gated windows of the homeless shelter and wondered, how in the hell did I get here...

MY LIFE

IT WAS THE beginning of April 2002 when I moved to the big city, fresh off the plane with a young spirit and big dreams. I was 19 and had a bank full of money due to the unfortunate loss of my mother to cancer the year before.

My mother's death was not sudden, but it was a shock to us all. She had gone into the hospital in Dallas to receive a bone marrow transplant and we were blessed to find that someone in the state was a perfect match for her.

During her five-month stay in the hospital, I was at home alone, going to high school, leading my show choir, taking care of the house and managing the finances. Being the only child from a single-parent home, it was a lot of pressure to put on a 17 year-old. But I was an intelligent youth, and my mother trusted me completely. She was a nurse and knew many of the doctors, so in my mind she was always going to be coming home.

Unfortunately, fate would not have it that way. In the last month of her hospital stay, after multiple rounds of chemo, she had the bone marrow transplant and she was cured. Our prayers were answered, we thought, but due to a post-operative infection my mother ultimately lost her battle with leukemia. She ended up on life support and, as her only child, it was now my decision to pull the plug. It was the toughest decision of my life, coming just twenty days after my eighteenth birthday.

I grew up very fast. I was urged to sell the house where I had shared so many amazing memories with my mom, to give up the place I loved and move into my own apartment, all before my high school graduation. My friends were a wonderful support in place of my real family. My mother's brothers dishonored the promises they gave to her on her death bed and disowned me.

At that time, being a gay kid in Fort Worth, Texas was not easy, especially when I felt so alone. Thank God for my grandmother, who always loved me no matter what, and those true friends who I am still blessed to have in my life to this day.

College was my next step. I was accepted to Texas Christian University, where I started to open up to who I really was. I joined the college choral, took drama classes and even got immersed in a music fraternity, where I got my first taste of the female illusion world. I was the first and only 'drag queen' to appear on the school's quarterly magazine. Talk about scandal! The magazine told my life story up to that point and it led to some wonderful opportunities for me and for the school. I loved going to TCU. Especially when the choir was asked to perform at Carnegie Hall, a trip that would be the turning point in the grand path that was to be my life.

If I wasn't already in love with the city enough, (I was a huge Sex and the City fan - totally a Samantha!) performing on that world-renowned stage sealed the deal. New York City was made for me and I was made for it. I quit school immediately after receiving an offer to move to New York and host a weekly drag show at a popular gay nightclub.

My first apartment was in the heart of Greenwich Village. It was a cute one-bedroom in one of those pre-war buildings right off the Christopher Street strip. I remember going to the Stonewall Inn and being so excited when they asked me to become a backup female illusionist for one of their show's hosts! Stonewall was the most well-known gay bar in the United States and was the epicenter of the gay revolution. Getting into the bars was a little difficult at first, being someone under the legal drinking and club going age. I was excited to find out that the flower shop on the next block just happened to make fake IDs and I immediately got one of those!

My first official New York City gig was hosting

my own 'drag show' at Kurfew, the hot spot for club kids around my age. Hosting the show as my alter ego, Sarah Summers, I started to get a lot of attention from the local gay magazines and TV producers.

One evening I remember someone praising my show and telling me they were a producer for the Ricki Lake Show. Having had people say things like that before, I took it with a grain of salt. But low and behold, the next morning in my AOL mailbox (it was 2002 remember) was a letter from the Ricki Lake Show asking me to come perform. This would be my first television gig and it turned out to be one of those breakout moments in my career.

It was early in the morning and there I was getting into full Sarah aka Britney Spears and feeling more nervous than I ever had in my life. This wasn't an amateur show at the Village Station, this was national television!

My alter ego Sarah looked like Britney Spears, danced like her and had all the same mannerisms (I watched hours and hours of footage to make sure of that). My connection with Britney Spears came about the second I heard her songs and started dancing to them. The first time I dressed up at TCU, my friends saw the resemblance before I did and told me I should impersonate her for a living. It wasn't just the visual connections. Britney's songs seemed to parallel the events in my life, even from the beginning. "Stronger" was her biggest hit when I was going through the death of my mother and I even performed it as Kaleb at my last show choir event in high school. I was ready to show the world what I could do as Sarah Summers!

Outside the hotel, I waited for the limo to pick me up at 6 a.m. When we arrived at the set, it all seemed so big and scary with the bright lights and the commotion of all the production assistants getting everything ready. The head PA came up to greet me, "Hello Ms. Summers, you'll be in this room with a Madonna impersonator and your Britney vs. Britney battle will be filmed second."

Yes, Britney vs. Britney, a battle to see who was the top Britney Spears impersonator in the country. After a few minutes of getting to know 'Madonna,' it was time to film my first segment. We each sang a chorus of "Slave 4 U" and then had to compete in a silly game of 'find the snake in the can.'

If it hadn't been so nerve-racking with the audience, the judges and Ricki watching, I probably would have been laughing at myself popping those cans with the rubber snakes flying out.

The judges chose me as the winner of that round of competition and told me I would have to face the three winners of the Tina, Whitney and Madonna battles in a final round.

At 19, and dressed like "Slave 4 U" Britney Spears, this was one of the most dramatic moments of my life.

Backstage before we went on, 'Madonna' and I were talking about the VMA kiss the real superstars had shared and how funny it would be if we kissed during the song.

We got in our places on stage and Cher's "If I Could Turn Back Time" came on. Tina's verse was first then me. I tripped up on the words and sang, "I don't know the words but I'm gonna win girls!" Manifesting much? Madonna, then Whitney sang their verses and we all joined together for the chorus right before the drag version of Madonna and Sarah Summers' kiss on national television.

Talk about crowd stopping. Ricki Lake tried to catch her breath as the music stopped and said, "that moment put me in talk show Heaven!"

After deliberating the judges had decided on a winner.

I couldn't breathe.

Cameras rolling, lights glaring, audience silent – the head judge then spoke: "Tina moves more like Tina Turner. Madonna looks more like Madonna." My heart stopped. "But Britney...she's got the whole Britney vibe. Britney you're the winner!"

Exhale. Tear up. Smile.

A gorgeous, shirtless male model walked on stage with a crown and red roses. After strutting down the runway and waving to the crowd, Ricki joined us on stage for her closing speech.

What a day.

"Making Britney Spears proud today. That kiss sent me over the edge!" Ricki said.

The cameras stopped rolling. The crowd filed out. The pride and excitement stayed with me for weeks, hell, years! I still show off that clip. In fact, it was one of the first videos I showed to Liam all those years later when we finally met.

New York life was all about Sarah Summers. Nightly shows, magazine photo-shoots, guest written articles for different publications and the Britney Spears body-double gig I had for the few months she had a restaurant open on Park Ave. The day we met, our photo went global and the headlines read: "Britney Befriends Drag Impersonator!"

It was true. There were nights when, after an event where I would distract the paparazzi for her, Britney and I would meet at this secret little restaurant on Lexington for food and a nightcap. One night after her driver had taken her home, he had to come back to pick up Britney's father. I'll never forget him saying, "Hey – how did you get back here so fast? I just dropped you off!" Her father, Jamie, and I laughed and I said, "No, no... I'm the other one." We all cracked up good at that one!

After her restaurant closed, I moved back to Texas for a couple of years. During that time, I made a bunch of really good friends who I could be seen dancing and drinking the night away with at The Black Dog bar in downtown Fort Worth. I even experienced one of the 'Great Loves' of my life. I met a guy named Shane and fell in love with the way he loved me. It was by far the most adult relationship I had up to this point in my life, but it ended because I wasn't ready to settle and I still had big dreams for stardom.

It was also during this time that I began to drink almost daily and started to explore the world of drugs. Shane got me into smoking pot for a while, which was not too detrimental to my life, and my other group of friends introduced me to cocaine, ecstasy and shrooms. The nightlife had not taken over my real life though and when the opportunities arose to get out and perform, I took them!

I continued to pursue my dreams when I was asked to be a guest on the Tyra Banks Show and when I flew to LA to film some scenes with Sandra Bullock for 'Miss Congeniality 2.' During that trip, I met and fell in love with a gay porn actor who convinced me I had to move to Los Angeles. I still had about $20,000 in my bank account from the money my mother had left me, so I was able to pick up and move with ease. Unfortunately, the relationship with the porn star only lasted about as long as one of his videos.

As amazing as these adventures were, I started to get a little burnt out on the whole female illusion thing. I started to feel like I was living Sarah Summers' life and not Kaleb's. My dream since I was a child was to act and sing. I wanted to get notoriety for being me, not Sarah. It was like I was Superman (or Supergirl, really) when I was Sarah. I got so much attention and did so many good things, but felt like I wasn't living the 'human' version of me anymore. I wanted to be appreciated for my talents as Clark Kent... Kaleb... and show the world I was more than just an alien in a fancy costume.

I started looking in new career directions, but still did the occasional Sarah gig when asked, as not to be completely forgotten. My next professional role was in Hollywood, my new home, working for a pretty famous cake shop.

Hollywood Cakes was a business started in 1976 by a professional artist named Glenn, who saw the uniqueness in the idea he had. Why not make cake into art? It could be molded, shaped, spackled with icing and painted. The best part about these works of art was the fact that you could eat them. He was a pioneer in the cake art world and he had the celebrity client list to prove it!

Glenn had a business partner named Tim who took over the company after Glenn got ill and passed away. He had been running this shop on his own for a while but had decided to try out the cupcake business while the craze was at its peak in 2006. That's where I came in!

I had seen a 'Now Hiring' sign in the window and went in with a resume and declared that I would be the manager. Tim, the owner, liked my self-assured attitude and I was hired on the spot. The bakery itself was more like an art studio the way the kitchen was set up. There were paint pallets, brushes of every size, every shade of food coloring created and a few pictures of celebrities with the cakes they had ordered placed in various parts of the shop. It was quaint, but I knew I could make it shine!

I went in as the manager, but as the years progressed I took it on as my own, creating a family bond with my coworkers. I did some amazing things, like coming up with creative ways to keep the doors open through the 2008 recession and delivering the wedding cake to the steps of the Beverly Hills courthouse for the first gay couple to legally marry in California, which got world press! Our little West Hollywood bakery was featured on NPR, NBC Nightly News, all the local channels and my photo was in a Russian newspaper and even the China Post!

My experiences at the cake shop made me feel as if I was part of the Hollywood scene because I actually was. I delivered cakes to the homes of big-time celebrities and to the sets of television shows and movies just about every week. I had some amazing Hollywood-style experiences, putting me right into the middle of the world I had always dreamed of being in.

I was asked to deliver and cut the birthday cake for an Oscar winner at the Playboy Mansion one evening. At the party, I got to share cupcakes with Hef and the girls, shared a dance with Joey from New Kids on The Block, took shots with Amanda Seyfried and served Courtney Love her first piece of cake after she sang 'Happy Birthday' to the Oscar-winning writer Diablo Cody.

I hung out with Tommy Lee in the beginning too, when he had a bar on Hollywood Blvd. with Dave Navarro. I danced in front of him and some girls from 'The Hills' before he invited me over to his table to drink vodka from the bottle and join the group. We exchanged phone numbers and would text each other often until I lost contact with him.

I was asked to donate and decorate cupcakes with Jessica Biel at the Children's Hospital Los Angeles one Christmas, which was one of the most touching moments of my life. Being there with her, and being able to give those kids a moment of happiness in a pretty bleak time, was beyond amazing. I remember her taking me to the side and telling me, "Stay strong for the kids and when you get into the car to drive away this afternoon, then let it out." She was absolutely right! I stayed strong while we helped the kids design their cupcakes, but the second I closed the door to my vehicle, I lost it. The tears flowed for a good twenty minutes and I was grateful for the experience.

The cake shop made cupcakes flaked with gold for the big Oscar parties in West Hollywood, which I got invited to as well. I rubbed elbows with many stars and even got to hand feed my 80's idol Tiffany a special cupcake. How amazing was that?!

I loved all these moments because I was definitely a ham when it came to getting attention, but I was also very smart which made me perfect to run a creative business like Hollywood Cakes. But I wasn't happy just doing one thing. While working at the shop, I felt like I was in the celebrity scene, but also realized I was not actually a part of it. I had come to LA to be a star, not serve the stars. So, when I wasn't at the cake shop, I partied pretty hard with my friends, tried to do a little acting on the side, was featured in multiple segments on the local news because of things I did at the shop and filmed a reality show pilot as well as wrote a blog.

I was daring, talented, courageous, determined, kind, generous, loving, intelligent and a little crazy. My creative juices were always flowing and, by the time this story starts, I was almost to my breaking point, trying to figure out what I really wanted and who I really wanted to be in this world.

This whole story really began the year that I met him. The year that changed my life.

MORE THAN
JUST FRIENDS

IT STARTED out a typical day. The birds were singing, the local gay queens were doing the walk of shame from the night before and the sun was shining over West Hollywood. After years of living in a cramped little studio on the other side of the city, I had finally found my perfect LA one bedroom – right between Sunset and Santa Monica Boulevards and steps away from my job at Hollywood Cakes.

At the cake shop this day, somehow, between answering phones, helping customers and decorating cupcakes, I had finally finished a post for my popular Facebook blog I had been working on all week. It was something to do with finding a lover using your inner magnet. Mostly fluff, I guess, but something I had always believed in but never truly experienced.

Feeling accomplished, I headed over to my favorite local pub for a celebratory cocktail. Whiskey and Coke was my go to feel good drink – usually Jameson or Maker's Mark.

As I entered the back bar at The State Room, I was happy to see a crowd of the local faces smiling at me. Behind the bar was Natalie, the tall, thin, dirty blonde, beautiful bartender buddy of mine who I frequently dished with about boys and drama. In front of Natalie was Jake, the long dark-haired, buff, handsome muscle guy with a big heart and some intense anger issues; and Dennis, my tall, plump, goofy but sweet African American friend who always had a good joke for me. I sat between the two guys and ordered my drink from Natalie.

"What's new, sexy bitch?" she said, handing me my Whiskey Coke.

"You know cakes, boys, singing, boys, and..." I said.

"BOYS?!?!" she interjected.

"Ha-ha no, no – I'm actually working with two guys who are helping me to get back into singing live," I responded with a playful little attitude.

"YOU? And TWO BOYS?! Sounds like your perfect situation!" she quipped.

"You know it, bitch!" I barked back at her. "We're going to be looking for a band for me and I'll be doing karaoke at the upstairs bar tomorrow."

"Well if I'm not working we will all be there – right fuckers?" she exclaimed, looking at Jake and Dennis.

"Hell yea!!" said Jake.

"Wouldn't miss it!" Dennis responded.

"Good, I'm trying out some new music and I know you will all give me your honest feedback," I said, sipping my drink, feeling kinda nervous just thinking about it.

The Dodgers game was on and between pitches and pitchers of Bud a few new patrons had walked in, including a table of two cute girls by the window which Natalie let me serve. (It was kind of fun for me – like a mini acting gig.) A few new faces also appeared: a pair of older gentlemen with their Guinness, a young couple probably on their second date, her with a Cosmo and him with a Manhattan, and at the other end of the bar was a guy I had never seen before. What was this dirty blonde-haired, great looking, tall, well-built guy doing sitting all alone with what looked like a full shot of fireball in front of him? I liked his style from first sight as he was wearing tight black pants and a black rock 'n' roll band shirt. I had to find out more about him!

A big fan of fireball myself, I walked over and sat in the empty seat next to him.

"Hey Natalie! Fireball for me please!" I yelled out like I owned the place.

"No problem, lady! Comin' up!" she yelled back from the other end of the bar.

"You like fireball too, huh?" the gorgeous man next to me asked.

"My favorite shot! It's like swallowing a whole pack of..."

"BIG RED!" he said.

"Yes, Big Red gum. How did you know?" I answered.

"It was my favorite as a kid," he replied, flashing his sparkling white teeth.

"Mine too! That's all my mother would buy!" I said with a smirk.

I mentally froze the world surrounding me for a minute. Did this ridiculously sexy man just finish my sentence and have something in common with me? If this was how the first five minutes went, this could be something really special.

Coming out of my semi-dream state, I looked over at him raising his shot glass.

"I'm Liam and you are?" he asked, looking into my eyes with his dark emerald green orbs of heaven.

"K..Kaleb..I'm Kaleb. Nice to meet – uh drink with you," I stammered.

We clunk shot glasses together and inhaled the cinnamon whiskey candy shots.

Minutes turned into hours and shots turned into drinks. I don't really remember what we talked about that first time, I just remember a feeling. A feeling I had never felt before: total and utter wholeness. I wasn't for a moment nervous or worried about what he thought because – I KNEW. He accepted me, every part, and every word, everything I was. There was no need to explain.

Maybe that article wasn't all fluff – maybe putting

it into words made me believe it even more.

Liam and I met the next day around the same time for more drinks, more conversation and more closeness. Two weeks later I had this great looking, funny, charming straight guy friend who wanted to be around me as much as I wanted to be around him. I kept the friendship a secret from most of my friends in the beginning, I liked having something that was just mine, something special.

It wasn't until that second week in our blossoming bromance that something changed.

We were sitting at the bar in the late afternoon, like we always did, his arm over my shoulder, laughing about something on the television screen above us. Liam excused himself to go to the bathroom. A minute later a patron who had been sitting behind us came up to me and said, "You know who your best friend is don't you?"

"Yea, his name is Liam – what about him?" I responded with a 'what the fuck' tone.

"That's Liam Sparks – the singer! All those hit songs in the late 90's early 2000's - he's so cool! Do you think I can get his autograph?" the guy said, almost salivating as the words spewed out of his mouth.

Who the hell was Liam Sparks? It sounded familiar... sort of. I opened up my laptop and YouTubed his name. There on my screen and in my headphones were some of the top songs of the late 90's. The songs of my generation. I instantly recognized the music, but I wasn't a huge fan of the band itself, so maybe that's why I never connected those dots. Once I knew the truth, I got a little upset. Why would he hide this from me?

Ten minutes later when he came out of the bathroom, suspiciously wiping his nose, I decided to call him on it. He sat down next to me like nothing happened, like a grand piano of knowledge hadn't just fallen on my animated head.

"Liam Sparks is it?" I said, like I was introducing myself to a stranger. That's how I felt. How could he keep something like this from me?

"Well yes. That's what the label thought sounded more profitable. How did you find out? You didn't know?" he said, semi-defensive.

"No, I didn't know! If I had known my best friend was a singer, a Grammy winner, we could have been singing together, making music. Why didn't you tell me?" I asked, feeling hurt and confused.

"Because you liked me for me," he said, looking deep into my eyes. "You were the first person in years to know and really care about Liam – not Liam Sparks."

At that moment, I realized how much our friendship really meant to both of us. We really were best friends – better than best friends. There was love starting to develop there.

After he exposed his other side, I showed him mine too. He was quite impressed with all my accolades as Sarah, and with both our true identities revealed, our connection only grew stronger. I really started to like Liam and hoped maybe one day soon we could be more than just friends.

THE BROMANCE

I'VE HAD my share of best friends over the years. Eva was my bestie in kindergarten who I used to play house with and, oddly enough, I was always the wife and she was always the husband. Fast-forward 18 years and I'm the out and proud female illusionist and she's an out and proud lesbian. Go figure!

Then in high school there was Christy. We both loved being in the choir, worked at the same coffee shop, went to the prom together and shared that awkward best friend kiss. We even ended up going to the same college in Texas. She played a big part in helping me deal with the struggle of my mother's death during that time.

But Liam, he was different.

He was not a girl or gay, like all my previous lifetime best friends. He was a legit man's man who possessed a great look, magnetic charm, quick wit, tremendous talent and a love for most everything I loved. This was also the first instance where I spent that much time with a gorgeous man and wasn't playing any naked games. In fact, the closest we ever got to sex in those first few months was cuddling at the bar and occasionally looking at each other's junk in the bathroom while at the urinals.

We were kinda like an old married couple, always together, obnoxious PDA and no sex at home.

Our relationship really began to blossom after opening up to each other about our many talents. I found out that Liam had been out of the music scene for a little while due to a nasty divorce and a less than stellar release of his latest album. He shared with me experiences of world-wide fame: top of the chart hit songs, screaming fans, music videos, world tours and many music awards.

It was almost hard to fathom that my bar buddy from those first two weeks had really done all these amazing things.

But when we were alone and he sang for me... when we sang together... it was beautiful. It's totally cliché, but in our case totally literal that we really did "make beautiful music together."

One day after watching Liam go to the bathroom for like the third time in an hour period, I decided to follow him. Not a complete stranger to drugs myself, having done a few here and there in the past, I figured that's what he was up to.

I walked into the unlocked bathroom to see him standing, back towards the mirror, looking at me like he had been expecting me to follow.

"I knew you'd be coming Kaleb," he said with a smirk.

"Oh, did you now?" I responded with one eyebrow raised.

"We've been hanging out for a few weeks – you're my best buddy – you had to know what I was doing," Liam said, knowing he was right.

"Well, stud, you are a rock star so I had my suspicions. You gonna share?" I said, smiling at him, pretending to be a badass.

"Of course, baby! What's mine is yours!" he replied in his sexy, cocky attitude.

I walked up in front of him, our bodies were so close that our jean-covered private parts were rubbing together. We were so close we could have kissed. He put his muscular arm around my neck, slowly revealing a key in his right hand that was now stopped in front of my lips. He lifted his left hand, grazing my arms as it rose, and showed me a small bag filled with snowy white powder.

He looked into my sparkling blue eyes then looked at the tiny pouch and dug a scoop from it. He put the bag in his pocket and moved his arm holding the key from around my neck to the area right below my nose. Touching my nose with his left index finger to stop the air in one nostril, he said, "close one side like this then sniff with the other."

I looked deep into his piercing emerald eyes and,

at that moment, felt safe enough to share this experience with him. He was the man in my life and I knew he would never let anything bad happen to me. I knew Liam would never do anything to hurt me.

So there, in the bathroom of the bar, standing package to package with a man who adored me as much as I did him, I sniffed.

The drug started rushing through my head and it felt amazing. Maybe it was the proximity of our bodies or the fact that we were so close emotionally, but it felt like we were having sex just standing there together.

Then a phrase I wasn't quite ready for spewed from my sexy friend's mouth, "Do you wanna suck my dick?"

HOLY SHIT! Did I? Of course I did. The naughty person inside of me wanted to rip off his jeans right then, fall to my knees and give him the best fucking blow job of his life!

I don't know if the coke or the booze or both had started to wear off, or maybe I felt like it wasn't the right time, but at that moment I stepped back and just laughed.

"Oh my God, Liam you are so funny! Come on, quit playing around, let's go!" I said, trying to hide my desperate desire to appease my big-dicked rock star best friend.

I headed for the bathroom door and grasped the handle. His hand came from around the back of my body and landed on top of mine, stopping me from turning the knob.

"Kaleb, I'm serious," he said, his warm breath tickling the back of my neck and ears.

I turned the handle and without looking back at him I said, "I'm serious too Liam, let's go."

I walked out first to try and avoid suspicion from the other bar patrons and to hide the tear that was welling up in my right eye.

Something in my gut told me that if I took that next step now – gave into our sexual cravings – that there was a chance that somewhere down the line, if not immediately after performing that act of pleasure, that our friendship would be compromised.

That was not a risk I was willing to take. I was not ready to lose my best friend over what I knew would be an amazing and mind-blowing blow job.

This little cat-and-mouse, complicated, sexy, comfortable, music-making emotional rollercoaster of a friendship continued this way all through the summer and it started feeling more like a romance than just a simple bromance.

THE PATH TO FALL

FOR THOSE few months after we met, it was just the two of us, the two amigos, "Husband and Wife," as the staff and patrons of The Twisted Rainbow bar, that we also frequented, had titled us. He even started to invite me over to his mansion, an invitation he rarely gave to anyone. The first night I went to his place I was nervous, extremely nervous.

We had been all over each other at the bar and in the bathroom, but there were always people around us and we were never really alone. Even when we got to the bar at noon when it opened, the staff was always there keeping close watch. We loved to be together and we loved to drink, so it felt like the most natural place for us to share and cultivate our growing relationship.

For months I had successfully evaded falling for his lusty, drug-fueled advances at the bar, but would I be able to control myself if we were to be alone at his house, in his room, away from the prying eyes of fellow patrons and the watering hole bathroom walls that seemed to talk?

It was time to put it to the test, but I was going to need backup so I asked my friend Lacy to drive with me to his house. Lacy and I had known each other for years, she was one of the only people I told about our relationship outside of the bar, and we were more than friends, we were like brother and sister.

We had met years ago working at a funky fashion boutique on Melrose for a spunky drag queen named Cosmo. We instantly connected. In our heyday we were going to the hottest clubs and getting photographed by the paparazzi. She was an actor and a performer like me and we looked strikingly similar. Everyone who saw us together asked us if we were siblings - EVERYONE! We finally got tired of telling the story of how we met and eventually just started saying yes. She was on an extended vacation in Los Angeles and she was the perfect person to be my safety net on this shaky rope I was about to walk.

As we circled around his Hollywood Hills neighborhood, trying to figure out which house was his, there were crazy and sexy thoughts circling in my head. Would tonight be the night? How would I react? Would it be romantic? Would it be special? Would it be rough? Would it be the end of our relationship or the next step into something even better? The thoughts kept bouncing around my mind and it wasn't until the car stopped that I realized we were actually there... that this was it. Time to find out!

We got out of the car and headed to his front door. As we walked, I took in my surroundings and saw that the house was really as beautiful as I had imagined it. The path to the front door was a set of stairs covered in gorgeous vines and greenery leading over the garage where his sexy black special-edition '87 Corvette was resting. Another thing I was desperately interested in taking for a ride.

We got to the door and I could hear drums being played in a masterful melodic way. I was intrigued. Lacy was excited to finally meet the rock star I had been talking about for months. I'm not sure if she even believed the stories I was telling her via phone and text, but she was going to find out the truth now. She knocked and we waited until the beating of the drums finally came to a halt. He opened the door and we went inside. The main living area was huge, with vaulted ceilings, but it was hard to see much from the entry way.

When we were completely in the main living area we were kinda shocked. This was definitely not what we expected. Blankets covered the couch and furniture was pushed up against the back door like he was trying to keep someone or something out. It was pretty dark in there, too. It all just seemed a little off.

He opened up one of the shades to let in some

light and, even though his house was kind of disheveled, he still looked like the man I loved. I gathered that he must have been up all night by the darkness visible under his usually glowing emerald eyes.

I introduced Liam to Lacy and he proceeded to give us the tour of his house. Swimming pool outside that needed a good cleaning, but the yard was pretty well kept. The kitchen was made for a chef but was littered with take-out boxes. The two guest rooms were mostly empty, except for remnants of what could have been a roommate at one point. We then climbed the stairs to his bedroom, which I was relieved to see was the most organized room in the house. His trophies from a once thriving career lined the shelves and his giant bed looked rather inviting. The best part of the house was his bathroom...it was immaculate. He had the biggest jet stream tub I had ever seen and his shower, which could fit at least four people, had like 12 different water spouts.

My mind automatically went to the amazing moments of pleasure we could share in that room. The bathroom was where we seemed to get closer at the bar...imagine how close we could get alone in this one!

Walking through his house, I started to do that thing that we 'girls' do... you know, visualizing myself living there and fixing the place up. Being the 'lady' of the house, cooking dinner, doing laundry, hosting fancy parties, relaxing in a bubble bath with a glass of champagne as my lover boy sings a song he wrote for me on guitar. Making it the best place for my man and me to live our married lives together, and, one day, have two perfect.... oh my god! I had to stop. We hadn't even gone all the way yet.

Lacy said something to me that brought me back down from the clouds of fantasy I had drifted away on. We went back into the living room and had some drinks and talked for a little while. Liam and I sat close together on the couch as he talked about his career and how we met. Lacy listened with attentive ears.

About an hour later, Lacy got a call reminding her she had a meeting with an agent she had to get to and that she had to leave.

Okay.

So we were finally going to be alone.

This was it.

As Lacy left, she told me Liam was nice but she felt like something was off about him. I brushed the comment aside because to me he always seemed a little off and that was just how I liked him to be... I am kinda an off character myself.

She left and, as the door closed behind her, I mixed us another drink. He pulled out his guitar and said he had a new song he wanted to share with me. He said it was like a sequel of sorts to his biggest hit song and he knew it was going to be an even bigger smash single. For months I had been trying to inspire him, to get him back to writing music and maybe, just maybe, it had started to work. He began to sing his new song and, as he went along, there was a feeling inside I had yet to feel in our relationship.

Pride.

I was so impressed with the song, with the lyrics and with his musical ability to find the hook that drew you in! It was a sexy pop rock song that was basically the story of his life... "I keep fucking up" being one of the repeated lyrics in the chorus. I could tell he really put his heart into this song and it paid off!

I vowed right then and there to help him in any way I could to get this song out to the public and get him back to doing what he loved. Knowing that I would be there, to share the journey with him this time, was like a dream come true.

Then he said, "Kaleb, I want to sing another song for you."

"I could listen to you all night." The words escaped my mouth sweetly before I could even think.

"Good. Let's see how far we get," he said as he started to strum his guitar. What did that even mean?

Then a familiar melody began to fill the room as he sang, "She packed my bags last night, pre-flight. Zero hour, nine a.m. And I'm gonna be high as a kite by then..."

His voice was glorious and it was a private

concert just for me. At that moment, I wasn't thinking about sex, I was no longer nervous ... I was happy. I was being serenaded by the man I had fallen in love with. I didn't need anything else but that moment. He sang, we sang for the rest of the night until the sun rose over the hills. It was magic. We didn't have sex that night or any night after that. It would be a little while before I got up the nerve to go for it once again.

I went back to his house a few times as the season began to change. And it wasn't until fall that things started to change in our relationship. He was still talking to some of the girls he had been involved with in the past and I was making new friends too.

I had a couple of close girlfriends I would hang out with when Liam and I weren't glued at the hip. There was Cheri, the tall, dark haired, smart, sexy, funny British girl who had become my best girlfriend. Cheri and I met through a mutual friend from the bar and we instantly clicked. There was Jackie, a dark chocolate Goddess, who was an uber talented singer and shared the same birthday as me! It was also during this time that I became very close friends with a new girl who had appeared at the bar, Anna Lynn.

If the name of the season that was upon us was any sort of prophetic sign from above, then we all were definitely on the path to fall.

ALL ON THE TABLE

FALL AND FOOTBALL season were upon the Sunset Strip and, even though I had never really been a big sports fan, I did appreciate how amazing the men looked in those tight uniforms! Liam was a manly man and we spent most of our time together at a straight bar where sports were shown constantly on every screen. Sports became something that really grew on me. It was a blast cheering for a team, engaging in bar rivalries and mostly celebrating a touchdown with the man I had fallen in love with.

The days the big games took over the bar were some of the best days in our relationship. We were spending most of our free time together, in fact he even asked me to move into his Hollywood Hills mansion at one point during the season. Even with that offer and the fact that we were still spending almost every day together, I started to feel our connection weaken.

Maybe it was the fact that I still hadn't given it up to him, despite all the times he asked, or that I had been hanging with Cheri and Anna Lynn more frequently. Maybe it was the increased amount of drug use, I'm not quite sure, but our once rock-solid relationship had started to erode.

It was a Tuesday night in West Hollywood and Cheri and I had decided to go out to our favorite crawfish restaurant, Hot n' Juicy. Cheri was in between jobs and had recently gotten back from a trip home to England to see her family. Cheri, like a few of the other girls from the bar, had known Liam prior to knowing me, and when I hung out with him she rarely came around. I didn't quite know why but I would soon find out this particular evening.

As best friends we usually tried to get one night alone to dish about boys, work and every other 'girl talk' type of discussion. We loved this crab place not only for the food but the fact that we were treated like VIPs, especially by the handsome, average height, dark brown-haired, fantastically in-shape waiter, Tad. He always had a big welcoming smile and friendly greeting for us upon arrival.

As we walked in, the uber good-looking Tad seated us at our regular table, laid down the menus and I swear to God he winked at me! He walked away to give us a minute to decide on our order even though we really didn't need it because we usually ordered the same thing every time. My eyes focused on his muscular back side as he walked toward the next table. "God, he is so fucking cute!" I blurted out.

"He is quite delicious!" replied Cheri in her lovely British accent.

"I wonder if he's single?" I pondered out loud.

"I wonder if he's even gay, Kaleb?" questioned Cheri.

"Who cares? I can turn him! Look at Liam, he's been trying to get me to do dirty things with him for months!! Did I tell you he asked me to move in with him?" I said with assured confidence.

"BLOODY HELL! Tell me you said NO?!" exclaimed Cheri, now fidgeting in the booth across from me. It seemed like this news had struck a chord deep inside her.

"Well, I did say no... but not at first exactly. I mean who wouldn't want to live in a Hollywood Hills mansion with your best friend slash love of your life?" I said, feeling almost uncertain about the decision I had already made. "I have a great apartment that I love and from what you and some of the other girls he's dated have told me it just didn't seem right ... right now."

"Exactly darling, it's also imperative that you stay focused on your singing, your cupcake classes, and your new business venture," she said, relieved, relaxing in the booth once again.

A few minutes later, the ever adorable Tad walked up to our table with the tasty-looking bucket of steaming crabs and a steamy smile on his tasty-looking face.

"Here you are, ladies!" he joked, looking at me.

"Thanks, stud," I replied in a cute playful way like always.

It seemed that in most of my relationships with my 'straight guy' friends, we always had that playful innocent flirtation. Sometimes I wanted it to be real, of course, but for the most part I was just happy to have these amazing friends and acquaintances that liked me for who I was, and treated me with respect.

I had a lot of these types of relationships in Hollywood. Hell, even with my girlfriends we'd flirt and goof around – I mean isn't that what friends do? It's a bond, a closeness, where you know you can say just about anything and the other person gets it and reacts accordingly.

As we began to crack the best crab legs in town, I started to really wonder what my next step would actually be. My mind got clouded with thoughts of what life would be like living with Liam and the craziness that would ensue. I had never even been naked in front of him, and now I'm supposed to move in and shower in the same place and cook breakfast? My mind just went off a cliff.

As I was floating down the mountain of crazy thoughts, I noticed Cheri had a strange look on her face, the look that said 'I really want to tell you something but don't know if I should.'

"What is it girl? What's with the face? What are you not telling me?" I questioned her with a half-eaten crab leg pointed directly at her.

"Well.... I never told you about it and now that you are, whatever you are with Liam, I never found the right time to mention it..." she hesitantly said.

"Spit it out, Cheri!" I said, literally spitting a tiny piece of crab out of my mouth across the table.

"Well.... Liam and I used to date a long time ago. It was pretty serious. I... I was asked to move in with him too... and ... I did. It was okay for a little while, but then it got weird. WAY WEIRD. He started acting crazy at night – playing his music at all hours... doing all sorts of drugs and drinking like a fool," she said, taking a sip from her glass of Pinot.

"I know he uses drugs," I replied. "I've done them with him. As sad as it actually sounds, that's where our relationship got even closer." As I said the words, I almost couldn't believe I was saying them. I mean we did get closer in those moments physically and emotionally. It was in the bathroom over a bag of cocaine that we started singing together.

"Kaleb... he got too crazy. One night I came home and he had thrown all my stuff over the balcony and locked me out. I had nowhere to go. He left me out there to fend for myself. Thank God I had a good friend at the time that let me stay with her," she said, with an air of warning to her words. I took a moment to let her words register in my mind.

Okay, so that was her experience with him and it was absolutely terrible, but our relationship was different, stronger, more meaningful. Right? He was a gentleman around me. He was a more inspired person with me and most importantly he truly loved me. I didn't know all the juicy details of their relationship, nor did I really want to, but deep down I felt like he and I must have a stronger connection. I began to tell myself that must be the case. Because I was the first guy he ever had a relationship with, it was much more special... maybe even destined.

Cheri's words, though, did start to seep into my stream of thought. She was my closest friend and I knew she only wanted the best for me. Like so many other people in my life who had tried to warn me about choices that I was making, I ignored her. I was going to see where this relationship was headed, even if I was potentially on a craft doomed to sink. I was in love with the captain and was willing to go down with the ship.

As we finished our dinner, Tad came by to drop off the check. His cute little-boy face and sexy grown man's body distracted me from my train of thought long enough to come to my senses and ask him to come to our karaoke night, which our favorite bar was hosting the following evening.

I was going to sing that night and it was set to be a big deal. I would be singing in front of an audience for the first time in years and in that audience would be my rock star, the man I adored, who I had been secretly singing with in bathrooms and other random places for months.

I wanted to show him my skills, but more importantly, I wanted to inspire him to get back to singing professionally. It killed me to see the man I cared so much for wasting his God-given talent sitting at a bar with me all day, drinking and snorting his life away. I didn't realize it at the time, but that situation was starting to happen to me, too.

Out of my head and back in reality, Cheri grabbed the bill and as she was fishing for her wallet, her phone and mine began to vibrate. It's a message from Anna Lynn:

'Hey bitches! We are at the spot! It's Game night! Beer Pong! Where are you? There are tons of cute guys here and Liam just walked in alone. Get your asses here a.s.a.p.'

"Oh boy, another exciting night at The State Room! What's the special tonight, 2 for 1? Not like it matters to you Kaleb... it's always like 5 for 1 for you and Liam!" Cheri rolled her eyes as she put down her credit card.

"Jealous?" I said, with a smirk, trying to sound funny but not to rub it in her face after just having that emotional conversation and her pouring her regrets and warnings out all over the table. As I glanced down at my phone, I still kept hearing her sad story playing over and over in my head.

I texted Anna Lynn back saying we were on our way. As we said our goodbyes to Tad, I had a brief moment where I stopped and thought that maybe a guy like that was better for me. Not necessarily Tad himself, but a man like him. Someone with a job, a drive ... a life that didn't revolve around a bar and cocaine.

Before I could get carried away on another heart-wrenching game of brain twister, Cheri had grabbed my arm and was pulling me out the door. We were off to the bar. Two adults going to join other adults in the glitziest city in the world, to play a plethora of drinking and board games! Ha! The night was just getting started, and I would soon find out that the games some people were playing, were not just the ones all on the table.

THE GAMES WE PLAY

WE ENTERED The State Room that evening to find all the familiar faces already in the midst of various gameplay. The upstairs lounge area had been converted into a game space and there was just about every type of drinking game you could imagine being played tournament style. Cheri and I found the girls at the bar holding two empty seats and two full glasses waiting for us.

"Hello Ladies! So what have we missed so far?" I asked as I took my first sip of my purple long island iced tea poured for me in a special glass.

"Not much, it's pretty much the same shit as usual... except Liam is over there talking to his tarty bitch of an ex," said Anna Lynn, pointing across to where Liam was sitting, drink in hand, with some dark-haired younger girl. Who was this? Another ex-girlfriend? How many girls did he have in his local rolodex?

"If you will excuse me ladies, I think I'll go say hello to Liam and good-bye to whoever the hell that is," I announced, while taking an extra big gulp of my drink. If I was sharing my spotlight with some hoochie, I wanted to be loosened up.

"Okay, Kaleb. If you need us, just motion," replied Cheri, looking rather concerned. I'm sure she was still processing the conversation we had at the crab place earlier that night.

I walked over and sat on the arm of Liam's chair, putting my arm over his shoulder. He introduced me and within a minute I had already forgotten her name. Her name was not important to me, getting her away from Liam was. She was probably 21, if that, and one of those annoying bitches who complained about everything going on around her. 'The music sucked, the drinks were crap and the coke was not strong enough.'

I listened to her ramble on about something stupid for a few minutes and soon the ramble turned into drunk babbling and over-intoxicated flailing of the extremities. This was my cue. I motioned for the girls, who brought the bartender over with them. My cute bartender friend with the glasses (who I always had flirty conversations with) came over and asked the little twit to leave. My hero!

Cheri sat across from Liam and on that night I realized even more what an amazing woman she was. She was pleasant with Liam even after everything he did to her. He was a good guy at heart and fun to be around, but could I hang out with someone who hurt me like that? She was definitely a bigger person than me. But she was not alone in the ex-girlfriend group.

There were a couple other exes of his that I actually liked and sometimes we would get together and they would tell me stories about their times with him. All of the girls in the group had met him at a bar and had some length of a relationship with Liam. They liked to drink and do the occasional drug, so it was no wonder they connected with him like I did. They all varied in looks and ages, but he was our common bond and it brought us closer together. It was like living the strangest version of Sex and the City where three of the girls had dated the guy and one was still in a relationship with him! I always chalked it up to research. I needed to know what I was getting into.

Anna Lynn sat on the other side of Liam's chair and I noticed them talking and exchanging something in their hands. Looked like Anna Lynn had brought the snow to the party tonight. Liam grabbed my hand and led me to the bathroom. We entered the dimly lit room and he pulled out the bag for us to share.

"Kaleb, I have an idea I want to share with you. I want to start working on a music video for my new song. Would you meet up with me and Ray tomorrow to come up with ideas?" he said, as he fished the bag of powder from his pocket.

"Of course, Liam. I would be more than happy to. You know I want you to get back out there and

I will help however I can! I love you buddy!" I quickly said as he finished portioning out two lines of cocaine on the sink.

Did I just haphazardly tell him I loved him? Oh Lord... Well, here was his moment to say it back. Would he?

"Awww... I love you too kid. You're so creative and stuff... I know you'll come up with some awesome ideas!" he replied, snorting one of the lines in front of us.

Okay, so he said it too. Looked like we finally got that out of the way, albeit not the romantic ideal version of the situation I had been imagining in my head all those months. It had been said and I felt closer to my rock star than ever before. I snorted the line he left for me and we walked out of the bathroom, his arms on my shoulders, laughing at some random quip I made.

As the night went on, there were many more trips to the bathroom and copious amounts of liquor being consumed. We were all playing a game of poker at the bar and at some point I realized I was sitting next to Cheri, while Liam and Anna Lynn were seated across from us oddly close. Maybe it was the booze and the cocaine, but I could swear she was totally hitting on him. But Anna Lynn would never do that to me, right? I didn't know her as well as my other girlfriends, but she had become very close to me in the weeks prior and I considered her to be one of my besties. I brushed it off as over-thinking intoxication and was pleasantly surprised when I pulled a three-of-a-kind and beat her that round. Three-of-a-kind... looking back on it now it was almost an ominous sign, but one I wouldn't recognize until a little later down the road.

As the night wound down, it was clear that none of us should be driving and luckily I didn't have to as I lived a block from the bar. I invited everyone over that night for a little after-party at my place. Liam was in no mood to join us and started asking everyone for a ride back up to the Hollywood Hills. The rest of us were almost out the door when he convinced Anna Lynn to drive him home. She obliged and said she would meet up with us later.

At my spacious one-bedroom apartment, I had the living room set up to look like a lounge. Black-leather sectional with glass tables on either side, a bar by the kitchen that was always stocked with various liquors and enough space in between the couch and tv for multiple people to dance.

This was the life! A 2 a.m. after-party at my place filled with friends playing dancing games on the Wii, singing karaoke songs at the top of their lungs, drinking and dancing in one room and snorting and sniffing in the other room. I had finally made it. I was popular. I was the cool kid. I was no longer that fat, glasses-wearing choir nerd who was constantly made fun of all those years ago in Texas. I was the Queen of the night and I had a rock star 'boyfriend.' My life was perfect, or so it seemed.

From the outside it looked fabulous, and for the most part on the inside it felt fabulous too, but there were other things going on in my life that were not so glamorous.

Things at the cake shop were not going well. I was constantly arguing with my boss (who had become more like a father to me) over tardiness and sometimes outlandish behavior due to coming in to work hungover or at times even drinking to excess on the job. It was not a stress-free job mind you; there was always some extreme drama falling on my shoulders that would cause a lot of people to want to drink. Obviously, that was no excuse for my actions. If the owner and I didn't have such a close bond, I would have been fired years ago.

Tim, the owner, was a good man. He was smart, caring, generous and always encouraging. When I started there 9 years ago, I told him the story of how my father went to prison for a life sentence when I was in seventh grade and about my mother's tragic death. I think that's when he took on that fatherly role in my life. He always saw the best in me and would tell me often that he knew I could make it big in show business if I really wanted to, if I would stop my partying ways. Just like in a real father-and-son relationship, I was determined not to listen to him and live my life the way I wanted.

Tim was never too approving of my relationship with Liam either. I guess he could see things from his 'fatherly' perspective that was oblivious to me at the time. Turns out as one relationship was growing another almost equally important relationship with my chosen father figure was wilting away.

Anna Lynn never showed up that night but the next day I was meeting with Liam to talk about a music video and I was too excited to care why she didn't.

Soon the stresses of my life would come crashing down on all of us. But for now I was blissfully unaware. With the Wii controller in hand, and a group of friends around me, I was content to continue playing the games we play.

THE THINGS WE COULD DO TOGETHER

I G O T U P a little bit earlier on this Wednesday afternoon. Yes, that was not a misprint. I said, "up early in the afternoon." At this point in my life, I was pretty much living the stereotypical rock star lifestyle, filled with continuous partying, drinking and doing drugs every night. I was working fewer hours at the cake shop and spending more time trying to come up with ways that I could make money so I could keep living this life of reckless irresponsibility on my own terms. This particular Wednesday would be a catalyst allowing me to pursue those new uncharted capital-making ventures. Some in a positive way and others... not so much.

It was about 2 p.m. when I arrived at The State Room. Waiting for me at the bar was Liam, already 2 drinks in. Ray, the bartender, was an old friend of mine who I had met working this same bar when it was under a different name and owner. He was one of those guys who possessed good looks, charm and a passion for life. He was an actor and actually did a lot of cool shows and commercials, but acting doesn't always afford us the lifestyle we desire until you actually make it big. He also really loved his job because he loved people and being a bartender was like being on stage – you always have an audience requiring constant entertainment. Hell, if that damn bar had ever given me the chance to officially work there, I would have made an awesome bartender. Maybe they were afraid I would drink all the profits or that I wasn't the 'right fit' for their 'straight bar' mentality. We will never know, as I was headed down a different path and bartending might have just gotten in the way.

As I approached the bar, Ray had already begun pouring my signature cocktail in my signature glass. My 'special' glass was made up of a giant mason jar, looking like one a Texan lady would drink her sweet tea from, attached to what could only be described as a large glass candlestick. It was my 'white trash wine glass' as some of the regulars coined it, but that was not the best name. Rarely did wine ever fill the glass, unless I decided to add it to the mix of my personal cocktail on a whim. If you want to get a feeling for how high my tolerance was at the time, just listen to the ingredients in my personal creation: Kaleb's Kool-Aid. Everything you would find in a Long Island: vodka, gin, rum, tequila, triple sec, a splash of Coke then added to that were splashes of blue curacao, midori, a ton of grenadine, a dash of fireball and topped off with some 151. For some reason, this ridiculous mix of liquors actually ended up tasting like Kool-Aid and, as time went by, other people started ordering it too. One of those would knock a regular person on their ass, but I was good through most nights by drinking about five or six of those accompanied by multiple trips to the bathroom with my Hello Kitty pocket compact where I hid my cocaine. That also became a term used around the bar. People always asked me if kitty was coming out to play or if I knew who had the kitty.

With my 'Kool-Aid' in hand and my laptop in front of me, it was time to get down to business. The boys had already started coming up with ideas before I arrived. I listened as I started to type what I thought would be the perfect music video for this new song that would be Liam's rise back to the top.

Our video would start with Sarah Summers and Liam coming home from a bar with a brief glimpse of intimacy before he realizes she is a guy. Another scene portrayed Ray sleeping with Liam's fake ex-girlfriend, whom he longed to get back with by serenading her outside her window from the grass below. I was going to be featured again as Sarah during the chorus dancing on top of The State Room bar, serving him drink after drink and seducing him. The finale featured Liam outside the ex-girlfriend's house where he is fighting with Ray's character. He eventually loses and falls to the ground where a cute little dog pisses on him as a last bit of comedic relief.

The whole video was going to be a parody of his 'fucked up' life and we all saw it as golden! This video was going to be his return to the spotlight and he wanted to feature me in it, too. Sarah Summers would finally get to be in the spotlight again, and this time it would be with someone I really loved and cared so deeply about. This time it was going to be a big deal and if we played our cards right, a very lucrative deal as well.

Feeling accomplished for putting into words this big plan, I closed the laptop and we all shared a few of our favorite fireball shots. We spent the afternoon drinking and smoking cigarettes at the bar like we did most days. This bar was one of those bars where you could legally smoke inside because technically it was a patio bar.

The room we hung out in the most was a beautiful room separated into two sections: the bar and the lounge area. Filling the lounge were leather chairs and wood tables, reminiscent of the fancy cigar lounges seen in the movies. We had a table in the back that was 'our spot' and it was rare that anyone would dare to sit there unless invited by us. I had a very diverse group of friends at The State Room whom I got to spend time with when Liam was out doing whatever it was he did those days. This room became my second home and as these new business ventures started to come up it became my office. The staff became like family to me and I genuinely deeply cared for all of them, even if we didn't always see eye to eye.

On this particular Wednesday, there was to be a new promo that evening featuring a group of cigar enthusiasts hosted by a woman I had yet to meet, but had heard good things about. I was quite intrigued by this idea of having a cigar night where people could get together and share their love of fine tobacco while conversing about politics and life itself. The bar was labeled a cigar bar but it had been rare to see more than a small group of businessmen smoking cigars in the lounge at one time. Not only was this going to be good for business, it was also going to open people up to a different experience and I was definitely going to attend and find out what cigar culture was all about.

It was getting later into the evening now and, after multiple drinks and trips to the bathroom with Liam, singing and playing touchy feely like we did, he decided it was time for him to go home. He suggested that I email the video idea to Anna Lynn because she was working at a celebrity gossip magazine, and somehow he thought that made her important in the entertainment industry. He thought she might be able to help find the right people to get it made. I obliged but didn't really see the necessity of bringing her into this matter. But if that's what he wanted, that's what I did. I sent the email and we hugged tightly as he left the bar.

The bar began filling up and I had been joined by some of my other friends, including a group of girls I was close to and a plethora of guys I had started to interact with. Most of the guys were just friends, but there were a few others I had started to acquire feelings for. It wasn't like I was cheating on Liam, because he and I were never officially a couple, and as emotionally attached as we were, I was still always keeping my eyes open for that special someone who could actually love me like I needed. I loved Liam and he loved me, but because of his 'celebrity' status as a 'straight' rock star we were never able to show our real affection for each other outside of private settings. I had dreams too. I wanted to have a boyfriend who would be out and proud about sharing his life with me. Not someone I constantly had to lie to everyone else to by saying we were just best friends. Doesn't everyone deserve a love like that in their life? As I stared out the window looking out onto Sunset Boulevard with my drink and cigarette in hand, I wondered if I did? What have I ever done to deserve a love like that? My relationship with Liam was the closest thing I had ever experienced to that kind of closeness and it still wasn't what I had always dreamed of.

It was 6 p.m. when the cigar group came into the lounge. Soon the air became sweetened by the smell of fancy cigars from all over the world. Seated at the head of the table in the middle of the room was an attractive African American woman smoking a full-sized cigar. When you think of cigar smokers, you usually think of some rich white dudes in suits huffing and puffing over convoluted conversations of business with maybe a woman or two smoking tiny flavored cigars, if anything at all. She was not one of those 'girls.' Michelle was one of those strong women who was just as intelligent and business savvy as she was attractive. She definitely commanded the attention of the room. Her aura filled the lounge and I was immediately drawn to her presence. I was very much the same kind of person and I knew if I got to know her we would have a lot in common. She might also be able to impart on me some life lessons she had learned about the world. I was right.

That first evening she allowed me into her group of practiced smokers and was more than accommodating to this novice by patiently showing me how to cut, light and hold the cigar. We shared many stories that night and she became like a mentor to me over the next few months. She introduced me to a culture I had never even really thought about. And I fell in love with it. The cigar culture, the history, the process of making them and the bond people create while sharing these fine products became something really positive in my life at a time when, even though I didn't realize it, things were slowly headed into major decline.

It wasn't like I was completely unaware of the things that were not right in my life. It was just that I had days like this where there was so much positivity and moments of creative ideas allowing visions of a fulfilled future, that I tended to ignore the signs. On this day I had come up with a surefire winner of a music video with the man I loved and met a woman who introduced me to something new that would later become an inspiring business venture. I was not worried about those negative signs because I had creative people around me and I was too busy looking into the future, distracted by the excitement for all the things we could do together.

UP IN SMOKE

WEEKS WENT BY and I started to find new and exciting adventures to fill my time. The work situation at the cake shop had become pretty volatile. I was continuously frustrated and mostly bored with the daily arguments and monotony. I used every excuse to avoid stepping into that place. I decided to take a chance on myself and put into action all the creative ideas for businesses I had conceived.

I had created two businesses that kept me occupied. My catchy confection company called 'Edible Elevation' with the tag line 'Taking taste to a higher level,' and my own cigar label for a barber pole cigar line called 'El Diablo Anjel Royale' (The Royal Devil Angel). Both fantastic business ventures that expanded my horizons led me to a deeper connection with myself and would very well have been quite successful had I not been distracted with all the partying, drinking, snorting and rock star cavorting.

I became obsessed with the cigar culture and learned everything I could about it. Michelle's Wednesday night cigar groups had inspired me to spend the hours I was not at the bar, researching on the web and meeting with and learning from the Sunset Strip cigar shop owners. It was almost surprising to me that right beneath my nose was a thriving culture of cigar enthusiasts with a wealth of knowledge that I was eager to learn. I thought I knew just about everything that the famous 1.3-mile section of West Hollywood had to offer, but I was constantly learning that there was so much more there than meets the eye. One owner in particular became another cigar mentor to me and introduced me to a 'dos copos' or barbershop pole style cigar. Because of its fantastical design and unique appearance, a lighter leaf wrapped around darker one, I was immediately drawn to it. Being somewhat of a spiritual person, I have always seen signs and felt strong emotional connections to certain things and this cigar was one unlike any cigar I had ever seen and it reminded me of... me.

This cigar, like me, had two different aspects to its facade and that comparison to myself was easy enough: Kaleb and Sarah. Like me, my feminine and masculine sides were always struggling to become dominant like the two leaves fighting to share their flavor between the time each one burned. Inside the cigar was a various blend of tobacco, grown in many different lands and environments, giving it a unique quality and taste.

Likewise, my stories were a blend of happiness and tragedy becoming the mix that created my intricate inner being. This particular type of cigar was known to most as a novelty cigar, unique for sure but not taken too seriously as it was seen as more of a gimmick.

Could there be a closer comparison to my life at this time? Even though I felt like Queen of the bar, the most unique character there by far, sporting my top hats, various coats, cane and one glove, there was a part of me that knew I was just a novelty to some. Was I letting my own gimmick get the best of me? I know it appeared to some that I was just the outlandish character that entertained and sometimes bothered people with my eccentric ways, but there was a deeper, more complex person in there just crying to get out. Yes, I loved the attention most nights, but it was nice to find some people there that took the time to get to know the real me and could separate the difference between the party version and the real one. That cigar was a perfectly wrapped tobacco version of my life and I aimed to share it with the world.

I spent a lot of time designing a beautiful label and name for my cigar because I am a creative perfectionist when it comes to something I want to put my name on. Michelle told me she was going to cut back on her Wednesday hosting gigs and that there would be a Wednesday free for me. I could now host my own event, so I immediately began the process of putting together what was going to be the fanciest, most entertaining and lucrative night the cigar lounge had ever seen.

I was on a mission to prove myself to the naysayers that only saw me as the drunk clown at the bar. I started with the product. My labels turned out beautiful, some of the best and most detailed graphic design work I had ever done. I was elated that I would be showing it off at my own event.

I worked with the chef at the bar, whose amazing appetizers had become my main source of food as I was spending most of my days and nights there. We came up with the perfect bite-sized menu to accompany the drink specials I had created with my favorite bartender.

I asked my friend, a brilliant musician, to play a few numbers on his saxophone throughout the night for that added touch of class. I even secured a professional cigar roller who would be making to-order fresh cigars for the patrons that evening. I had a popcorn company agree to set up a promotional table to give out their products and other unique giveaways. I came up with an amazing name for what was going to be my magnificent new cigar group, 'The Rolling Gallery Cigar Club,' its name deriving from the place cigar rollers gather to put the products together during production.

I took ample time designing a professional image that was featured on posters, postcards and flyers promoting a free drink, an appetizer plate and one of my own label's cigars upon ticket purchase. I even had Liam commit to making a rare evening appearance to show support and solidarity.

This was looking to be a big night for me,

securing my place at the bar I so desperately wanted to be involved with on the business side. I would finally seal the deal on my way into actual employment there, finally being an official member of the team, finally fitting in, finally earning a living at the place I enjoyed spending my time. Most importantly, finally getting the respect I deserved from the bar staff and patrons who saw my existence there as a gimmick, or nothing but a parody of a person. I had put so much work into this night I thought there is no way it could fail. Boy was I wrong.

The set up was beautiful, the drinks and the food were prepared, my cigar roller was busy setting up his table and my talented musician pal was ready. The first hour went by and a few people came in. The next hour only a few more. The cigar roller who I had commissioned to hand roll cigars and give me a portion of each sale, was now selling his cigars on his own, blatantly disregarding our agreement. My friend who signed up to be the doorman had left his post to get drunk. People who did not have tickets began coming into the lounge and partaking in the musical show and the free giveaways. To top it off, my 'dear friend' Liam never showed up and Anna Lynn was nowhere to be found either.

I was frustrated and saddened by the fact I had put so much work into this event, so much of my soul and my time and now it was blowing up in my face. I felt betrayed by so many people that night. If the managers and staff had been more supportive by helping me promote the event, it could have been such an amazing and lucrative evening for everyone, instead of the disastrous failed attempt that it ended up being.

I went upstairs to the other bar and drowned my tears in booze. I realized my dreams of finally doing something right and being the successful entrepreneur I always knew I could be were squashed. There would be some good times after this disappointment, but there was an even more devastating event just around the corner. At this very moment though, my dreams for my cigar company had gone up in smoke.

TIME TO CALL
THE DEALER

" W I N T E R " was upon us in Hollywood and I use quotation marks because it is rare even in winter for the temperature to dip below 70 degrees. A rainy day is so infrequent that when it actually happens the locals act like a hurricane is approaching.

I was still dealing with the feelings of disappointment after the major debacle of my cigar event, but I decided to pick myself up and focus on my other business ideas. By the middle of October, my personalized chocolate bar business 'Edible Elevation' was going full steam ahead, with some very interesting prospects on the horizon. One of the projects was a promotional deal with the West Hollywood Chamber of Commerce for their annual Creative Business Awards Ceremony (an event I had attended every year and had won an award representing the cake shop).

The holidays were rapidly approaching and I had to find another way to make money since I had basically quit the cake shop. My nightlife had almost completely taken over my 'regular' life and I was determined to make that my full-time gig. I wanted to be in that environment all the time, I was almost addicted to the lifestyle. The addiction to alcohol and drugs mirrored the need to be out at the bar or in the scene at all times.

My job at the cake shop, the job I had held for 8 years, had come to a close. At this point I was not going into the shop at all anymore and had cut my involvement down to only doing computer work from home. This was the month I also put into effect the severance package I had earned after working tirelessly those first few years to keep the doors open and the company afloat during the recession and later to help it to really thrive again by creating new products and establishing lucrative business partnerships. I was owed that much I thought!

The severance package I had planned out with the owner would basically keep my bills paid for six months while I would find another job and get my company off the ground. The money was just enough for bills, but I had to have more in order to keep up my rock star lifestyle. I had become good friends with all sorts of people at the bar: actors, businessmen, servers, computer geeks, sports stars, rock legends, and my fair share of shady characters, too. I even considered some of the shady characters my friends and, of course, they were also my suppliers.

There were a couple of guys who I bought my stuff from most of the nights. Richie was one of them. He actually hung out with our group and he wasn't particularly shady looking, in fact he wasn't imposing or scary looking at all. He had even dated one of the girls in our group and it seemed like they had a good relationship while it lasted. Having a dealer in our group, having one of your besties dating one, made it a lot easier to continue living this fantastical life we had all chosen to live.

I watched him closely and was intrigued by his business skills. Aside from the dark alleys and bathrooms he used as his office, it seemed like he was running a pretty lucrative business. Being an entrepreneur myself, I thought that selling my own 'kitty' was the logical next step. Everyone was always asking me for some, or asking if I knew where to get it. I knew I would make a killing from the start. So I asked Richie (when we had a moment alone at the bar) how he got into it, how much profit did he make and how I could get into the drug-selling business myself?

He explained to me that I would have to buy a large amount and put it into bags myself and then I would decide how much to sell it for. Was I really thinking about becoming a drug dealer? It sounds like a very bad idea now, but at the time, living a life where cocaine and other drugs were just as common as booze, it didn't seem like such a bad prospective side gig. I took particular notice that everyone was always really nice to the dealer and he was by far the most popular guy in the room when he was there and fully stocked up. I wanted to be that guy! I wanted to finally be the cool guy... the most popular person in the room.

It seemed like ever since high school that had always been my dream: to be cool, to be popular. My relationship with a rock star and the life we were all leading at the bars and in the nightlife was sometimes just like being back in an adult version of school. At the bar, there was the popular group, the band peeps, the cigar clique, the stoners, the girls from other countries, the nerds and the jocks. I was a part of the popular group of course because of my ties to Liam, but I was definitely more of a social butterfly at this bar version of school. I was involved with the most popular guy and close friends with all the popular girls, but I hung out with everyone and treated everyone like equals. And for that reason alone I knew I would make an excellent dealer.

My first taste at dealing was through a guy Richie had referred me to and I guess for the most part it was a successful run. I bought the goods straight out so I didn't owe him any money because we have all heard the stories and seen movies of what would happen to those who were dumb enough to cross a higher-up drug dealer. I was, for the week that the product lasted, the most popular kid at the bar and I even made a slight profit selling the powder. It also felt powerful to be the one holding the goods and the one with the power to dish out 'gifts' to my friends and the love of my life. Liam was very excited when he found out I started selling because he knew he would be getting a good deal. Our bathroom encounters became even more frequent with additional instances of sexual passes. Being the dealer made my presence at the bar feel important. I was in demand more than ever and, even if all those people were using me or getting close to me to get something out of me, I didn't care, I loved the attention. In fact, I reveled in it!

Halloween was always a favorite holiday of mine. This year I had planned it to be even more meaningful for me, my friends and, most importantly, Liam.

For the first time I was going to introduce everyone to Sarah Summers in the flesh. I was hoping that maybe as Sarah I would have enough guts to finally go all the way with Liam. He and I were still playing touchy feely in the bathrooms and he always told me how even more attractive he found me as Sarah from the videos and pictures he had seen. We had talked about sex. He had asked me numerous times before and I thought maybe the time was right. I wasn't worried any more about it ruining our friendship because we had become so emotionally connected that, if he had let me, I would have been calling him my boyfriend. So in my mind Halloween night, dressed as Sarah, would be the night to really take that next step in our relationship.

I had to get ready for the evening so I invited all the girls over to my house to pre-party and get dressed up in our costumes. Cheri, Jackie and some of the other girls in our group were confirmed but

Anna Lynn said she wouldn't be able to make it due to other obligations. This had become a regular shtick of hers as she always seemed to be blowing me off for some random reason or another. Whatever, we didn't need her anyway! The bar was stocked and the 'kitty' was in the house and ready to be unleashed on what I was planning to be the biggest night of the year!

Jackie was the first to arrive already dressed up as her version of a pretty punk thug girl complete with a bandana, long pigtail braid and a fake gun of course. My girlfriend from the bank came too and I helped her get into her sexy vampire makeup and costume. We were about three drinks and a bag of 'kitty' in when Cheri and her friend showed up to get into their pumpkin costumes and joined in on the pre-party shenanigans. I had decided to go as 'Country Hick Britney Spears,' donning my trademark blonde locks, perfectly done makeup, a tied-up plaid shirt, blue jean short shorts and my favorite cowgirl boots with a black trench coat on top to keep warm in the "chilly" 60-degree weather. Ha! I had told the girls of my plan to finally take Liam up on his sexual advances and that tonight would be that night. We finished off the last bottle of liquor and headed out the door on our way to The State Room and my big reveal to everyone as my alter ego Sarah.

We arrived at the bar and I was feeling nervous, waiting for Liam to arrive. But the awestruck reactions from the crowd at the bar and the free drinks that followed were enough to keep me distracted for a while. A while being the key words. It seemed like the hours were flying by and Liam still hadn't shown up and miss Anna Lynn was a no show, too.

At that time, I was starting to get a slight inkling that it may be more than just a coincidence that the two of them never seemed to be around at the same time anymore. It was this night that the real thoughts of worry, possible betrayal and regret started running through my head. What was going on between them? Were they sleeping together on the side? Would they have the nerve to sneak around behind my back? Was it my fault this was happening? Had I waited too long to make my move? Had he gotten past the idea of being with me and traded me in for a real female version of Sarah? Was it lust...or was it more?

Before I could go off into full-on murderous mode, the girls who cared enough to show up for me that night handed me a drink and calmed me down enough to take a breath and enjoy the evening. I sold a few bags of 'kitty' at the bar and we shared one between us before Jackie and I split off to head down to Santa Monica Blvd. to hit up the gay clubs, where I was once a staple character. I figured I might even have a shot at meeting a guy to take home and fuck me into forgetting the fact that Liam and one of my best girlfriends might be having an affair.

That didn't happen though. I met plenty of guys that night who were interested in a one-shot sexual escapade, but I just wasn't feeling it. I was too emotionally connected to that rock star douche bag. I wasn't ready to give my body, that had gone untouched waiting for the right moment with

Liam, to some drunk guy who I would never see again and most likely regret the second it was over.

Jackie and I headed back to my apartment and had more drinks and talked for hours about the potential drama that we were sure was soon to rear its ugly head in our lives. Jackie left as the sun was coming up and I had finally decided it was time to put Sarah back in the closet for now. As I dropped the jacket to the floor, I had a brief moment of what felt like déjà vu or maybe it was a premonition, either way it shook me to my core. As I washed my face and took off the blonde wig, I wondered if he was in bed with her, grabbing her real blonde hair as he screwed her from behind. That thought enraged me.

Looking back at me in the mirror was Kaleb, once again stricken with a look of hurt and dissapointment the likes of which I had not seen in years. I left the outfit on the floor, an unintended symbol of how low I felt, and went into the kitchen to make myself a drink and have another hit of kitty to get my mind off of it all. I opened the ornate cigar box where I kept my inventory to find that I was all out of cocaine, out of any other drug I may have had in there, and that would not do. It was time to replenish my stash which meant it was time to call the dealer.

WHAT AM I
THANKFUL FOR?

NOVEMBER is the month when the retail holiday displays go up far too early and we are supposed to start putting together lists of all the things in our life we are thankful for. On my personal list this year, I was thankful for my 'whatever we were' relationship with Liam, my beautiful apartment, my severance package, the adventures at The State Room and my close friendships with people like Cheri and Jackie. Those two girls had been by my side through all the up-and-down drama of having a rock star as the love of my life. They would prove to be invaluable friends throughout the next few months.

The Chamber of Commerce event went off without a hitch. I owe a lot of thanks to those two girls for helping me get it all done in time while still partying every day. The Chamber was gracious enough to give my business a full page ad in the event program and even mentioned my freshman company during the awards ceremony. I knew I had a good thing going there and if I had been able to kick the bad habits in my life, I know my company would have been an even bigger success.

I was finding success in other areas of my life that I thought were more rewarding for much more personal reasons. I was good at being a coke dealer at first, but had given up selling 'kitty' as I had started to lose money on the deal because my generosity started to get the best of me. I had become like the Robin Hood of Cocaine, stealing from the rich person's stash and giving it to the needy, except the rich person I was stealing it from was me and the 'poor' people were my cocaine-using 'friends' who could have bought it from me if they wanted to.

The State Room had become a lively place and more and more new characters were entering the scene almost nightly. The upstairs bar had turned into a live music venue, evolving into a wonderful place where I was introduced to new types of music and the people who made it. The restaurant below was also becoming very busy as the word got out about the chef's cooking and the amazing happy hour deals. In the cigar lounge though was where I held court most of the nights. I loved the way it smelled, the way it vibrated with energy and I loved the many different people I had come to know.

There was the motorcycle guy who was ruggedly handsome and tough on the outside but, when we were alone together at my apartment, he was a real sweetheart with a penchant for karaoke. He was straight. There was another guy who played guitar and was closer to my age. He loved to smoke his pot and when he would come over to my house we would sing together like Liam and I did. But this cute guy wrote a song for me and that was something really special. But he was 'straight' too, of course. Then there was the cigar-smoking scientist who was just as adorable as he was smart with whom I had many a wonderful and inspiring conversation. He aroused me mentally, something I found so utterly desirable in a man, but in this environment pretty difficult to find. I fell for him pretty hard and I definitely thought that there was something there. But he was 'straight,' too, he claimed, even though everyone around us thought otherwise.

I was basically tearing my own heart apart trying to love and be loved by these men surrounding me. Maybe I was clinging too hard to each subtle word they spoke to me that always seemed like flirtations. My girlfriends, on the other hand, saw things as they were. They saw the looks of confusion some of these guys gave me as they struggled with their feelings for me and, maybe even deeper down, their own sexuality.

Even if one of the few guys I had really opened up to and started to have feelings for had said they wanted to be with me out loud, there is a chance my connection to Liam probably wouldn't have let me. I couldn't totally give my heart to them anyway, so maybe it was better they retained their 'straightness.' I still didn't feel worthy of a real loving relationship and maybe I sabotaged these possibilities myself without ever realizing it.

As the middle of the month approached, the crew and I had all started to make plans for Thanksgiving. LA is one of those towns where a lot of people come from far away to try and make their dreams come true, meaning they usually leave their family in some random state or country. Jackie had made plans to go back to Texas to see her family, another reason we were so close. Not only did we share the same birthday, we also were from the same home state. My lovely 'husband' Cheri, as I referred to her, would be staying in town this week and so the two of us made plans to go to the Irish bar on the Sunset Strip that was hosting a traditional Thanksgiving style meal during lunch with their specialty whiskey drinks at a very reduced cost. So that was the plan...or so I thought.

It was midafternoon on that day when my phone rang and to my surprise it was Liam. He was one of those guys who actually called people instead of texting. I doubt he even knew how because I had to show him how to use new phones just about every other week as he was always losing them during his nightly benders. He started the call off like usual with his "hey you, what's up?" The conversation continued on in a normal fashion; deciding what time we were going to meet at the bar, who had the 'stuff' and questions asking if I had any new ideas for getting him back into the limelight. Before we were about to hang up, he tried to sneak in a question that I wasn't really expecting and said, "hey, do you want to meet my parents on Thanksgiving? They are coming to visit me at my place and I have talked about you a little."

Woah... Woah... What?

He was asking me to meet his parents? Where the hell did this come from? I mean I know we were close, as close as you could be to someone without actually being a couple. But this was just out of the blue. He never talked about his parents or anyone in his family and, to be honest, I hadn't met the parents of someone I loved since my boyfriend, Shane, back in Texas.

If I remember correctly, that was on Thanksgiving too, and it turned out quite nice. He was one of the 'Great Loves' of my life as Carrie Bradshaw coined it. He was the man who loved me beyond the meaning of love. He accepted every part of me and was so loyal, so kind and so intelligent. I wasn't ready for that kind of love at the time and my youth and wild ways led to the ending of that relationship. I could have married that guy if I had been more mature, but that wasn't part of my greater plan, I guess. But it did teach me a lot. Was I ready to take that next step with Liam now? I had become what I thought was a mature adult. (What did I know about maturity? I was partying every night.)

I agreed to meet up with him and his parents that weekend and I immediately made a distress call to the girls. Cheri, sweet Cheri, was there to calm my nerves and give me some advice to not get my hopes up about this because it wasn't like he was going to come out or anything! He was going to introduce me as his best friend, which we were, and that was it. Was that good enough for me though? Maybe the drugs were adding to the heightened intensity of the whole situation, but either way, emotions were running high. Drugs or not, meeting the parents in any relationship was a big deal and he wanted me to meet his.

Thanksgiving day arrived quicker than I had hoped and by morning he had not called to confirm the time for dinner yet. Cheri and I kept our plans to meet up for Thanksgiving lunch at the Irish bar and were pleasantly surprised to find it wasn't too busy and we could actually talk.

The lunch conversation focused on what we were thankful for and the looming meeting with the people who came together and bore the beautiful fucked-up mess of a man that I loved and that she had once been involved with. What a twisted web of loves and lies this man had created. And we had both fallen into his trap. Maybe that added another level to our friendship, but I tended to stay away from bringing up her involvement with him, as it seemed like a soft spot for her. She had gotten over him and was good at being civil with him, but still held some residual feelings.

Thanksgiving lunch was pretty good but the drinks were better! We had our fair share each and I finally got up the nerve to call Liam. No answer.

I called again later and again there was no answer. What a fucking flake! What the hell was he doing to me? My heart was already in a twisted mess because of this man and this just added to the carnage. How had I let myself get so attached to a man with such a heinous track record? My friends were always trying to tell me that it was a bad idea. Hell, they told me that about a lot of things. But I didn't listen to the warnings about any of it! I wholeheartedly believed our relationship was different, magical and beyond compare. I had a once world-famous rock star questioning his own sexuality for me and I was willing to stick by his side while he figured it all out. I guess the 'woman' in me believed, like so many do, that I was going to be the one to change him, to fix him. But what I failed to realize was there was no possible way I could fix anyone before I fixed myself.

Thanksgiving night came and went. I don't remember much of it because I drank myself into a blackout, overcome with emotions. I didn't call him or hear from him for almost a week and I was okay with it. He had hurt me pretty badly. But I was not a weak enough person to go crying back to him for his attention. I wasn't necessarily trying to prove a point or hurt him back, but maybe I was. The expression 'hell hath no fury like a woman scorned' came to mind. Ha! But what's the saying for a gay boy with the heart of a woman scorned?! What's scarier than hell and more vengeful than the devil? Whatever that is, was what you would find if you hurt me. So maybe, just maybe, my cold shoulder resonated all that towards him because later that week around 3:30 a.m. I got a call. This call was different than any other because it was the first time I heard him really sound sorry and like he missed me.

"Hey... Hey... What are you doing Kaleb?" he said with a slur.

"I'm at home with a friend hanging out enjoying the sounds of the rain... What do you want?" I said, trying not to let the anger sound over apparent.

"I've been up for a few days and I can't stop thinking about... that... that video ... idea...," he said, taking a moment to take a drink of something then continued, "I want to see you... to... to uh... uh... to try out that part in the video..."

He was barely audible and his slurred speech was almost uninterpretable, but I was getting most of what he was saying. Still a little confused, I asked for clarity, "What the hell are you talking about Liam?! You do know it's almost 4 a.m. and pouring rain outside? You want to come over and do what part of the video?"

Again his voice was quiet and I could tell he was struggling to put into words the thoughts that were circling in his head. I had heard this voice before. Usually after days of drinking, multiple bags of cocaine, and any other drugs and pills he could get his hands on.

"Kaleb, I want to drive to your apartment... and turn the radio up loud ... and...and sing that part... You'd be like the girl in the video I'm trying ... trying to get back."

Really?! Was this actually a conversation that

was happening? If this wasn't my real life I would swear it was a scene from a movie or Lifetime channel show. My inner Juliet wanted to let him come be my Romeo outside the window. But the logical person on the outside, who had already been getting looks from his neighbors for hosting late night after parties just about every night, knew that it was not a good idea to let it happen. I didn't want to set off any more red flags with my building. Having a man come and sing at the top of his lungs with music blaring in the pouring rain at nearly 4 a.m. would surely have been an instance where the cops were called and a real possibility that the apartment management might take advantage of the situation to get me out of there. That was not something I was willing to let happen because I loved my apartment and my life at that very moment, no matter how fucked up it seemed to everyone else.

So I talked the rock star out of coming to my place that night in fears of repercussion from the law. But what I didn't stop to think about at the time was, maybe I was holding back this man I loved from trying to really express his inner feelings for me for the first time in the only way he knew possible. A friend and I were discussing the call later and she helped me take a step back and think about what was actually going on there. He was a bonafide rock star who, throughout his career, made music geared towards hard-core type men. He was known for his womanizing and bad boy ways and undoubtedly had never had feelings like this towards someone like me. He was more than likely fighting the demons in his head on a daily basis as to whether or not to show me... to show the world. What would the fans think if one day he just came out as bisexual and started dating someone who was well known for their Britney Spears impersonations? The publicity really could have gone either way, but I believe the backlash would have been incredible and the hard core straight male fan base he had accumulated would not understand.

This was something I had been thinking about too, as our relationship had grown into whatever it was. I was trying to help him get back into the music business and I knew that he needed to be perceived in a certain way, even if that meant I would not be getting the relationship I had always dreamed of.

I LOVED this man and I was willing to make whatever personal sacrifices I had to make in order to get him back to the top. The next month would produce one of those great sacrifices as I would soon find out, but as this month known for 'thankful' thinking came to a close, I tried to put my life into perspective. I thought about all the beautiful craziness that surrounded me and had to stop and ask myself, "Is this all really worth it? Is this what I am thankful for?"

THE GIFTS I'D
BEEN GIVEN

DECEMBER is a month full of holiday cheer and wonderful moments of closeness with the people we love. I was always a big fan of the holidays growing up because my mother was the best at throwing our family holiday party and she always worked her ass off to get me the best presents every year. I missed those easier times: the good times with a family who loved me and a childhood with no stress or responsibilities. When my mother died it was like Christmas died for me too. I had spent many a Christmas with good friends, but I had yet to find anything truly similar to those Christmas Eve get-togethers enveloped in the love of my mother, grandmother and cousins.

This year I had a stronger group of close-knit friends then I had ever had in West Hollywood. I was looking forward to putting together an event for the ones who would be staying in the city for the holiday. I was still living off my severance package and doing a few digital print jobs for the cake shop as well as producing holiday chocolate bars through my own company for new clients and people I knew.

On the financial books, it appeared as though I was doing pretty well, even though I wasn't quite to the point of being able to pay all my bills without my severance package just yet. I was going to live it up and enjoy the holidays and when the fourth or fifth month of my six-month severance package came up, then I would really start worrying about rent and bills.

At the beginning of the month, I went to my favorite crab place with my favorite German friend Annette. Our friendship came about in such a random way and it was one of those meant-to-happen friendships. My grandmother and my mother were 100% German, so I had always been around the German language and traditions. Becoming friends with Annette was like becoming friends with an estranged family member. She would always try and teach me more German than the naughty words I knew and turned me on to some interesting German music.

We met through a mutual bisexual ex-fling and, though we tried to remain friends with him, he got a little crazy on us and started talking some neo-Nazi type bullshit that really turned us off. Even though our relationships with him didn't end well, it was amazing that we had found each other as a result; one of those Universal happenings I didn't quite understand at the time, but would become more educated about in the months to follow.

When we arrived at Hot n' Juicy we were pleasantly surprised to see our buddy Tad there, looking just as cute as ever but in a new outfit. The owners had promoted my flirty man-crush to manager and the promotion was well deserved. He was just as good an employee as he was a dreamboat! Annette and I ordered our usual buckets of custom crab wonderfulness and the usual girl talk ensued. She had never met Liam and it was actually kind of nice to have a friend I could talk to who was outside of the party scene. She was like an older sister to me and our bond was very strong. She was mother of a lovely young girl who I had become close with as well. When Annette and I talked, her motherly instincts would sometimes take over and she was always there with the logical advice.

This evening the conversation centered around how Liam had hurt me on Thanksgiving by giving no real excuse why he invited me to meet his parents and then it never happened. We also discussed the odd call he made to me about wanting to sing outside my window and of course our Christmas party plans.

"I hate to see you get hurt, Kaleb, especially by a man like that. It sounds to me like he doesn't really know what he wants and you are extra confusing to him. Are you going to invite him to our little get together?" she asked, as she delicately placed her napkin on her lap.

"Sure, I'm going to invite him, but just to be nice. He's been such a flake lately, I'm sure he won't show up. I won't get my expectations up or anything. I've done that too much already," I said, taking a sip from the glass of Chardonnay Tad had dropped off as a VIP gift.

"That's the best thing to do. Don't let that guy get to you! Rock star or not, you don't deserve to be treated that way by him or any man!" Annette said in her comforting German accent.

I knew she was right and I knew I deserved better than the quasi relationship we were in. But I was holding out hope that maybe something would make him change and eventually he would be able really give 'us' a shot.

We discussed the plans for the holidays and decided we would get together Christmas Day instead of Christmas Eve like my family used to do. That was something I was really pushing for but the majority of the group already had plans for that night. So we scheduled Christmas afternoon at my place for the get together and everyone would bring a dish to complement the turkey dinner my 'husband' Cheri and I would be making.

We said our goodbyes to Tad and the crew then to each other. I was going to head home but decided to meet up with Jackie at The State Room for a couple of drinks before calling it a night. On the cab ride from LaBrea to San Vicente Boulevard, I got a call from Michael, one of my best friends from Texas. He and I went to junior high and high school together. Michael told me he was finally going to come and visit me for about a month like we had been planning for a long time. He said he would arrive in February, a few days after my birthday and was looking forward to it.

I was super excited about this because he was a lifelong friend. I still called him almost every night to just talk. We were so close when I lived in Texas. He was there to keep me grounded when the whole Sarah Summers adventures were taking off. Now with the Liam drama, he was always there with the right words to not let it all go to my head.

Excited with that news, I arrived at The State Room with a happy-go-lucky, let's party attitude. Jackie met up with me and there were of course a bunch of the regulars already enjoying their evening. I ordered a Kaleb's Kool-Aid and filled Jackie in on the Christmas plans and the Liam drama she had missed while she was home visiting family. Jackie was always one of those glass half-full gals and her advice was always congruent with my emotional needs. She always told me to stick it out cause, "You gotta fight for what you want!" And "if it's meant to be it will all work out in the end."

I loved her for that attitude and we always had a good time together. Tonight would be another one of those fun evenings, but with an added twist that neither one of us quite expected to affect us the way it did.

We drank and carried on through the night and at around midnight we went on the hunt for 'kitty,' but were unable to find it as readily as usual. A guy we knew said he knew a guy that could get something for us, but it would be a little stronger. As long as it wasn't heroin or anything with a needle, I didn't see a problem with trying it. That was something I had promised my mother years ago. Being an emergency room nurse at the beginning of her career, she often told me of the horrific things she had seen come into those rooms due to heroin and drugs of its caliber. She made me promise to never do any drug that used a needle and also promise that I would never do acid. I have kept those promises ever since.

What this guy had to offer us was crystal methamphetamine. I was sort of familiar with this drug as I had tried it back in Texas a few times and didn't remember it having many bad side effects. I remember it had made me stay up for a long time but didn't remember much more than that. We agreed to purchase some this night, just to give it a try, and then we would go back to 'kitty' when our guy came back around.

We stayed up all night and late into the afternoon working on artistic projects and computer cleanup. We got so focused on whatever task was in front of us that we forgot to eat and didn't drink many fluids. By the time it wore off, we were tired, thirsty and very hungry but we were pleased with the fact we had done so much work on our individual projects and had a good time doing it. Maybe this crystal stuff wasn't so bad after all. We were strong-willed people who wouldn't get addicted to it, right? Wishful thinking. The drug became something I would do pretty frequently and Liam even started doing that along with cocaine and drinking with me, too.

It didn't really seem like a big deal to me, as I always went out and presented myself in a pretty coherent manner, or so I thought. I was still running my business and taking care of the side jobs for the cake shop, so it appeared to me that I had mastered being a functioning addict, although there were some nights when it really was more apparent that I was not as 'functioning' as I thought I was. This realization didn't come until a few months down the line.

As Christmas was approaching, I was going about my normal routine of partying daily and working on my business. I had also found a new love for digital painting, which I had become rather good at! I had even made a special painting for Liam that I was going to present to him on Christmas or whenever he decided to show his face.

Liam and I had still been hanging out but it was no longer an everyday thing. I don't know if he was upset with me for not moving in with him when he asked, or the fact that I didn't let his crazy ass come sing to me that night. It felt like he was getting further and further away from me. I knew he still had love for me though, as we did talk on the phone pretty often. But it seemed a little strained.

It was Christmas Eve before I knew it and I was all alone at home feeling rather sad and lonely wishing for those days of the past spent celebrating with my family. I hadn't seen Liam in about a week and the way things had been going between us I hadn't expected to hear from him this night of all nights. But I did.

This was one of those rare moments when he became exactly the man I wanted him to be. A man that showed up for me when no one else would and would find a way to show how much he cared at exactly the right time. He made it hard for me to stay mad at him, especially when he did something as chivalrous as he did that night.

He must have known I was alone and feeling down because I had told him about how important Christmas Eve was to my family. I was surprised when he called me around 7 p.m. to check on me and ask how I was doing, but the real surprise came with his second question, "Kaleb, do you want me to come over so we can spend some time together tonight on Christmas Eve?"

This would not seem like a shocking question to most people who had been involved with someone for as long as we had been, but this was the man who had never been to my apartment and was rarely seen outside his house or the bars. All of a sudden he was asking me if he could come to my place to see me... on Christmas Eve! Had he finally decided to step up and be the man I was dreaming of? Was this my Christmas gift from the Universe?

"Of course you can come over Liam... I would love that. What time should I expect you?" I said with a glimmer of hope welling up inside.

"Within the hour," he replied and hung up.

Since these words were coming from the same man who just last month asked me to meet his parents and then totally flaked, I obviously had not really put much faith in him actually showing up. But he did. Like he said he would.

He rang the buzzer and I granted him access to my building and, in a way, was granting him access to my heart once again. He knocked on my door and I was relieved to see he appeared to be sober and put together, which was another welcomed surprise. He sat next to me on the couch and our bodies relaxed next to each other with a sense of security that we both had been missing as of late. It was one of those moments where every indiscretion, every let down and every bit of pain disappeared and all was forgiven.

For that moment, we were the two people who met at the bar all those months ago. The unlikely duo so infatuated with the each other, the pair so comfortable just being ourselves together, it was all I could ask for right then and there. It was perfection, just being close to the person I had come to love, and him feeling free in the privacy of my company.

I made us some drinks, we did some 'kitty' and we talked and sang for hours before we decided to exchange gifts.

I had ordered a large print of the digital art piece I had done for him as a Christmas gift, which was a heartfelt expression of how I felt for this man. The artwork I created was a painting of his face with tears in his eyes and swatches of red covering up different areas of the canvas. It showed his constant struggle with so many things, but also the softer side that only I was allowed to see. He was very touched by the print and was moved to present me with a gift of his own. He had been wearing a red scarf nearly every day as the weather had dropped into the 60s. I had worn it a few times at the bar, taken directly from his neck. He gave me the scarf that night as a token of affection. Maybe in the back of his mind he was really giving it to me so I would wear it often and everyone would know that it, and I, were his. I could never tell where his thoughts were, as he was never completely open with me. More importantly, he was never really open with himself. The gift meant a lot to me, but him showing up for me that night meant even more. As we grew tired, he called a car to take him home and I went to bed happy for the first time in a long, long time.

The next morning was Christmas Day. Cheri was there bright and early with all the groceries and we started to prepare the meal. Our cooking experience was very husband and wife-ish, but being true to our relationship, she was in charge of the meat and I was in charge of the baking. We had a blast getting all the food prepared and during the preparations I informed her about the previous night's encounter.

Cheri was pretty shocked to hear he had actually been so sweet. She almost didn't believe it until I showed her the scarf.

"That's his scarf alright... Seen him wear it a million times. I am glad you had a good experience last night, Kaleb. Believe me it's rare," she said, as she basted the turkey.

A few hours later, Annette, her daughter and our other English friend Rupert, arrived to enjoy the festivities. We exchanged Secret Santa-style gifts as we ate the traditional Christmas meal and drank copious amounts of wine. Rupert shared with us a video he said was a traditional viewing event in England around the holidays. Annette recognized it too, as something she had seen in Germany. We searched the Internet for the video entitled, "Dinner for One." What I saw was a mixture of slapstick humor with a hint of sadness.

I may have been oversensitive watching the video of a woman sitting at a table eating a holiday dinner with imaginary friends. Her sweet butler, pretending to serve each guest, got progressively more drunk as the clip went on. Made me think about the direction my life might actually be headed. Would I eventually wind up all alone in a fantasy world where no one was really there for me? I had felt that way for years, but at this moment I had a group of real friends around me and I felt loved once again. My darkest hour was just around the corner, but that night, the vision of a sad lonely future was nowhere to be found. For that I was grateful, and even more, thankful for the gifts I'd been given.

PERFUME

WITH CHRISTMAS behind us, we all started preparing for New Year's Eve. Our plan was to share the night with friends at The State Room. It was one plan that would actually come to fruition, but not without a few dramatic turn of events.

The day started out like any other in West Hollywood, with the sun shining down on a chilly winter afternoon. I had just completed some edible graphic art for another local cake shop and was paid upon delivery, meaning I had plenty of money to party the night away. Jackie and I were hanging out, getting all the necessary party supplies put together for what was going to be another exciting evening with the crew. Britney Spears had just released her latest album and I had it on constant repeat. Loving every second of it, I didn't realize that this album was actually a storybook background track to my life at the time.

"Work Bitch" came in handy as an anthem for my chocolate bar company. When you are focused on making money to continue living a certain rock star lifestyle, it is a very motivational song. "Alien" was a retelling of how I felt at The State Room most of the time and my relationship with Liam. "The light in your eyes lets me know I'm not alone, not alone..." being a string of lyrics resonating quite deeply in me as a comparison with the way Liam and I felt for each other. "Lived a wasteful life in a hateful city ... Til I found you" from another song spoke to the openness and love I found when I was with him. The song "It Should Be Easy" represented my willingness to open my heart to him and, even though I had been warned, give him the benefit of the doubt that he would not "break my heart, break me apart..."

The song that my life ended up becoming a real life music video to was "Perfume." But I can't say I didn't have a hand in the instances that lead to it happening that way. I'll fill you in on the song and how it became a battle tactic of mine a little later, but let's take a look back at the last few months and put together the pieces of a twisted puzzle that would finally come together on this night. The night we are supposed to celebrate the new year ahead with the one that we love.

Liam and I had been growing further and further apart as the past few months flew by. My dear friend Anna Lynn had seemed to have almost vanished from the bar scene. She had been giving him rides home and he had been insisting that I include her in our musical comeback plans. There were events they were both scheduled to come to, but both coincidentally had 'emergencies' to take care of. On top of those instances, he had been inviting me less and less to his house when I asked to stop by and see him. It wasn't until early that afternoon when I got a text confirming all my suspicions. The text read:

"I wanted to tell you because you are one of my good friends and you deserve to know. Liam and I have been hooking up for a while now and we are gonna make it public and I just wanted you to be prepared. <3 Anna Lynn."

BITCH.

I guess I had known all along. But maybe because it was always behind closed doors, I never had to see it. I tried to pretend it wasn't happening. Like people always say, "What you don't know can't hurt you." Right?

Wrong.

I had been preparing for this moment for a while. I was gonna kill that fucking tramp! Blonde, big boobed Sarah Summers wannabe!

While malicious thoughts cruised through my mental highway, so did thoughts of regret and what ifs. What if I really was Sarah Summers? If I had been born a girl or transitioned all those years ago when I had seriously considered it, would he be public with me right now? But if that was the case, would I even be with him? He can't possibly feel the way he does for me ... for her? Was she trying to use him to get a story for the gossip magazine she worked for? Should I have put out when he asked me to? Had I been the one actually holding back what could have been? No. He wasn't ready to admit to anyone that he had feelings for me. I guess, for him, it would just be easier if he started seeing a girl so that the rumors would cease

I wasn't going to let them get away with this betrayal though. They would never know the plan I was cooking up. I was going to give them my blessing and we would become the three amigos. Perchance the rumor mill might really start going on a three-way relationship? I was going to keep my friends close and my slut of an ex-best friend, now frenemy, even closer. Kill them with diabolical kindness.

I didn't text her back immediately after receiving her message though. I gave them time to stew on what they had just done to me. Make them think I was completely furious. Which of course I was. But I had a party to attend and I was sure the news had already begun to spread. So I prepared for the worst. I was not going to cry or be weak. The actor in me was ready and, with a couple of puffs of the glass pipe, I was ready to take on the night!

Jackie, one of my lead partners in crime, and I downed a few drinks at my place then headed up the half a block walk to The State Room where Cheri and the crew were already waiting for us. Liam and Anna Lynn were a no show and I was okay with that. I wasn't quite ready to deal with that whole situation anyway. It was New Year's Eve damn it! We were gonna have some fun!

The night was a blast from what we all can remember. I think Jackie, Cheri and I gave one another a friendly kiss and then Cheri, sweet drunk Cheri, was making out with our friend Samir and he was trying to get her to go home with him! I was trying to be protective and was able to talk her out of it. We all went back to my place for a little after party before passing out.

January was the month I put my plan into action. I was not going to lose my relationship with Liam to some real-life version of my alter ego. I made sure throughout the month that the three of us got together as much as possible. When we did, I was always the one with the 'kitty' or sitting next to him or making him laugh and finding any excuse to take him off to the side to have some alone closeness.

The song "Perfume" by Britney Spears had become my anthem and my biggest weapon in the war of love. "So I wait for you to call and I try to act natural. Have you been thinking about her... about me? While I wait I put on my perfume... I want it all over you. I'm gonna mark my territory. I'll never tell, tell on myself but I hope she smells my perfume." Of course there were moments of jealousy, but I was ready with this plan laid out for me in song. Everyone knew my scent, especially him, and her. I wore 'Fantasy,' the perfume by Britney Spears. Maybe that too was another sign I had never seen because my life was sort of a Fantasy, with a rock star as my Prince UnCharming.

Before every outing where I knew I would see him, I made sure to put on extra sprays of my perfume, in the pink fantastical bottle, in the areas of my body I knew I would be touching him with. I got some sense of winning, knowing that when she would go to kiss him, hug him or anything else, she would smell me all over him and maybe for a second have a feeling of insecurity.

These games we played continued as the football season was coming to a close with one of the most public expressions of our three-way 'thing' planned for the big play-off game that would be shown at the bar. Our appearance was sure to make people talk.

The NFC Championship Game was a big game for our group of friends as it was a battle between the San Francisco 49ers and the Seattle Seahawks! Our friend, the bartender, was a huge Seahawks fan and he and I had a playful bar rivalry when it came to sports. Why? Like I said before, this bar had brought out the sports-loving man deep inside me that really got into the games when I was there. I guess watching the games had become just as fun as playing the emotional ones. This day ended up being a hearty mix of both.

The game had already started when I walked in, fashionably late of course. Waiting for me at the bar was an empty seat next to Liam and Anna Lynn. I almost couldn't believe there was a seat open at all, because the bar was completely full, almost overflowing! It was kind of awesome to see it this busy! Whether the staff liked it or not, I took a lot of pride in that place and was happy when the successes came. I sat next to Liam as Anna Lynn ordered us a round of drinks and shots. He commented on my look for the day, "You look good, rock star butch! Haha"

I guess I had been 'butch-ing' it up lately, wearing a baseball cap turned sideways with my all black shirts, jeans and leather jacket. I loved that jacket and so did Anna Lynn. She was always trying on all my outerwear. This day she decided she wanted to wear my hat and jacket for a selfie we took together.

"Bitch get your own look... Hell, get your own man!" I thought, while flashing a fake smile for the camera and motioning the bartender for another drink.

The game went on and it was great, but my team lost (not without playing a hell of a good game though) and I gave congratulations to our bartender friend. As the bar started to slowly clear out, I had to prepare myself for the last game I would play that evening. Before I said my goodbyes to the crew, I took a solo trip to the bathroom to do a line of 'kitty' and reapply my 'Fantasy' scent. As I left, I gave Anna Lynn a quick hug barely touching her but paused for a long, very hands on, full body contact hug with Liam. If I wasn't going to be wherever they ended up that night, you better believe that bitch would be smelling my perfume.

LAST CALL

F E B R U A R Y is always a special month for me. I kind of consider it MY month! My birthday is on the first, the Super Bowl is on shortly after, and of course the day of love is on the fourteenth. What is there not to love about February? This month, normally associated with everything happy and love-filled, would turn out to be one of the hardest months of my life. February would also hold the ending of many, very close, relationships.

February 1st, my birthday, seemed to come and go pretty uneventfully. The rent was due, but like every other previous month of the last few years my old boss at the cake shop who wrote the check for my rent was late with it. He usually got the check to me by the third, which was the cutoff date. So I wasn't too worried. I put the thought out of my mind and prepared for my birthday evening.

My partying ways had been getting the best of me, meaning my pool of friends had been dwindling. I hadn't really planned anything special, so it was no real surprise when not many people came to celebrate my day of birth.

In the afternoon, I had a few drinks alone at the bar with Liam, which was surprising and nice. It had been our first real me and him time since Christmas Eve. It was pleasant, although he had forgotten to get me a present. But at that point in our relationship, just stealing him away from Anna Lynn for a few hours was present enough. You better believe he left with the lingering smell of 'Fantasy' all over his clothes!

That evening, Jackie was off celebrating our shared birthday with her other friends, but my bestie Cheri and our mutual friend Britta were there with thoughtful gifts and a lovely dinner at The State Room. I was lucky to have such an amazing friend as Cheri. She was one of those people who had been through a pretty rocky time in her life, survived, and never judged me on the life I lived. She was my best friend. If I had been born a straight man (or if she had been born a gay man) we probably would have been married. Everyone should have a friend like that.

The Super Bowl was the next day and it was also the day that my other best friend would come into town. Michael and I had been friends since junior high and we had been involved in choir together as well as in a lot of the same honors classes. Our favorite class was PEAK English, which was part of their Gifted and Talented program. We were both very gifted and talented, but we were also social outcasts. I was a plump kid back then with big glasses and my hair parted in the middle. He was a bookworm with glasses even bigger than mine. He always had his head down, wandering off into the make-believe world of his many different books.

I was able to get him out of those books for a while. He would come over to my house after school and we would take part in role-playing games in my front yard. We didn't play those dungeons and dragons board game type role-playing games, we actually played roles! We would become our favorite characters from 'Buffy the Vampire Slayer' and make up live action adventures of our own. I was always Buffy Summers of course, she was the star, and one badass bitch (this is where I would get my name for my female illusion alter ego later in life). He was always Giles, the well-educated watcher and teacher of the slayer. As we grew older, these character relationships kind of became our real-life relationship. Michael was always there with educated advice and a watchful eye over me as my star began to rise. I was a real-life Buffy, a young person going out into the world all alone, battling through circumstances that most normal people never had to experience. Thankfully, I always had my Giles to watch over me and aid me in the fight.

He arrived on the 2nd day of February, just as the super bowl pre-game show had started to air. It was wonderful to see his familiar face at my door once again. Michael's arrival took me back to that safe place in my heart where I felt like I was that young kid full of extreme dreams with hopes of a brighter future. Having him in LA was also like having a piece of my past "regular" life haphazardly inserted into my current "rock star" lifestyle.

We hugged and as he sat his bags down on the floor, I began to get dressed up to go to the bar to watch the game. I hid smoking the glass pipe from him that first day as I wasn't quite sure how he would view it. So I got my high on in the bathroom as I got ready for us to head out of the apartment. I don't know what it was about that new stuff, the crystal, but it made me feel more alive, more creative and gave me a sense of being present without any fears. I was also able to drink more than normal amounts of liquor without feeling drunk, so I was able to actually carry on conversations with people and take notice of what was going on around me.

Before I started using crystal and cocaine, I was the blackout Queen of West Hollywood. Friends told outlandish stories of crazy things I had done after a night of binge drinking that were almost impossible for me to believe. I didn't remember any of the events they would tell me about and after looking up the definition of a blackout online I understood why. "The receptors to the brain that make new memories are blocked but you still have all of your previous knowledge and can function." Scary. But my question was why did I act out so much when I was blacked out? I guess I was an angry drunk. I had been holding back so much pain and regret for so long that maybe my subconscious or my dark side was finally able to free itself during those blackouts. My friends did not like the person I became. They compared me to Jekyll and Hyde on numerous occasions. I had that under control for now, but it was just more addiction on top of other addictions. It never seemed like it would end. In fact, none of it seemed like it would ever end. The partying, the lifestyle, the "friendships" at The State Room and the beautiful fantasy of reckless abandon that I thought I thrived in. But it did. And it all came crashing down hard and fast.

We went to the bar and watched the game. It was a pretty lackluster Super Bowl as the Seahawks annihilated their opponents with a sense of ease. We still had a good time. I had fun introducing my old friend into this new world I had been sucked into. It was worlds away from my life he had seen the previous year when he visited for a week, and universes away from our old life back in Fort Worth, Texas when we were younger.

He got along pretty well with most everyone. When I told them that he was a world-class masseur, they liked him even more. Some poked fun at the way he dressed and the length of his hair and nails, but I tried my hardest not to let those hurtful words get to him. I didn't care what they thought, because he was my best friend. I knew he would be there for me when these 'friends' were not. I hoped he would any way.

As the month went on, one of my favorite holidays was approaching. I was hoping to celebrate it with the man I loved and with my best friends by my side. I hadn't really planned anything special, but I was holding out hope that maybe

Liam would surprise me like he did on Christmas Eve. He didn't.

I got word from my circle of "friends" that Anna Lynn had moved in with Liam. I was immediately devastated. Wow! That bitch moved fast. Of course, all my thoughts of regrets started to return. I became overcome with a feeling of hopelessness I had never felt before. I knew she was no good for him, but he was too blind to see it. Now I could do nothing to stop the imminent poisoning of his easily susceptible mind. I left Michael at my apartment that night and went to The State Room to drink the pain away alone.

I was sitting with a couple of guys I knew and we were going on like always. But after a few drinks, I wanted to sit at my usual table to relax. When I ventured to the lounge area of the bar, my table had been taken by some rough-looking guys. I sat down at another table close by. I guess I was giving them the stink eye or something because one of the guys started yelling at me!

"What the fuck are you looking at, faggot?!" yelled one of the men.

"Yo! Chill out... I'm not looking at you, man," I said, half-drunk and kind of bitchy. "That's just my usual table. How long are you guys gonna be there?"

"As long as we fucking want, you little bitch! Fag!" the other guy responded, as he started to get up and approach me.

What the fuck? That escalated quick. The other guy got up and moved towards me, too. Once they were both standing directly over me, one of the guys decided to flip the hat off my head in a sign of aggression. That was not cool. I didn't touch those guys and believe me they could have easily kicked my ass. But at that moment the angry drunk she-devil inside of me came out!

I jumped out of my seat and onto the table in front of me and screamed, "What the fuck, man?! There's no reason to fucking touch me!! I'll fucking kill you!!"

Thank God my buff friend Jake and the bartender had been keeping an eye on me because they ran over to take the guys out of the bar before anything really bad happened. Overcome with anger and confusion, I threw the contents of my drink at the attackers before they left. I hadn't been called a faggot in years, and even though that bar was considered a straight bar, I was never offended like that in all the time I had been going there. Jake and the bartender came back in to calm me down. I guess the news of the encounter had already made it up to the office as the manager came over to the table too. I was pretty good friends with the manager, as I had known him from his last job and we had all become pretty close since this new place opened. But even friendship wasn't enough to save me from the bad news about to come out of his mouth.

"Kaleb, I'm sorry this happened to you, but I'm gonna have to ask you to leave, too. Unfortunately, we won't be able to have you back for a while either. So as of right now, you are 86'd," he said with a hint of sadness to his voice. He did let me have one last drink as it was nearing last call, but that would be the last night I was officially allowed into The State Room.

What a shit-show of a Valentine's Day that turned out to be! Anna Lynn moved in with Liam and I got banned from the one place I truly loved going to. Could this month get any worse?

Yes...yes it could. And it did.

The next morning came around and I filled Michael in on what had happened. He was a little shocked and said, "I thought they loved you there? Hell, I thought you worked there the way you carried on at that place!" I did feel love at The State Room. I did a lot of promoting and helping out. I assisted in putting up the Christmas decorations for Christ's sake!! I guess my larger-than-life character was sometimes more than they could handle. To be honest, it wasn't the first time I had been banned from a bar, but it was the first time it affected me so deeply.

I got pretty depressed that first week and was doing more crystal and kitty than ever before. I even started doing it in front of Michael and persuaded him to try it. He tried it a few times but did not get addicted to it like the rest of us. I still didn't think I was addicted. But looking back, at one night in particular, the signs were obvious and quite sad.

It was a few days after Valentine's Day. Jackie, Michael and I had just gotten back to my apartment after spending the night out at The Twisted Rainbow and had a few more drinks. Jackie and I were smoking our glass pipes. Michael decided to go to bed in the other room while we stayed up and hung out. We had been smoking and playing games for a while before we noticed we were both out of the stuff. Our dealer was not answering his phone, so there was no way to get more right then. Or was there? I came up with a new game for us to play. While it was fun at the time, being high, it was actually very, very sad. I suggested we pretend we were treasure hunters and start searching everywhere for crystals! Each equipped with a pair of tweezers, we moved couches, turned over pillows, inspected all the surfaces we had broken it up on, checked every drawer and old glass pipes.

We searched for an hour or so, yelling out to each other after we found each tiny rock. At the end of the 'treasure hunt,' we had about enough for a bowl each and this time we took our time with it. How could two smart, creative, loving people turn into such drug-obsessed, weak, time-wasting people? The drug was stronger than our will at the time and, in my case, I was already so broken inside that it was easy for the addiction to take control. It wore off hours later and, over-exhausted, she left. I went to bed to sleep for most of the next day.

The following day came and I went to the coffee shop up the hill from my house to work on a couple of different projects for the cake shop. While I was at the café, which faced The State Room, I was overcome with grief. But I took that pain and was able to make some beautiful digital art after finishing my projects for the shop. I left the coffee shop feeling better. The walk down the block in the cool breeze lifted my spirits even more. I was in a good mood until I got home and found Michael sitting on the couch with an envelope in his hand and a worried look on his face.

"Someone came by and knocked on the door and said to give it to you. I didn't know what to do so I just answered the door and took it... I'm sorry," he said, as he handed me the letter.

EVICTION NOTICE was written in red across the front of the envelope. My heart immediately sank back into the pit of despair. This had to be a mistake, or for another apartment, because I had turned in the rent check the week before, even though it was a couple of days late.

I opened the envelope to find a returned check and a letter stating that I had to vacate the premises on the grounds that since my check had been delivered late every month (I knew that Tim's lateness each month was eventually going to come back to haunt me!) and the fact that this check bounced, the management no longer saw me as a fit tenant. I freaked the fuck out. How could this happen?! How could a check from this thriving cake shop have bounced?! I instantaneously got on the phone with Tim, the owner of the cake shop, to ask him what had happened. He said there was a bank error and some fraudulent activity on the business account and that must be why it got returned. He said he would get me a new check immediately. The building management, however, was not going to have it. They wanted me out.

It finally happened. All those late-night parties, the rumors about drugs, the complaints from neighbors were all coming back to kick me in the ass. I knew why they were really trying to kick me out and it wasn't because of late rent. It wasn't like I was the only person in that building doing drugs and having loud parties all the time. But for some reason, I was the one that got the short end of the stick this month.

I really didn't know what to do at this point, so I turned to the internet to see what my rights were as a tenant. I found some interesting facts that put my mind at ease for a little while. I was going to fight this however I could, so I wouldn't lose the apartment I loved so much. Michael was no real help during the whole process either. He had come to Los Angeles to see if he could start a massage business here, maybe seeing himself moving to the city to inspire a new purpose in life. But that didn't happen. He became lazy, slept all day and had no drive to help me find an answer to my problem. He wasn't looking for a job or following any of the leads on potential clients and ideas I was giving him. I was actually awaiting the day when he had to go back to Texas now, as I was becoming more and more frustrated with him every day. This was the person I considered to be my lifelong best friend and here he was just sitting idly by watching my world come crashing down. This was the situation that would end our friendship. For that I was truly sad, but when he finally left that month, I was glad to see him go.

Tim was no help either as it seemed he had really given up trying to help me, too. This was the man

I considered a father and he, too, seemed to act like there was nothing he could do. Maybe he was trying to teach me a lesson or something but, in the state of mind I was in, it was an act of betrayal. It put a huge cloud of darkness over our relationship, too.

I found a lawyer online and my dear friend Jackie, who had been let go from her job too, was kind enough to loan me $300 from her severance package to pay the lawyer fees, giving us a little more time at my apartment. My world was crumbling all around me and the only thing I could do was drink and use drugs to mask the pain. At one point, I even traded my old laptop and my Nintendo to my dealer so I could get enough drugs to last me through the end of the month. I thought it couldn't get any worse. But it did.

Early one morning, near the end of the month, I got a call I never expected. A Texas phone number I hadn't seen in a while flashed across my iPhone screen. I answered it with hesitation.

"Kaleb, good morning, this is Chaplain Brown down here at the prison in south Texas. I have some news about your father and I wanted you to hear it from me," said the man on the other end of the phone.

I had talked to this man a few months earlier when I received a letter from my dad. Instead of writing him back (which I rarely did) I decided to do some research and get the number to the chaplain and see if I could actually talk to my father. My father had been in jail since I was in 7th grade. Being so young at the time, my mother kept most of the details of the trial a secret from me. I knew he had done something bad and was sentenced to prison for a very long time, but I was never told why his punishment was so severe. In the letters I had gotten from my father over the years, he would tell me about his life in prison and how he had become a man of God. He said he was the director of the church choir and leader of a group of prisoners that would put on shows for the prisoners' families and groups that came to visit. He always did have a wonderful singing voice and loved to act. I guess I can thank him for some of those gifts.

Knowing all that he told me over the years, I figured he had a good rapport with the religious figure at the prison and I was right. The chaplain spoke very highly of my father the first time I spoke with him and even allowed me chances to speak with my dad a few times via phone. This was a privilege not given to most prisoners or their families at this particular facility. This call was different though. His voice seemed to have an air of sadness and urgency to it.

"Hello, Chaplain Brown, this is a surprise," I said, knowing something was wrong.

"Kaleb, I'm sorry to have to be the one to tell you this but your father has prostate cancer and the outlook is not good. We think he is on the last leg of this journey and I wanted you to have the chance to get to talk to him one last time before the inevitable."

"I understand," I replied out loud, but inside I felt the exact opposite. I had always dreamed that maybe one day he would get out and I would have a real parent again. I always hated him for leaving me when I was young. I hated him for what he had done and the pain he caused to the people I loved. I always hoped he had truly changed and one day I would get to see that new man in person. Fate decided it was not to be. This was my last chance to hear what he had to say and my final opportunity to speak the words I had been reluctant to speak.

"I'll put him on the phone now, Kaleb, and give you guys a few minutes," the chaplain said, as I heard the phone switching hands.

"Hey, number one son, it's your daddy. I just wanted to tell you how much I love you and how proud I am of you. You've come such a long way since your mother died and I just wish I had been there to experience it all with you. I know I messed up bad in the past and all I can do is ask for your forgiveness this one last time. I'm not going to be around much longer and I want to know that you are going to be okay and that you forgive me. I love you, son."

I took a moment to wipe the tears from my eyes and lifted my head up with as much strength as I could muster and said, "I forgive you, Daddy. I love you, too."

The call went on for a few minutes more before I heard the Chaplin say it was time to go. It was then that I realized that everything in my life was changing and, for so many things in my life, this truly was the last call.

HIGH HOPES

"IT'S TIMES LIKE THESE that you find out who your real friends are" was a commonly used quote that kept running through my head as the month of March began. Where were all these so-called friends that seemed to disappear when situations got rough. I had let people stay with me when they were in between homes. Yet when I was in danger of becoming homeless, there was no one there to offer me a room or a couch. Was I really that terrible of a person that no one felt safe enough to have me in their home? I'll admit my drinking and drug use was a problem I was unwilling to acknowledge, but the people I helped had the same problems when they came to me. These same people looked the other way now that I was in need. It broke my heart. I guess that block of ice in my chest that used to resemble a heart was still able to be chipped away at by these constant let downs and disappointments.

It was the first week in March and the last week in my lovely apartment. I had to take a hard look in the mirror at the person I had become. I was no longer that bright-eyed, cheery, hopeful person with grandiose dreams excitedly stepping off that plane from Texas all those years ago. I was a skinny, drug-addicted, hopeless mess of a soul who, at times, felt the only answer was ending it all. I thought about committing suicide often (especially when I realized that I was losing everything I had), but deep down inside there was still a tiny spark of hope in there, begging to once again be a roaring flame. It was that spark that kept me going through all the past hardships and the spark whispering to me that I wasn't done yet. Maybe the spark was actually my mother's voice reminding me of another promise I had made to her years ago.

"Only God can decide when it's your time to die. If you take your own life you will not get to experience all the gifts that God has to give you when his chosen time to take you from this planet comes. Promise me you will never take your own life; I want to see you in Heaven one day," she said, looking at her child on the edge of the bed in my childhood home.

"I promise, Mommy," I remember saying so vividly.

I've kept all the promises I can remember making to my mother and this one always seemed the most important to uphold. She was not a religious woman, she was more of a spiritualist, which is something I began to understand and cling to later in my life's story.

So it was decided. I would not give up! I would find a way to make the best out of this situation, however difficult it may be. I had exhausted all the possibilities I could think of to fix the problem at hand. I asked every person I knew if they would take me in until I found a new place. No one had room for me and my invisible lawyer turned out to be a scam, or so it seemed. As the move-out deadline rapidly approached, I could not get a hold of anyone at the law office. It looked as though my fate was sealed. I would have to move out... but where?! Was I going to be forced to sleep on the street? For the first time in my life I was going to be homeless and that idea really scared me.

During the week before my move out date, I made a couple of new friends up on Sunset Boulevard who turned out to be exactly what I needed at exactly the right time. Leah and Wendy were two spunky, edgy, beautiful and talented chefs who co-owned a swanky restaurant in between the rock 'n' roll nightclubs that lined the Sunset Strip. I met the two of them outside one evening when they were taking a smoke break. I was immediately drawn to their auras. I asked one of the girls, who looked very familiar, if she could spare a cigarette and she kindly obliged. We introduced ourselves and quickly became well acquainted with one another. It was so easy to talk with them and the entrepreneur spirit they possessed was akin to mine, making me like them even more. They invited me in for a glass of fancy wine at their mahogany bar placed against the wall in the dimly candle-lit room. I felt very comfortable with these two ladies from the get go and it was easy to be open with them about my story.

They told me about themselves, too. Leah had been a finalist on a very big cooking series and Wendy had studied abroad to learn her amazing French pastry skills. It wasn't long before the three of us bonded over our troubles with men, while consuming a deep red wine from a part of France I had never heard of. They seemed intrigued by my life story and were especially interested in the stories about Sarah Summers and her rise to fame as well as the most current drama with the rock star.

"I would have killed that backstabbing bitch!" Leah said, referring to the story involving Anna Lynn.

I left the girls that evening with a promise to come the next day for dinner. I headed to The Twisted Rainbow where I was to see an all-girl band I had heard good things about. Anything to get my mind off the looming storm of doom that was getting closer and closer as the days wore on.

When I arrived the group was already mid-show, and I was instantly impressed the second I saw them on stage. The lead singer was also the drummer, which was an impressive feat itself, but their music was what really got me. The music set off something inside of me, rekindling that faint flickering spark a bit more. At that moment, I realized I wanted to sing again like I had done in high school. To sing with a live band at one of the most famous rock 'n' roll bars on the Sunset Strip.

I made friends with the lead-singing drummer of the all-girl group. She mentioned that the bar had a house band on Wednesday nights and occasionally would let people sing an open mic song. This was great! It was also the perfect distraction to get my mind off of Liam and every other drama that was plaguing me.

The following night happened to be Wednesday and I was actually excited to get out of bed a little earlier that day to prepare for the show. My new drummer friend said she had put in a good word for me with her friend who was the drummer for the house band. They would allow me to do one song that night to see if I was any good. I knew exactly what song I was going to sing: "Creep" by Radiohead.

I don't remember how or why I first listened to that song, but I do recall it being later in life. My music choices throughout my life were usually centered heavily around female pop artists like Tiffany, Madonna and Britney Spears. But I occasionally got sucked into the work of artists like Evanescence. The song "Creep," however it eventually crept into my music library, was one of those songs that I felt a deeper, soul level, connection to. I was the person the song spoke of and had been for most of my life. It resonated with me and apparently my soul-melting performance that night resonated with the crowd and band as well.

One of the original Power Rangers was in the audience that evening. He came up to me after the set to show me the pictures he took and tell me how impressed he was with my song. I was a huge fan of the Power Rangers, as all my childhood friends could attest to, so meeting him was a pretty big deal and the fact that he was moved by my performance meant even more.

The band also must have been pretty impressed as they asked me to join them again the following week with an additional song. This was the one thing that gave me joy in the midst of all the life-shattering occurrences happening all around me. I immediately started thinking about another song to show off more of my vocal range.

Another couple of days went by and I still had no exact plan as to what I would be doing when the hammer finally fell on the whole eviction process. I had been hanging with my two new chef BFFs and they suggested I introduce myself to the owner of the building next door. I thought, "Why not? Couldn't hurt...and what other options do I really have?" So I walked over and introduced myself to the character next door and that is exactly what he was ... a character.

His name was James and he was an all-out yogi. The building he had leased next to the girls' restaurant was a large, completely empty, 3-room space that he intended to turn into a yoga studio/massage center. We got to talking that afternoon. We actually had some common interests and seemed to get along. I told him about my situation and he told me about his plans for the building. The light in my brain went off almost immediately with an idea that would help us both! I would move into the back room and we would use my gorgeous living room furniture in the front area as his reception area. Then I would help him turn this empty shell into his dream yoga studio! Helping paint, organize, website building and promoting would be my way of paying rent until I could find a real apartment or roommate situation. I was thrilled when he said yes. It came at just the right time, almost like it was meant to be.

When I returned home that evening, there was a note on the door stating I had one more day to move everything out or the sheriffs would escort me out with force. That was a scary thought that really began to worry me. How was I supposed to get everything packed and out of my apartment in one day?!

Then that other thought crept back into my brain. It was even louder than before: "You can't keep going. You have nothing left. You are a failure. No one wants to help you. If you end it now everyone will be free of your craziness and drama. If you kill yourself now... you will be free."

It was so loud that no amount of liquor, kitty or crystal would silence it. It was now the most viable option. I started thinking about the easiest and most dramatic ways to go. Everything else in my life had been such a show, why shouldn't my death?

But that damn spark found its way to the microphone and slowly began to overpower the fortissimo of the dark thoughts. The voice in my head said, "You really want to be dramatic? How about you be that person that makes it through all this unthinkable crisis and hardship and come out on the other side better, stronger and more inspirational than anyone ever imagined." As an Aquarius, I was always up for a good challenge and that was actually a challenge I was willing to accept.

I started packing that night, all by myself. The next morning, I packed more and it was pretty difficult to have to sort through my whole LA life and decide what I could keep and what had to go in such a short period of time. I had most of it packed when I made a call to Tim at the cake shop to ask him for help. Even though I wanted to do this on my own, there was no possible way that I could.

He did agree to help me that day after a pretty heartfelt talk on the phone. I didn't know exactly why he did it, but maybe he felt sorry for me or felt responsible for the fact that the late payments and the bounced check had led to this situation. Or maybe it was just because he truly saw the best in me and had never really given up.

Whatever the reason, I was grateful for his help at this crossroads of my life. He quickly arranged for a moving company to come pick up everything I was taking with me to the empty yoga studio just a few blocks away.

It was a bittersweet moment taking that last look at my mostly emptied apartment I had made so many memories in. There was sadness, naturally, but there was also a hint of excitement as that little spark began to burn a little bigger and whispered that there was something better on the horizon. The horizon was Sunset Boulevard and I headed into it with high hopes.

THE END

THE FIRST FEW DAYS living on the Sunset Strip were pretty amazing. I was close to the places I liked to go to and was living next door to the restaurant my two new friends owned. At this point in my life, it seemed as though I was in a good position to get back on my feet. If I had been able to focus my energy towards that goal, I probably would have achieved it.

I soon became distracted by this yoga guy and his weird requests. He didn't seem to really have a plan for getting his business up and running. Sometimes it was uncomfortable just talking with him. He made all sorts of rules for me to follow. I felt they were a little harsh, but I understood them because technically I was living at a business. Not being able to bring people over and cleaning the place from top to bottom were two of the rules I found a little annoying. I did help him clean though, because he was letting me stay there for free. But it was what happened on the fourth day I was staying there, in mid-March, that rocked my world once again.

I was hanging out with my friend Jessica, a staff member from The Twisted Rainbow, at her apartment. While we were having some beer we somehow got on the subject of Sarah Summers. I had been promising everyone at The Twisted Rainbow I would make an appearance as Sarah for months. For some reason I finally got up the nerve to do it this day. Jessica and her cute guy friend came back to the studio with me and we decided to play dress up. It was quite fun putting her into my wigs and outfits as I got ready to show the rock'n'roll world Ms. Sarah Summers for the first time.

Jess and her friend wanted to smoke some pot. I said they could but they would have to do it on the back porch because the guy who was letting me stay there was pretty strict on the rules of not having drugs used in the building. They went out on the back patio area and lit up a joint and asked me if I wanted to join. I declined as I was not a big pot smoker. I realize it sounds odd that I didn't smoke marijuana because of all the other drugs I had been doing. But when I smoked pot now, it made me feel different, like I was God or the second coming of Christ or something. When I was stoned, I felt like I could read people's minds and what's worse that I could transfer my thoughts to them. This was not a feeling I was comfortable having. It made me feel quite crazy just thinking about it. I used to smoke pot every day when I was dating my 'Great Love,' Shane, back in Texas. But now, with the amount of time that had passed and the many different hybrids of marijuana, my body was just not enjoying it the way it used to.

So I let them smoke while I continued to get dressed up. In between applying my eyeshadow and lipstick, I turned on the Wii U to play my favorite 'Just Dance' game. Jess and her friend grabbed a controller each and joined in on the fun. We continued to have a blast until we heard a noise in the other room. Mr. Yogi forcibly burst through the 'bedroom' door in shock.

I can only imagine how strange it must have been for him seeing a Britney Spears looking character and her two cohorts turning around to face him with a lingering scent of weed in the air. Not only were two of his rules being broken, but maybe he was even more weirded out by the fact that he had let a female illusionist move into his once empty studio. Hell, maybe he was attracted to me as my alter ego and he couldn't handle the feelings. Either way, the outcome was no good.

"What the hell is going on here?! What's that smell? Who are these people?? You know what?! I can't have this in my business, in my life... I'm gonna need you out of here! Tomorrow at the latest!" he screamed in what can only be described as utter disgust and sheer panic.

I was appalled by his outrageous reaction and his demands that I be out the following day. How could this be happening to me again?

I tried to tell him I had not been doing the drugs

he smelled, and that my two friends had just been there for a few minutes, but he did not want to listen to any of it. His mind was made up. I even pleaded with him to let me stay, telling him I would have nowhere else to go, nowhere to put all my belongings I had just unpacked a few days before. No luck. He was not budging on his decision. So I had to make an emergency plan. I knew I would have to relinquish what little pride I had left and go to Tim, once again, and see if he would be gracious enough to save me from this latest travesty.

Thank God for Tim and everything he was as a person. That man had saved my ass more times than I could count and gave me more chances than anyone truly deserved. God may have taken my real parents away from me but he had given me an even better father figure in this earth angel that was Tim. He arranged for the same quick-moving company to come back and pick up my belongings and put them into storage. I kept a few pieces of personal memorabilia with me as well as a box full of clothes and once again watched as everything I owned and all my memories were boxed and shipped away.

Leah and Wendy heard all the commotion as they were getting the restaurant ready to open. They instantly came to my aid. Leah was kind enough to suggest that if I really had nowhere else to go that she would let me sleep in the upstairs office at night as long as I helped out at the restaurant and never let anyone in after hours. She also insisted that I cut back on the drinking. After what had just happened at the yoga studio,

I made a promise to them and kept it. The first night I slept at the fancy French restaurant on the floor in the very small upstairs office with a single pillow and fleece throw blanket. It wasn't the most comfortable situation but at least it was safe and secure.

The next day I cleaned myself up and put my culinary skills to use. I soon became an asset that helped my relationship with the girls grow even more. I had been a baker/cake decorator at this point for nearly 8 years. As much as I enjoyed baking, I had always been interested in cooking, too. Working with the girls while I stayed there allowed me to train under two of the most brilliant chefs in Los Angeles and their lovable Spanish sous chefs! Leah even taught me how to grind meat and make handmade sausages and charcuterie. That process was very interesting and fun as we squeezed the freshly ground meat into the slimy pink intestines. I made a number of crude jokes, naturally, garnering uproarious laughter from the girls.

The girls taught me new skills I had only seen on TV and their trust in me (shown by allowing me to stay there) meant the world to me. If it hadn't been for them, I think those dark thoughts of 'the easy way out' would have returned with a vengeance.

I had been staying there for almost two weeks and found a most needed sense of joy in cooking while still dealing with the drama of finding a new place and more work. The ability to get up in the morning and cook a chef-worthy breakfast in a

5-star kitchen was a wonderful perk, but I knew it couldn't last forever. I needed to find an apartment or a room soon. Wendy was nice enough to let me shower at her place daily and wash my clothes there so I could feel fresh and motivated to get back on my feet.

During this short time at the restaurant, I had cut back on the drugs and was not drinking as much because I hardly had any money at the time and I was trying to be respectful of the girls and their rules. The three of us had a good time and Sarah even made an appearance with a special performance one night in that two-week period for chef Leah's birthday.

It was the first week in April when I got asked to perform with the house band at The Twisted Rainbow again. But this time it would be a special performance for the owner and his friends. I was so excited about this opportunity and even more excited that the owner was interested in hearing me sing! He knew everyone there was to know in the rock music business and, if he thought I was good enough, maybe he could introduce me to the right people.

It was Wednesday before I knew it. I felt pretty confident as I had been practicing my song selection for the girls at the restaurant all day. They wished me luck and told me they would be leaving at around midnight or maybe earlier and if I was going to sleep there that night I should try to be back before then. I assured them it would be no problem and began to get ready to head to the bar.

I donned the most rock 'n' roll outfit I could put

together with the wardrobe I had available. Wearing my skin-tight black jeans, a black fitted Johnny Cash t-shirt, my cowboy boots, fingerless gloves and a fitted leather jacket, I felt like a bonafide rock star. I was ready to sing as though my life depended on it. Perhaps it truly did.

The stage was up a set of creaky wooden steps that had seen the bottom of many a rock legend's boots over the long history of the famous bar. On the second floor was the stage area that was made of the same aged wood glistening under the spotlights and seeming to beckon me with its glory. The drum set was fixed up close to the back wall, the guitars sat against it looking forward at the microphones on their stands. The bustle of the audience, drinks in hand, permeated the room, as they sat a few feet from the stage, patiently waiting for the show.

The band began playing and the sounds of authentic rock music overtook the room, filling the air with raw energy. My performance had been pushed back towards the end of the set as the owner and his friends had yet to arrive. At this point in the evening, I began to get slightly nervous as I listened to the rapid beats of the drum and watched the hands on the clock inch forward almost in synchronicity. This was a massive opportunity for me and I was determined to perform that night even if it meant I was going to be late getting back to the restaurant.

I made my way up to the bar in the back where I sat with the other regulars at The Twisted Rainbow while we listened to the band play on. I had a few drinks before the show to calm my nerves, but didn't drink to excess like usual as I wanted to be professional and put on a good show. A little while later the owner and his crew arrived and after getting settled into their seats, with glasses of beer in hand, the stage manager motioned for me to come over. This was it! My big chance.

Since it was getting late, I decided I would only do one number for them and that song was 'Creep.' As I stepped up to the microphone, the audience seemed to hush and in the near silence of the room, now filled with stage smoke and spotlights, I could only hear my heartbeat as it pounded in my chest. The first chord played and the intro began and I let the emotions take hold as I started to sing:

"When you were here before,

Couldn't look you in the eye.

You're just like an angel

Your skin makes me cry...

You float like a feather, in a beautiful world.

And I wish I was special

You're so fuckin' special

But I'm a creep, I'm a weirdo

What the hell am I doing here?

I don't belong here..."

My performance that night was the most

heartfelt and heart wrenching I had ever given. The sound of applause from the crowd, from the people I respected, made me feel alive again. When I was singing, that song especially, I could take all the pain and drama from my life and turn it from burden into power. And for the minutes that it lasted, be free of it all. I wasn't thinking about Liam or the fact that I was basically homeless at that moment. I was just able to let go and...be.

The owner was impressed and very complimentary, which was all I could have asked for because it meant my performance was a success. Maybe the wheels in his head were turning on ways he could help further my career. We all shared a drink as he told us stories about some of the rock legends who had graced that stage before they made it big. I got so enveloped in the moment that I forgot to keep track of time. I looked at the time on my phone and was shocked to see that it was already 1:30 a.m. I immediately got worried. I hadn't checked in with the girls at the restaurant because I was so distracted by the performance and everything else that was going on around me. I called and texted, but received no response. I figured they had left and were more than likely already home and in bed.

"SHIT! What am I going to do tonight? Where am I going to sleep?" I thought.

I waited around the bar and had a few more drinks hoping that someone I knew might let me crash on their couch for just one night. It was nearing 2 a.m. and I had not found anyone I knew well enough to ask for that favor. So I left the bar defeated with only one option in mind: I would have to go up to Liam's house in the Hollywood Hills and ask to sleep there for the night.

As I walked down Sunset Boulevard in the unseasonably chilly air, I thought about what I would say when I got to his door. If he still cared for me the way he said he did, it would be no problem for me to stay there one night, right? Why did I feel nervous about this? I was nervous because he had been spending all of his time with Anna Lynn. Who knew what kind of brainwashing she had been conducting on his fragile mind. She was an opportunist and she had been taking advantage of this situation since the day she met me. Or so it seemed. She had pushed her way into his life and ultimately pushed me further and further out of it. He still had love for me though because he told me when we talked on the phone. And I was there first! I was HIS first. That had to count for something.

As I reached the corner of Sunset Boulevard and Sunset Plaza Drive, I prepared myself for that long walk up the dark and winding road. The walk to his house was not an easy feat as it was about two miles up into the hills of West Hollywood. I had no cash for a cab and what balance I had left on my credit card I was saving for an even 'rainier' day, so I decided to walk. Maybe it was a form of self-punishment making myself walk that long path in the cold. Thoughts filled my head as I trudged up the dimly lit street. "What was I doing with my life that meant anything real? Why was it so hard to say the things I wanted to say? Had

I made a mistake not moving in with him all those months ago or would he have put me out like he did Cheri? Why couldn't I find real love? Did I even deserve it?"

It was nearing 2:45 a.m. when I got even remotely close to his house. I checked the time on my phone and realized it was running out of power. At that moment I felt just like that poor little iPhone. I, too, was running out of energy and I definitely had no power left over my life. The phone died as I heard a car making its way up the hill. I could hear the muffled sounds of rock music blaring from the inside. The car zoomed past me with no sense of acknowledgment, but I knew exactly who was in that vehicle and I began to follow it up the hill.

Liam and Anna Lynn must have been out at some bar partying the night away like usual and were finally on their way home. They made it up the hill way before I did as I still had about a half-a-mile walk up that twisted road before I reached the house. When I finally reached my destination, I took a second to catch my breath and sat down on the curb by his car. How low had my life gotten that I had to come ask this man, who had broken my heart more times than he melted it, for this demeaning favor? I took into account that Liam had come through for me before in some very special ways. If the man I fell in love with all those months ago was still somewhere inside of him, he would never turn me away. Especially in my darkest hour of need.

I got up off the curb and climbed the stairs up to his front door where I had been invited many times before. But this time as I went to knock, there was something different in the air. Fear. I was afraid of which version of him might answer and afraid of how he would react. What I didn't realize was that he was not the person I really should have been afraid of because it was her who had poisoned his mind and her that opened the door that night.

"Ugh. What are you doing here, Kaleb? It's like 3:30 a.m. We are going to bed," said Anna Lynn, with her smudged makeup, wearing pajama pants and a tank top.

"Well, I... I need to stay here in one of his three empty rooms for the night. I have nowhere else to go and it's cold," I said, as I shivered in my lightweight black leather jacket still covered in the scent of rock 'n' roll stage glory.

"I don't think so... I mean... I don't know if..." She started to say as he walked up behind her still in his white tank top and black torn jeans with his long blonde hair disheveled across his tired-looking face.

"DUDE! You can't stay here tonight!" he yelled, as he approached her from behind and put his hand on her bare shoulder.

What did he just say to me? What did he just call me? DUDE? Really? He had never called me a dude in the year we had known each other. I was anything but just another 'dude' to him and he knew it. He made a mockery of our whole relationship by uttering that one word as he stood behind her like a human shield.

"What did you just say? Are you serious? You won't let me stay in one of those empty rooms for ONE NIGHT?" I replied with a confused and hurt tone, trying to keep a tear from falling that was welling up in my right eye.

"I said you can't fucking stay here, dude!" he yelled, still standing behind Anna Lynn as she began to smirk slightly.

"Are you serious? If you fucking do this to me Liam, I will NEVER fucking forgive you!" I screamed back at him with intense rage as tears now trickled down my cheeks.

He stepped around her and closed the door. He closed the door in my face.

COWARD! BASTARD! FUCKER!

As I heard the door lock and the chains go up I felt the last piece of my frozen heart shatter inside of me. He had done it. He had crushed every last dream, squashed every ounce of hope I had left. I was all alone, with nothing and no one.

What was I to do now? My phone was just as dead as my soul and I could barely stand to walk as I was weighted down with pain and agony. I couldn't just stand in front of his house and I still had enough self-worth to not go back to that door to plead with him. I meant it that I would never forgive him and that promise went into effect the second he slammed that door.

The chilly air on that long walk back down the winding hill was but a reminder of how cold he and that bitch had been to me just minutes before. When I finally reached Sunset Boulevard again it was nearing 5:30 a.m., as the clock in the middle of the street was so kind to point out. I figured I would go to Mel's diner, and have a cup of coffee, and try to figure out what my next plan was.

I sat down in a booth by the counter and a waitress I had seen before came over with a cup of coffee.

"You look like you've been crying. What's wrong, dear?" said the dark-haired woman in the Tiffany blue colored diner dress.

"My life is shit," was all of the answer I could muster as I reached for the sugar packet, tearing it open to pour it into the coffee.

"I'm sorry, sweetie. Let me get you a menu," she responded with a hint of empathy splashed across her wrinkled face.

At this point I was so tired and so defeated, all I wanted to do was sleep, but knew that was impossible because I had nowhere to go. I knew I had to stay awake and since I didn't have any 'kitty' I thought maybe a little Splenda pick-me-up might do the trick. I didn't know if it would work or not, but I figured the sugar would go straight to my brain if I snorted it and would keep me up for little while longer while I tried to piece my life back together.

I opened the yellow package and dumped the contents out onto the table in front of me. I used my only credit card to cut it up and put it into a line then grabbed a straw from the canister next to the table-sized jukebox. I snorted it like it was 'kitty' and felt a little tingle. Maybe it had actually worked! I did another line of the saccharin sweetener and awaited my menu.

I drank my coffee and patiently waited for the waitress to come to my table to take my order. She never did. The next two people to come to my table were LAPD officers with questioning looks upon their faces.

"Sir, we got a report that someone was doing cocaine on a table here. We're gonna have to ask you to step outside," said the portly male officer with a stern look on his face.

"Are you kidding me? This has to be a joke! I would never do cocaine on a table in a restaurant!" I said, laughing at them, truly thinking I had to be getting punk'd or something.

"No sir, this is not a joke... please step outside," said the thinner, blonde female officer with a furrowed brow on her kind face.

I obliged the officers request and stepped outside with them as I tried to explain what had just happened with Liam and that it was just Splenda that I had snorted on the table.

"It was really just a joke! I wanted to see if I would get a sugar rush from it," I said, as the lady officer patted me down and searched my pockets for drugs. They didn't find any because there was nothing to find.

"You're going to have to come with us sir," said the male officer, as he put the cuffs around my wrists and placed me in the back seat.

Oh my God. Could this night get any worse? I had just had my heart demolished by the man that I loved, I had nowhere to sleep and now I was getting arrested for snorting sugar in a restaurant. My life had officially hit rock bottom and there was no way out.

The car drove out of the parking lot of Mel's and down Sunset Boulevard towards the restaurant I was staying at. I pleaded with the officers and told them I had to be there when the girls opened up so I could get my belongings. I didn't think they heard me until they turned right on San Vicente and then left into the alley behind the restaurant.

The female cop got out and came to open the back door. She assisted me out of the car and removed the cuffs from my wrists.

"Listen, sir. Kaleb, is it? We are sorry you've had a rough night and we realize it was only sugar. It still was not a good idea to be snorting anything off a table in public though, so we had to cuff you and cart you off to show the diner we meant business. We are going to let you go with a warning this time but please try and get yourself together so we won't have to arrest you for real," she said, with a warm pat on the back, before she got back into the car and drove off.

I couldn't believe all of this had happened in such a short period of time. It was more drama than I could take and I was over it! Over him! Over Hollywood! I couldn't stay here anymore. And as the sun rose over Sunset Boulevard, I had made my decision on how I would fix all these problems once and for all.

I walked from the alley back onto the street and hailed the first cab I could find. I opened the door and with the most assured voice said, "Take me to the airport, I'm going back to New York City!"

As the car drove down the long stretch of road leading towards the airport, my mind began to race. Maybe this plan would actually work. Maybe once I got back to the city, my life would finally change for the better. I was going to leave Los Angeles and I marked this day as the new beginning I had been searching for. But, like everything else in my life, there would be a few more hiccups before I would get to start over in the big city and finally be able to write in my life chapter titled "LA" those final words...the end.

THE MILE-HIGH CLUB

I ARRIVED at the airport around 7 a.m. and hopped out of the cab before I could try and talk myself out of this brash and unprepared plan. I didn't have any luggage, my computer or a change of clothes. Nothing but my wallet with that single credit card and a hope that a trip to New York City would be the break I needed to pull my life together. I wasn't going to stay there forever, I just needed to get out of LA and away from all of the drama that had made me think seriously about ending it all.

Standing outside LAX watching people trickle through the open doors leading to the airline desks, I knew that this was what I had to do.

I entered the first door I found leading into the giant airport and was overwhelmed by all the bustle inside. How was I going to pull this off? I had about $360 left on that one credit card I had in my wallet. I figured that would be enough for a round-trip ticket. What I hadn't taken into account was that I was trying to buy a ticket for the same day and it was almost impossible to book a flight that late without it costing through the roof!

I walked around that huge airport for a couple of hours going up to every single airline desk and asking them for their cheapest price. Six hundred at one of them, $550 at another. Virgin America had a flight for the next day for $300 but I was not going to wait until then. I couldn't. I couldn't risk the chance that I would talk myself out of it or worse, someone else would talk me out of it. My phone was still dead so I had not been able to tell anyone where I was or that I was going to leave. To some it may have seemed like I was running away. Perhaps I was. But what was I running from? Liam? Homelessness? The suicidal thoughts? Or was I really trying to run away from the sad, pitiful version of myself that I had become those past few years in Los Angeles? I thought if I could just get back to NYC for a weekend I would have time to breathe, to think and most importantly, have some time to find myself again.

I knew this was the only choice I had. If I stayed in Los Angeles one day longer, if I had to go back to sleeping on an office floor and if I had to face that heartless asshole and his bitch of a girlfriend, there was no question I would kill myself. I didn't want my life to end like that (as juicy of an evening news story it would have made). No, I was going to get to New York City one way or another. So I continued my walk down the long hallways of the airport to try and find the perfect ticket.

It must have been around 11 a.m. when I finally reached the desk of Southwest Airlines, on the opposite side of where I had been dropped off that morning. I was tired and I looked it as I stepped up to a friendly looking airline agent dressed in her pencil-skirted, dark navy airline uniform. As this defeated young man with a tear-stained face approached her, I was shocked to find that instead of a scowl or look of judgment, she presented what could only be described as the warm, glowing smile of an angel.

"Rough night, sweetie? How can I help you?" said the older, blonde woman who reminded me a little of my mother with the plumpness in her face and her bright brown eyes.

"You have no idea..." I muttered as I began to pull my wallet from the back pocket of my tight black jeans.

"Well, I hope wherever you go next will be better for you. Are you going on vacation? Do you have a ticket?" she asked, already knowing the answer to that last question. I'm sure she had seen people like me before. People who had been broken by life in Los Angeles and ran away to get back in touch with reality or went crying home to their parents. That wasn't an option for me. My parents were gone and my grandmother was now in a nursing home going through severe dementia. She was no longer a viable option to 'run home crying to.'

Sure, there were some cousins and some old friends I could have asked to stay with in Texas, but it had been over 10 years since I had been home. And really, who would want to take in a drug-addicted, alcoholic mess from Hollywood? I didn't want to burden anyone else. I guess my ego was still too big to let me go back to Fort Worth until I had accomplished the goals I had set when I left all those years ago.

I left Texas to become a star and follow my dreams. You better believe I would not go back there a failure, especially after everything I had gone through in that state and since then!

"I need a ticket to New York City for today, please," I said with a smile. The light in the blue of my eyes shined into her soul as I pulled the credit card from my wallet.

"You look like a sweet kid, let me see what I can do okay? I can't make any promises but I will try," she replied, with a sense of compassion in her voice I had not heard in many years living in Hollywood. She must be from the south.

After a few minutes of typing she looked up at me with a big smile and said, "I found a standby ticket I can sell you for $250, but it's only one way. Will that work?"

Without hesitation I blurted out, "Yes!" At that moment I didn't care if it was one way, I just knew I had to get out of there and thought that when I was ready to come back to LA I would call Tim and he would help me get a ticket. I wasn't planning on calling him, or anyone, until I got to New York because I didn't want them to try and talk me out of it. I had made up my mind and when I make up my mind, I rarely can be told any different or falter in my decisions.

I handed the sweet-faced older woman my credit card and she swiped it with confidence. The transaction was accepted and as the ticket was being printed, I could feel a sense of relief wash over me. I was going to get out of that toxic twinkle town for a few days, or a week, and I would finally be able to breathe. I didn't know where I was going to go once I got to the city, or where I would sleep, but I felt like it was still a better option than staying in Hollywood.

"Have a nice flight, dear. May God bless you on your travels and whatever ventures lay ahead," the woman said, handing me the ticket over the airline counter. The ticket was made of white card stock paper, but in my hand at that moment it felt like she was handing me a magical golden ticket. I smiled warmly back at her and began to walk towards the security check-in line. I felt a momentary burst of happiness and it began to fan my much needed second wind. I was tired and I had been up all night, but at that moment, as I trotted up to the TSA security station, I was alert and ready to take this giant leap of faith.

Entering the boarding area would not be an easy task though. Like everything else in that extended 'day,' there would be drama and another hurdle to jump.

I finally got to the front of the line after a 20-minute wait (without my phone to keep me busy). I was already pretty frustrated when I placed my shoes on the conveyor belt. The attractive male security officer took me through the scanner and then asked me to wait on the side. Oh my God, really?! I realized I looked pretty haggard from the lack of sleep, but did I look suspicious too? I didn't have a bag or anything so maybe that set off a red flag.

They moved me to the side and asked me to remove my jacket and then began the pat down. The movement of his hands all over my body felt like a massage after the trauma of the last 48 hours. After being felt up by the attractive TSA guy, the next agent then asked to see my boarding pass and ID. My California ID was expired and it didn't even have the correct spelling of my last name due to an error at the DMV when I signed up for it years ago. I had bought the ticket under the name that my ID had on it, so that was not an issue, the fact that it was expired seemed to be one though. So I sat and waited as they did some sort of background check using my social security number to verify my identity. It must have been 20 minutes before they came back with some sort of paper for me to sign. Undeterred, I signed and was finally able to make it into the boarding area part of the airport.

The drama! If I hadn't been so determined to get out of Los Angeles, I probably would have given up at this point, but I kept pushing through the obstacles because the goal line was so close.

As I arrived at my gate, I noticed a little bar on the other side just steps away from where I had to wait. I still had money left on my credit card and thought that after EVERYTHING I had been through recently, I really deserved a drink...or 5.

The bartender smiled as I saddled up to the bar. He placed a drink menu in front of me, but before he could even say hello, I blurted out my order, "Manhattan please. Straight up!"

My stand-by flight was not for another hour and a half so I figured I would unwind and get a little tipsy so I could fall asleep the second I got on the plane. I hadn't been on an aircraft since I arrived in Hollywood back in 2005 and my nerves were pretty high. I also had not done 'kitty' or crystal for over 48 hours and maybe was having a hint of withdrawals. The alcohol took care of that problem. After the 3rd Manhattan, I was feeling pretty numb, ready to get to the actual Manhattan.

As I sat there with the bartender, I told him my story. He was in state of utter disbelief. He even mentioned at one point that I "should write a book about it." He wasn't the first person to tell me this and he wouldn't be the last. But he was right: all the drama of my life could be a book or a movie, especially these last two days.

The hands on the clock above the airport bar moved forward and the time of departure was nearing. I said my goodbye to the bartender, who had taken a couple of the drinks off my bill as a kind gesture.

Thank God for that! That meant I still had enough money on my credit card to survive for a day in the big city...or so I hoped.

I sashayed my way to the boarding area as they called my group number. I was thrilled to be getting on the plane. I already felt myself getting sleepy and knew that once I sat down in that seat the next thing I would see would be the night sky overlooking the glow of the Manhattan skyline. I was ready. This was it.

The plane seemed more crowded and tighter than I had remembered, but since I didn't have any bags, I thought I would be okay with the space. I sat down in row 43 seat B and began to relax. The city was calling me and I was going to answer!

I closed my eyes as I rested my head on the seat back and prepared for my first flight in years, but before I could actually get to sleep I was disturbed by one of the flight attendants and one armed guard.

"Excuse me sir, can you come with us please? We believe there is a safety issue here," said the Southwest flight attendant with her dirty blonde hair in a braided pony-tail and a stale look on her plain face.

"What's going on?! I'm not doing anything! I'm not talking to or touching anyone or anything! I'm just trying to sleep!" I screamed and probably slurred at the same time. I couldn't believe I was this close... I was in the seat... And now even more drama! This was starting to get ridiculous. If I had believed in seeing signs or listened to bad omens, I would have given up, then and there.

I begrudgingly got out of my seat as the flight attendant made way for me to stand in the aisle behind the Air Marshal. He began to walk and I began to follow. My spirit sank even deeper than it had before. I couldn't even imagine that there was any lower or broken I could feel after everything that had already happened, but again I was mistaken as this event really topped the cake!

Back in the boarding area, the Air Marshal told me, "Sir, we believe you are too intoxicated to fly and may be a safety issue to the other passengers. Unfortunately, we will not be able to have you on this flight and you will need to work this out with the airline if they decide to give you another flight."

Part of me wanted to blow up at him. But I stopped my inebriated self when I realized where I was. Never a good idea to go ballistic at an airport especially since 9/11. So instead of an explosion of anger erupting, a waterfall of tears sprung from my eyes and I fell to the ground. This had been one of the most exhausting, dramatic, earth shaking, heart shattering days of my entire life. I was just lost. I had a loss of words, a loss of direction and mostly a loss of hope that immediately put the microphone back in front of the 'dark voice' once again. It was louder this time as it said, "You can't take any more...you're weak... you're beaten... you are done. So just do it. What do you have left to live for?"

I didn't know exactly what I had to live for at that moment, but at that moment I knew I had to live!

I walked out of the airport with my head held high and just kept walking until I reached the Hilton LAX. The hotel looked like a heavenly palace that was calling my name. Once inside, the chairs in the lobby looked like comfortable clouds.

I sat down for a moment, putting my head into my hands. I felt so defeated. I wanted to cry, but my reservoir had run dry. There were no tears left, there was no strength left to fight...until that little spark decided to speak again.

"There is still hope, Kaleb...don't give up," it quietly repeated in my ear. That soft angelic voice always gave me faith. It must be my mother's.

I picked my head up and walked over to the front desk. I asked if there was a courtesy phone I could use. The bellhop pointed me in the direction of the lone phone in the corner. I walked over, knowing that there was only one person I could call to help me in this situation. I dialed the numbers I had dialed so many times before and wasn't sure what to expect when he answered.

"Hello?" said the reassuring voice of Tim on the other end of the line.

"Tim, it's me. I'm in a bit of a bind and I really need your help," I spoke timidly.

"Kaleb? Where are you? What's going on?" he said with a worried, fatherly tone to his voice.

I explained the whole situation to him, every detail of the last 48 hours. I told him of my plan to fix it all. "And that's why I can't stay here any longer. I can't face Liam or the people who refused to help me. I just need to go to New York for a little while. I feel like it's the only option left," I said, trying to hide the immense desperation in my voice.

"Are you 100% sure this is what you want to do? I will help you in any way that I can Kaleb, but you don't have a plan. You have nowhere to go when you get there. You have very little money. What are you going to do for work? This just sounds so drastic," he said, trying to figure out what was going through my mind.

"I've never been more sure of anything in my life Tim. I have to do this. I don't want to stay in LA and die," I said with a seriousness to my voice I'm not sure he had ever heard before.

"Okay, Kaleb. We will get you a room at the hotel for the night. You call me when you find a flight and I will purchase it for you. This is crazy though, you know that, right?" he said.

His voice was telling me he thought it was crazy, but I think he knew that it probably was the right decision. Tim always wanted the best for me. I think his position as my father figure gave him some sort of innate intuition that told him this was exactly what I needed.

He arranged for my stay at the Hilton that night and I was beyond grateful. When I went back to the reception desk, I told them my name. After a few clicks on the computer, the clerk handed me a key card.

When I reached the beautiful room, I was beyond tired. I was thrilled to see my first real bed in about a month. I couldn't believe I had slept on a floor for the last few weeks because I had always had my own apartment and money since I was 18. I was going to enjoy this night in this swanky hotel. Tomorrow I would find my way to Manhattan. Sober.

I crashed the second I hit the bed and the sleep was amazing but short. I woke up a few hours later, realizing I needed to charge my phone. So I went down to the hotel store and bought a charger. I stopped off at the hotel bar and asked the bartender if he could charge my phone while I had a drink. I was going to be sober the next day, but not tonight. I figured I'd have my last few drinks in LA and charge them to my room. I thought I might as well enjoy my final night in Hollywood since I was awake at this point and was energized by the excitement of finally traveling again the following day.

I had the bartender make me a 'Kaleb's Kool-Aid' as a tribute to the drama of the last year. It tasted even better miles away from that bar and those bad memories. I was finally able to relax, and momentarily, let go of all the pain I was holding on so tightly to.

As I was in the middle of consuming my second 'Kool-Aid', I saw a stream of sharply dressed people starting to make their way into the hotel. Shiny dresses, slick suits and tuxes paraded into the building, filling it with energy and laughter. "It must be a wedding party" I thought to myself. I had helped make tons of wedding cakes and delivered them over the past 8 years, but I had not been to a real wedding party in all that time. I had been to the history-making first Gay Wedding in Los Angeles, but that was more of a publicity thing and there was no reception like this.

Feeling pretty good about myself at this point (the 'Kool-Aid' had started to kick in), I thought maybe I would just go in there and join the party.

I snuck in alongside some girls I had started to chat up at the bar who were friends of the bride. They told the door guys I was with them. Once inside, we split up and I helped myself to some fancy food and free drinks. At one point in the evening, I introduced myself to the lovely mother of the bride and twirled her around on the floor for a sweet dance before I was finally asked to leave. Ha-ha. What a way to end my time in Hollywood! Crashing a wedding party and dancing with the mother of the bride! Who does that sort of thing?

I made my way back to the bar and picked up my now fully charged phone. I thanked the bartender and headed back to my luxurious room. I opened up a bag of chips from the basket above the mini fridge, but before I could take my first bite, I was asleep.

I woke up early that morning, surprisingly without a hangover. I immediately started looking online for tickets to New York and I was happy to come across a flight on Virgin America that was in the $300 range. I called Tim with the good news. He was gracious enough to give me his credit card number over the phone so I could place the order then and there.

He asked me one last time if I was sure of my decision and if there was anything I needed from the shop or the girls' restaurant.

"Well, I could use a change of clothes, my laptop, my skin care stuff and anything else you think I will need for this trip," I said, barely able to put together in my mind that this was actually happening now.

"Okay, call the girls and see if they can open the restaurant to get your stuff together. I'll have our messenger service run up there and pick it up and bring it to the hotel. Kaleb, I hope you know what you're doing here kid. I just want you to know that when you are ready to come back, I'll get you a ticket and we will figure it all out. But until then, be safe. I hope you find what it is you are looking for out there," said Tim, his normally reassuring voice tinged with a bit of sadness.

"Thank you. You don't know how much this means to me. I'll call you when I get there," I said, getting a little emotional. It wasn't like I was just saying goodbye to Tim, I was saying goodbye to LA and everything that was my life up til now. I shook it off though. I was only going to be in New York for a week or two until I cleared my head and knew exactly what I wanted my life to be like when I got back to Hollywood. That was my plan. But my plans rarely seemed to work out the way I designed them.

I called Wendy and she went to the restaurant quite quickly (her apartment was only a few blocks away). She was able to throw a bag together with all of the stuff I had asked for and a few things more. The messenger must have arrived the second she was done packing because he arrived to me just minutes before I had to leave for the airport.

The clock was winding down as I ran up to the front desk at Virgin America and got my ticket for the flight. The atmosphere of the ticketing area was more like a nightclub with pop music playing and strobe lights flashing on the walls. I immediately had a feeling of confidence wash over me, almost like a sign from above, that this was meant to be. This was exactly where I was supposed to be and exactly what I was supposed to be doing. I hadn't felt that sure of anything in a long time and my little spark started to flicker even brighter.

I had to go through the TSA line yet again, but this time it was a lot less dramatic. There was no massage-like rub down or trouble with my ID. I was in the boarding area in no time, which was a blessing because I literally had no time until my flight.

My group was the second to be called and as I walked up to the gate, I took a brief moment to reflect on my life in Los Angeles and what I was leaving behind. There were some good things and good people I would miss for those few weeks I planned to be gone, but there were also things I desperately had to get away from before they tore me apart. I was leaving so I wouldn't have to see Liam's face. I wouldn't have to be reminded daily of how low my life had gotten and I wouldn't be around those drugs and druggies that I had become obsessed with. This was the right decision. Now it was time to see it through.

I boarded the plane and sat between a lovely middle-aged African American woman and a gorgeous, young, short-haired, blonde father with his infant daughter on his lap. We all began to converse as the plane moved forward. Before we knew it, we were up in the air. There was no turning back now.

A little later as the fasten seatbelt sign went dim, the flight attendant came by and asked if I'd like a cocktail. As much as I wanted one at that moment, with all the crazy thoughts running through my head, I declined. This was one flight I would take sober and, even though the gentleman next to me was uber delicious, I had to stay focused on getting to New York. So I kept from flirting and squashed any ideas I had of joining the mile-high club.

THE BIG CITY

AS THE PLANE touched down, the wheels began to squeal against the runway. I was overcome with excitement! I had finally made it! I was finally in... New Jersey?! What the hell? This was not part of the plan! How did I end up in Jersey?!

I pulled out my ticket to check it, thinking there must be some sort of mistake. The destination clearly said Newark, New Jersey. I then vaguely remembered the airline booking website had said it was cheaper to go through Jersey to NYC than flying straight into LaGuardia airport in the city.

Well, that was a lackluster beginning to what was supposed to be my big, mind-clearing, life-changing, vacation to New York.

I got off the plane and looked at the time on my phone. It was already around 8 p.m. I had forgotten

I would lose all that time and daylight on the flight across the country. Even though I could see it was dark outside, through the giant glass windows of the waiting area, the light in my soul was burning brighter and I was ready to take on this adventure.

My next step was to get into the city. My first thought was to take a cab. I looked into my almost emptied wallet and quickly realized a cab ride was not the best choice. I was now going to have to start budgeting like never before.

I approached one of the airport staff to ask him what was the cheapest way to get to Manhattan. He kindly pointed in the direction of the AirTrain. I hadn't been on a train in a long time. The last time I was on a subway was when I traveled from Hollywood to Pasadena to attend a Power Rangers Convention (which was a lot of fun!) and I hadn't been on a train in New York City since I left back in 2003. My memories were littered with cab rides because I avoided the subway. My bank account was overflowing back then, so riding the train like a real New Yorker, a working-class citizen, was an exciting and new adventure for me.

I purchased my ticket from the airport kiosk, got a free map of the city and made my way to the train tracks. I hoped once I got into the city, into the West Village, I would still recognize the places I had called my home, all those years ago. A lot can happen in 10 years. Places change, people change, but I held out hope I would feel at ease once I stepped back onto Christopher Street.

The train ride from Newark to Manhattan was pretty interesting. There weren't very many people in the car I was in and it gave me time to think. The minutes went by like hours as the sounds of the train skipping over bumps in the tracks sang in my ears. These noises and the faint whispers of the small group of passengers, seated a few rows ahead of me, made me feel alive. Just 48 hours ago I was seriously thinking about ending it all. Now, with less than an hour into my New York adventure, I was already feeling more alive and more present than ever. This had to have been the right decision. I knew it.

The NJ Transit train connects to the Manhattan trains at Penn Station. When I got there, I was really thrown back into life! I had never been here the first time I lived in New York City. It had been ages since I had seen that many people at one time. A 'big group of people' to me, in the past few years, would have been when 100 people stuffed into the bar on the playoff game day. This was insane! There must have been at least a 1000 people, it seemed, whisking and whirling past me with determined looks on their faces, obviously in a big hurry to get to their final destinations. It was thrilling to see all this action around me. As I stood in the middle of it all, I was overcome with emotion. At that moment, my little spark became a tiny flame. I knew what I had to do. I headed to the subway station clerk and purchased my first Metro Card, my metaphorical ticket to freedom.

I knew I wanted to get to the West Village, but being unfamiliar with the subway system, I found myself kind of lost. The trains were named by letter and some by number. There were colored lines crisscrossing the giant map next to the turnstile. It was quite confusing, but after a few minutes trying to decode the jumbled map, I finally decided West 4th Street would probably be the closest stop to the Village from where I was. So I headed over to the A train.

This train was a lot more crowded than the last and it was shocking to see people standing shoulder to shoulder with strangers, huddled into the train car so close together they looked like sardines in a can. As comedic as it was to watch at times, it also gave me a rekindled sense of community and comradery I don't think I had ever felt in Los Angeles. People were on top of people, but there were no fights or angry looks. It was as though, for that few minutes of the ride, the people were one. It was inspiring to see, and I felt it deep inside.

As the train approached the 4th Street stop, I took a sip from my Diet Coke that had been resting in my bag since I left LA. It was a little warm, but it was still carbonated, and for a brief moment, it made me think of Hollywood and everything I had run away from. I wondered if Liam was thinking about me at that very moment and if he even knew I was gone. I asked myself if anyone else actually cared I had left or would they be happy when they heard the news? It was pretty shocking to most, I imagined, to hear the boy who rarely left a quarter mile area of West Hollywood had just up and left on a cross-country adventure, ending up in Manhattan to brave it all alone. "He must be insane," some would say. Or "damn, he is ballsy!" others might think. I thought of myself as being a little bit of both. But at that moment, as the train began to slow to a stop. I thought, above all else, I was brave.

The train screeched to a halt and the car doors opened. A throng of people entered and exited all at the same time causing a complex congestion. I forced my way out as I was bumped and nudged by strange-looking characters. I had forgotten how it felt to be around this many people at one time. It was like being in a mosh pit at the Whiskey a Go Go back in Hollywood.

I found my bearings once outside the train and on the platform underground. I sat down on one of the old wooden benches to look at my map and I noticed there was a certain smell wafting through the air, not good, not terrible, but city-like. It was an interesting smell that excited my senses and added even more flame to my little spark inside, getting stronger by the minute.

I checked the map until I was pretty sure I knew the path I was going to take to get back to the Village, the path that would hopefully lead me out of this total life funk I had been in for the past few years.

I stood up from the creaky old bench as another train rolled into the station. As the people trickled out of the train, I followed them towards the exit. What I saw next would shake me to the core. Something that changed the way I thought forever. And this sign was exactly what I needed at that very moment. It was the confirmation I had made the right decision to leave everything I knew behind and take this trip to the other side of the continent.

I walked up the long hallway towards the exit. Lining the walls were giant Diet Coke ads, seeming to speak to different kinds of people. The first one I saw was the one that seemed like it was written just for me. I took it as a sign from God, telling me I was on the right path. The sign read:

"You moved to New York with the money in your pocket, the clothes on your back and your eye on the prize."

And in the corner it stated: *"You're On!"*

I had finally made it to New York and it was as if the Universe was welcoming me with this sign. I did come here with only the money in my pocket and the clothes on my back! That part of the sign rang true. But what was my prize? Maybe my prize was taking the time to find myself again before I went back to LA. I didn't plan on staying in the city for very long, just long enough to figure out what I needed to do with my life. I didn't realize it at the time, but it wasn't MY plan I would soon be following. It would be the one my Creator laid out for me from the beginning. The plan would involve more than just a vacation to the big city...

EXTENDED VACATION

I WALKED OUT of the train station on West 4th Street and found my way over to Christopher Street where the world famous Stonewall Inn was located. Stonewall was famous for being the place where the gay revolution really took form in an age when being openly gay or transgender was illegal and bars like it were constantly raided by police.

When I lived in New York City, in 2002, just steps away from this landmark, I was privileged enough to get the opportunity to fill in for one of the house drag queens a few times and hosted her bingo show when she couldn't make it. At 19, I didn't even realize how big of a deal it was to host a show there, or how important that bar was to the very reason I was allowed to be exactly who I was. Those nights were some of the most fun nights I could remember spent in the Village. I hoped the magic of the past would still be there for my first night back in the city.

I walked through the large wooden doors to find the familiar sights of the bar I had once called home. Wood paneling covered every inch of the walls and the floor. The pool table was still situated in the back right corner like it had been all those years ago. To my surprise and relief, everything looked exactly the same! It was like time had frozen this sacred place while I was off living life on another parallel plane of existence.

My mind goes to that place sometimes and I wonder if maybe there are different planes where different versions of ourselves live. How many varied paths are there in these other realms our lives could take? If we make the right choices on this plane, do we realign with our correct path when the time is right?

My life, or the Universe, lead me to New York City when I was very young. It was in the big city that I gained fame and had success at a young age. The year and a half in Manhattan was but a fleeting moment of glory. When I abruptly moved back to Texas, did it knock me off the destined path?

Now, I thought, what if the Universe had brought me back here to have a second go at it? Does life work in circles? Or was the Universe allowing me a second chance, with a different outcome?

It was now 1 a.m. on this Sunday night and as I approached the familiar bar, I noticed the room was kind of empty. There were other customers there, of course, but it didn't seem to be as rowdy as I remembered. When I was going there back in 2002, I was young and the group of kids I hung out with stayed out until 4 a.m. every night and would go to after parties when we could. I remember my first best friend in New York was named Ladiss. He and I were the dynamic duo. He was always there to record my appearances as Sarah Summers alongside the big time New York Queens, like Shequida, at Barracuda Bar. He was my partner in crime on those evenings when we would climb to random rooftops to have drinks in the middle of the night. I lost contact with him when I moved back to Texas. I often wonder how he is and where he is now.

This evening, sitting alone at the bar, I wished my old best friend or any one of my LA companions were here to keep me company and tell me it was all going to be okay. I needed some physical comfort after the last few days of drama, but it had been ten years since I lived in the city and I didn't know anyone here anymore.

Looking at the wall of liquor and listening to the mix of light rock music, I suddenly realized I did have a few friends in the city still. Actually, they were my closest companions in any city and they were staring right at me: Johnny, Jack and Jim. They always knew how to comfort me. This night was no different. I slid one of the ancient-looking wooden stool-chairs out from underneath the long oak bar and placed my bag around the back of it. I scanned the room for the bartender and saw a dark-haired woman who looked vaguely familiar. She approached me at my end of the bar and I wondered if she could possibly be someone who had worked here ten years ago when I was experiencing the city for the first time. The shorter lady with the dark shoulder-length cut and glasses came up to me with a big smile and asked for my order.

"Welcome to the Stonewall Inn darling! What can I get for you?" she said, motioning to the wall of liquor behind her.

"Welcome back, is more like it! And I'll take a Jack and diet please," I said, as a big grin began to appear on my face. I guess it was at that moment I realized I had actually done it! I was actually back in New York City and, even though I had very little money and nowhere to go this particular night, I was beyond thrilled just to be back. I was back in the big city. Thousands of miles away from that rat bastard Liam and all the problems that had almost defeated me in Los Angeles.

"Welcome back, huh? When was the last time you were here? Where are you from? Just visiting?" asked the bartender rapid fire as she handed me my drink.

Taking the first sip of my first official New York City cocktail, I replied, "Wow, strong! Well, I was here ten years ago... I basically lived at this bar before I would go out to do my female illusion shows. I even performed here! I just arrived from Hollywood and I think I'll be staying for a few weeks. Just need to clear my head, ya know?"

"Ah! Drama back home, huh?" she said, as she poured two shots of fireball and placed them in front of her and I. (How did she know that was my favorite shot? The first shot Liam and I shared?

Was this another one of those strange signs from the Universe?) "Welcome back, this first round is on me. I hope you find what you are looking for, kid."

"Thank you so much... umm... I'm sorry I forgot to ask your name?" I said, holding my shot glass next to hers.

"I'm Mal, pleasure to meet you...if we haven't met before. You do look sort of familiar, though. I have been here forever so we could have met! HaHa," she said, with a chuckle, clinking glasses with me as we both downed the shots of cinnamon whiskey goodness.

Wiping a drop from my chin, I responded, "Thanks, Mal. I'm Kaleb. I'm not sure if we met before but you have a familiar energy and I hope I see you more while I'm in town."

Mal continued to work the bar as I took out my phone and pondered if I should call someone. My first thought was to call Cheri, but I knew she would be shocked and probably pretty sad at the fact I had left without saying goodbye. I knew she would be one of the few people who would actually miss me and one of the people I would miss dearly. I decided to wait and call her the following day because I needed to just take in this evening for what it was and see where my journey would lead me next.

The bars in NYC stay open until 4 a.m. and I knew that I would have to hang out at one of them until that time. After the bar closed, I would go find a diner somewhere to gather my thoughts and devise a plan to find a cheap place to stay. I would also have to wait until noon, New York time, before Tim would be at the cake shop and I could ask him for his help and suggestions.

With nothing but time, I sat and I talked to the random guys at the bar, who bought me drinks as I told them the harrowing tale of the last 48 hours, my love affair with a rock star, and my escape across country. Like most people, they couldn't believe my story! When I showed them pictures of my life in Hollywood, pictures of Liam and I together, their jaws hit the floor. The free drinks continued to be poured.

As last call came around, I was still surprisingly cognizant. I knew I had to find my next location to camp out at until the sun came out. I thanked Mal as the lights came on and gathered my stuff to head out the door. I turned to take one last look at the familiar place and a feeling of security washed over me. It felt like I was home.

I walked back towards the train station in the dark as the chill of the wind began to hit my face. It was still winter in New York City, it seemed, and I was not really prepared for it. When I left LA it had been like 58 degrees and I had been shivering. My first night back in NYC it must have been 30 degrees and the black leather jacket I had brought with me was doing all it could to keep me warm.

I jogged over to 8th Avenue to try and warm myself up and that's where I saw a 24-hour diner and immediately made a beeline towards it. I sat down at the first open booth I came across and ordered a coffee when an older Spanish man in a white button-down shirt and green apron came to my table. It was warm here and I had enough room to pull out my laptop and play some video games to kill time. I had refill after refill of coffee and eventually ordered a small plate of breakfast so they wouldn't kick me out. I was running low on cash so I think 'breakfast' consisted of a bagel and cream cheese, which I ate very slowly.

It was about 6 a.m. when I got the 'it's time for you to leave look' and I figured since the sun was shining now I might as well head out. I had found a hostel while online at the diner that sounded like a good price and looked like it had a pretty good quality room situation. I had stayed at a few hostels in Los Angeles when I first moved there. Before I started working at the cake shop, I had been living in a specific one for an extended period of time, so I knew what to expect. If this one was like the ones in LA, I would be sharing a room with a few people and the whole floor would share a few bathrooms. I couldn't book a room there until I talked to Tim, because I would have to ask him to pay for it and I was hoping he would say yes.

I left the diner and began to walk around the city for the first time in ten years. It was just as magnificent as I remembered it. The tall buildings were all I could see as I walked up 8th Avenue, but the sun found its way to my face between them. As the warmth enveloped me, I could feel my spark burning even stronger than before. There was something in the air, a magnetic force, I hadn't felt in years. The little voice started to speak again, "This is exactly where you are supposed to be at this very moment. You made it. Now your next adventure begins..."

My next adventure? How much could happen in two weeks?

I continued to sashay down the now-bustling avenue filled with the sounds of taxi cabs blowing their horns and people talking loudly on their cell phones, as they power-walked past me. The morning rush had begun and I was in the middle of it!

I picked up my pace a little bit to keep up with the hustle when I remembered how much I detested the slow moving people on the sidewalk when I had lived here before. I had to keep pinching myself every few minutes, every time I saw another New York City landmark come into view!

Madison Square Garden was the first big building I came across while walking, starting a flow of memories into my mind. Beautiful memories of my youth and those big dreams I had been able to accomplish in the city. The enormity of the building made me feel small, but also made me feel like the biggest person in the world at the same time. I had an energy rushing through me I could only equate to the feelings I had the first time I was in New York. I felt a tinge of happiness hit my chest, working its way into my soul. By the time it got there, I realized what I was really feeling... I felt alive...for the first time in years. Thank God.

I continued to walk up the avenue until I came to 42nd Street. I decided to take a right and head towards Times Square, but before I could get there I noticed it was 11:30 a.m. (time had seemed to fly by in this city) and thought I'd go ahead and give Tim a call, just to see if he had arrived at the shop early. So on the corner of 42nd and 8th I made the call and to my surprise Tim answered.

"Hello?"

"Hello, it's Kaleb. I'm here in New York, I actually made it! I found a place that looked reasonably priced for a week or a little longer stay. It's a hostel in Chelsea," I spoke quickly, excited to hear a familiar voice on the other end of the line.

"Well, I am glad you made it there safely. You can use the credit card number I gave you and charge a week to it, okay? Let's keep it at that though, and then we will talk about getting you a ticket back here. You really shouldn't have left like that; you have responsibilities here, Kaleb. I'm going to put some cash into your bank account too, so you won't go hungry. Be frugal with it. I'm not going to be your personal bank account all the time," said Tim with a sternness to his voice, but also a slight tone of relief mixed in.

"I understand, Tim. Thank you for allowing me to do this. I know it was crazy to just up and leave, but I honestly couldn't stay there one more minute," I replied, sitting down on a bench in what seemed to be a new open public area.

"Alright, Kaleb, call me when you get settled. Have a good day in the city. Maybe you can find a job for the week and make some money. You ARE in New York City after all!" he said, with the old 'Tim optimism' in his voice I had become accustomed to.

"Thanks again, Tim! You really are the best!" I said with a smile, as I pressed the end call button. With the phone still in my hand, I immediately opened up the website for the hostel and booked the room for a week. I was relieved I was going to have a place to stay and take a shower. But what I didn't know was I was about to meet a character who would come into my life, change it, and my view on this little NYC vacation.

After hitting up an ATM and walking back down about 20 city blocks, I arrived at the 'hostel on the water' located at the corner of 23rd and 8th. The Chelsea High Line Hotel was a pretty plain looking building, but the view of the Hudson River was beautiful. I walked in and thankfully the check-in process was pretty easy compared to the ordeal I went through at the airport. The tall, well built, African American man behind the counter handed me my room key and pointed me in the direction of a door behind him.

I walked into the beige room to see 2 bunk beds set up with the sheets of three of them undone. I figured mine must be the top bunk of the one closest to the door since the bed was still made. The room itself was pretty plain looking and bare, besides other people's belongings strewn across the floor, but what had I expected? The Hilton LAX? I climbed to the top bunk and before I knew it I was asleep. It had been another exhaustingly long 'day.'

The next thing I knew it was around six o'clock in the evening and I heard two of the other roommates walk in and change clothes. I didn't say hello or even let them know I was awake. I just laid still until they left. I wasn't planning on making friends this trip because I was here to figure out what I was going to do with my life once I got back to LA and to get reacquainted with myself.

After a few minutes, I got up and got out of bed and headed to the shower. There was complimentary shampoo in a basket which I used as body wash, but I had to use my sheet as a towel that evening because I obviously hadn't prepared for this trip and the hostel did not provide one.

Once back into the room, I changed into the other shirt Wendy had thrown in for me, put on my black top hat and decided to go back to the village to see who I would meet. The evening was fun (what I could remember of it) but I didn't make any new friends or go home with any of the older male suitors vying for my attention.

I made it back to the room at the Chelsea High Line around 1 a.m. and I must not have been as sneaky as I thought when I entered. I stumbled to the ground and when I looked up from the floor a beautiful girl was staring down at me from her bed with a perplexed look on her face.

"Oh hey! You must be my roommate!" I slurred slightly with a smile as I tipped my top hat in her direction.

"Who are you? What time is it?" said the surprised young lady, with a heavy Spanish accent, who slowly began to rise from her bed.

"I'm Kaleb. It's 1 a.m. Let's go get a drink! They serve liquor in New York until 4!" I stammered cutely, as I reapplied the pink lip gloss I had found in my pocket.

"I'm Maider. Let's do it! I need to get dressed... then we go," replied the dark-haired girl with big boobs as she fully sat up and faced me.

Maider quickly got dressed and we headed out the front door of the hostel. We didn't know exactly where we were going so we walked around the area looking for an open restaurant or bar. The first one we came to that looked open sold wine and beer so we went in to get our drink on.

Maider told me she was from Spain and was visiting America for the first time. She let me in on the details of her trip to New York thus far and we bonded over being new to the city. Even though I had been here before, it felt like it was my first time all over again and it was nice to have someone to experience it with.

We ordered a plate of food to share and a couple of glasses of wine each. I told her my story and tried to explain the meaning of some of the words to her as her English was still at the early stages at this point. She was pretty good though and I understood everything she was trying to say. I think it was because our friendship was another one of those 'meant to be' occurrences the Universe would drop into my lap.

Around 2:15 a.m. the waiter brought the bill and by this time we were both pretty tipsy. The total came to $42 and we pooled all the cash we had together and it came up to $32.56. We offered it to the man and, being silly (and partly serious,) I picked up the broom I had seen in the corner and began to sweep the floor. I cleaned up a small area and then burst into the kitchen and started to wash dishes. I got about 4 1/2 dishes washed before the gentleman came and escorted me out of the kitchen and said it was okay. He told me that I could come back to pay the remaining balance the following day.

We laughed the whole walk back to the hostel and our friendship was instantly bonded over an event that could only happen to me! Who else washes 4 1/2 dishes and sweeps a floor to pay for a meal? Classic Kaleb.

We were shushed by the front desk guy as we entered the building so we stifled our laughs as we made it to our room. Before we got into our respectful beds, we exchanged a big hug and phone numbers. I put her in my phone's address book as MAIDER HOSTEL BESTIE and then we went to bed, passing out the second our heads hit the pillows.

My second night in NYC and I had already made a new friend who I felt some real attachment to. Maider told me she still had a little over a week left on her vacation in the city. I thought if she was going to be here, then this little adventure of mine might be more fun. I decided that maybe a week away from LA wasn't enough. So it was looking like I would turn this supposedly quick trip into an extended vacation.

MY TRIP TO CHINA

THE NEXT WEEK with Maider was filled with excitement, entertainment and new experiences. One of our most memorable events occurred on the third day we were together when we explored Little Italy. This was another part of Manhattan I had not stepped foot into when I lived here back in 2002, so I was, in theory, seeing it with the same virgin eyes as my companion.

The streets were pretty busy as it had warmed up slightly in the city. When we arrived we saw tourists taking pictures of the giant illuminated sign hanging high and stretching wide over Mulberry Street, which read: *"Welcome to Little Italy!"*

I had always loved Italian food and I had heard Italian men were supposed to be just as tasty! I thought maybe I could find one while I was in the area to get my mind off of Liam. It had only been a few days since my heart was ripped from my chest and I was still thinking of him quite often.

Maider and I took pictures and tasted some of the bread and marinara that one of the Italian places had out to sample. We stopped by the cigar store, with the life-size Native American Chief statues out front, and I bought myself a 'dos capos' cigar that reminded me of my own brand back in LA. The walk down Mulberry Street was fun. It eventually led us to a quaint little restaurant named Paesano's where we met some characters who would soon make us part of their special "Italian family."

We entered the homey Italian restaurant decorated with authentic Italian paintings and trinkets. The wood-paneled ceiling matched the wooden pillars running down the middle of the room, appearing to hold the whole place up. The pots of ivy dripping from the banisters, along with the chandeliers and wine bottles hanging from the rafters, made us feel as if we had landed in a small town in Italy. "New York, New York" by Frank Sinatra filled the room as a kindly older gentleman led us to our table in the middle of the room.

His name was Dimitri and, from what I could tell, he looked like the owner or the general manager. He was a sweet man with kind eyes and a welcoming face. I had never met my grandfathers, but if I had, I would hope they would be like this guy. He was entertaining and very friendly with me and Maider and, really, who wouldn't be? She was a gorgeous Spanish girl fresh off the plane and

I was a young man from Hollywood, sporting a top hat and looking like a million bucks!

He showed us the menu full of Italian delicacies I had never heard of. There were things like Fusilli Amatricana, Fedelini Puttanesca and the Seafood Cartoccio, which was a mix of every amazing seafood on top of a pile of linguini. Although it sounded extra delicious, it was a bit out of our price range. I still had some of the money Tim had given me the day before and Maider had money she had saved for her trip to New York. So we figured we'd be okay to enjoy a meal here.

We bought the house bottle of wine that was sitting in the middle of the table and ordered the fettuccine alfredo along with a plate of manicotti. The meal was delicious and the wine had us feeling pretty loose. All the waiters were coming over to talk with us and took pictures for us when we asked. Dimitri gave us some shots of fireball on the house, which left Maider and I having the lunch of our lives!

We came up with crazy 'inside' jokes, put cream sauce on the corner of our mouths to take naughty looking photos and snorted sugar lines from the table in a very mob movie style way. This time I was not kicked out for the sugar sniffing. These guys had a sense of humor and chuckled along with us. We caught the whole afternoon on video and it was something we would watch many times before she left.

Nine days into my trip to New York and Maider's trip had come to an end. It was beyond sad when we had to say our last goodbyes at Penn Station as she waited for the train to take her to the airport. In nine days I had made a new best friend from another continent and felt a lust for life again. Thanks to her and this city, I regained a sense of hope I had all but lost when I was trapped in my rock star, drug fueled, world of LA. Don't get me wrong, she and I had partied like rock stars as well. We did a little 'kitty' and went to a strip club, but for some reason it felt different... innocent almost. I believe it was her youthful spirit and the newness to the city, that we both shared, that made this experience, this new friendship, so much more special.

Just as quickly as she came into my life, she was gone. But thanks to Facebook messenger we were able to keep in contact every day after she returned to Spain. For me it was about time for a change of scenery as Tim was not too pleased to be paying for more time at the Chelsea High Line. I had a few more days left at that hostel, so I figured I would enjoy them. I would figure out my next step when the time came.

I don't know what had come over me in that last week but I was more spontaneous and daring than I ever was before. Something had lit a fire under my ass and I was content to go with the flow.

It was in those few days that another odd variable would pop into my life's already jumbled equation and become a catalyst for an event eventually leading me to another 'family' away from home.

It must have been a Thursday when I met Houston, sitting alone having a cocktail and reading a book at a gay bar in Chelsea called XES. He was rather skinny and tall, but he had a handsome face and long brown hair. He reminded me a little bit of Liam the way he looked and the way he sat on his bar stool. I quietly slid out a stool next to him and asked the bartender for a drink as I scanned the guy sitting next to me up and down. He was cute, so I decided to see if my flirting skills still had any prowess.

Houston was from Texas, naturally, and we immediately hit it off with that commonality. He was also a video game nerd and loved comic books. He mentioned that he also played guitar. Oh, goodie...another musician. Ha! Houston was also very interested in the fact that I was a female illusionist. He was engrossed in the stories of my past when I told him I had performed on TV and stage. The afternoon was lovely and there was some heavy flirtation at the bar. I thought maybe I had finally found a guy that I could see myself developing a REAL relationship with. He was all the good things about Liam but he was gay! Or so I thought...

As we got to know each other, the sexual chemistry was pretty hot. I could tell he was really interested in me because when we moved to the patio his hands seemed to find their way to my inner thigh where they proceeded to rest... then caress. It was the first time in months I had felt attractive and the first time I let another man besides Liam get close to me. I wanted to kiss him badly, but I resisted as we talked and shared a few more drinks.

He told me he had to run to a meeting and that he really wanted to see me again. He said I should come out to Brooklyn to hang out with him and his wife on Sunday.

Wait. What?!? His wife?!

He had to be joking. Right?

I looked at him very puzzled and then he told me he and his wife were both bisexual. They had been married for a few years with an open relationship. Great. All I needed in my life was another confused man, and this one came attached with a wife. What was it about me that seemed to attract bisexual men or heterosexual men who were curious? Maybe my feminine aura was constantly letting off vibes that screamed, "I need the most emotionally unavailable guy in the room to please like me!" But I can't put 100% of the blame on my magnetic feminine appeal because I seemed to be just as drawn to these men too. There was something about them: their looks, charm, mannerisms ... and maybe something else. Maybe I was subconsciously attracted to the challenge that these men presented. Maybe I secretly reveled in their confusion. Or maybe, I just wanted to be loved by a man the way a woman was, fulfilling the Cinderella dreams in my mind. I wanted a butch man's man. A guy's sexual preference never stopped me. I figured I could go for any man I wanted because really it's my soul they are going to end up being attracted to, right? That's what I told myself anyway.

The New York, spontaneous version of Kaleb, immediately said yes and so we made plans to meet in Brooklyn on Sunday afternoon. He left the bar and I continued to drink and chat with other people before eventually leaving an hour or so later. As I headed back to the hostel, I tried not to let my mind go to that place in the distant future where I saw myself with him and how good things could be. I tried to tell myself to take it easy with this one because I had just been hurt and this one came with baggage. Actually, I guess a wife might be considered an everyday accessory.

Sunday came before I knew it and Houston called me with directions to his place in Brooklyn. I had never been to that borough when I lived in New York before, so I was excited to get to finally see it and him. Only a few days had passed, but I was ready to see this man and get that sexual energy flowing again.

I traveled from the hostel in Chelsea down to Canal Street in Chinatown (a place I had actually been often) and found my way to the J train that would take me to Brooklyn. I was already confused just looking at the jumbled subway map and tried to follow Houston's directions as best as I could. I headed into the subway and boarded the train headed to Myrtle Avenue, my first stop in Brooklyn.

As the train rolled into the station, on this very cold night, I was really wishing that I had prepared a little more for this trip. It's not like I had real winter clothes in my storage in LA though, because in Los Angeles it rarely gets below 60 degrees. If I had known I would be staying a little longer, I would have had time to buy some winter gear before I left. But that's what happens when your heart gets crushed. You run away... across the country... on a whim. Oh, everybody doesn't do that? Ha. My bad.

I exited the station into the unknown land of Brooklyn. From the get go, it had a weird vibe to it. It was dirtier than the city and the locals seemed a little less friendly, if you can imagine that! I walked a few blocks under the train track following the directions he had given me. After about an eight-minute walk, I was at his apartment. I was excited to see him again so I popped a mint into my mouth and sprayed a little bit of my travel 'Fantasy' on my neck. Just in case.

I walked up a small flight of concrete stairs in front of his building and knocked on his door. He answered it pretty quickly and grabbed my hand to guide me in. The 2-bedroom apartment was kind of messy and looked very lived in. The kitchen was in front of us as we walked in, the living room with the long brown couch to the left and a hallway leading to the bathroom and bedroom to the right. That's the room I was interested in. It had been too long since I had been with a man and I thought maybe he might be the one to fix that.

He showed me to the couch and served me a cold beer from the fridge. He sat next to me and we began to talk about life and the future. He then asked, "Do you want to smoke some pot? I want to ask you something and it might be more fun if we are high."

I don't usually smoke pot, but I figured if he was going to ask me to do what I thought he was, then being stoned might make it even sexier. So I agreed and he began to roll a joint. He passed it to me upon completion and lit it in my mouth. What a gentleman! My body started tingling as the marijuana took effect and I could sense the sexual vibes between us growing stronger. It was like I could read his mind or maybe he could hear my naughty thoughts. He stood up, grabbed my hand and led me towards the bedroom.

Before we got to the door he turned around and grabbed me by the face and kissed me. Talk about a romantic, sexual, steamy moment! He continued to kiss me, letting his tongue dance with mine, as one hand moved to my lower back then began to feel me up and down. I was in heaven when he tightly grasped my behind in one hand. Suddenly he stopped all action and led me the rest of the way to his room with a smile.

This was it. I was finally going to have sex with another man again. I could put that asshole Liam out of my mind for good. I was here with Houston and we were about to make love so why couldn't I get that jerk in Hollywood out of my head?

Houston turned around and unbuttoned his plaid, hipster-style shirt to reveal a very ripped stomach. I immediately got weak in the knees as I started to walk toward him staring at his body. Before I could get close enough to touch him, he picked up a bra from the bed and started to put it on.

Woah... Woah. What?!

I had seen the women's clothing when I walked into the room, but I had just assumed that it was his open-relationship sharing wife's belongings laying there. I was in shock. He seemed pretty butch to me and I was definitely attracted to him, but this added another layer of complexity to the whole ordeal.

"Whatcha doin' with that?" I asked, with a surprised look on my face while forcing a fake smile.

"Oh, I didn't mention this to you the other day? My wife and I are having a re-commitment ceremony next weekend and I will be wearing this dress..." he said, as he pulled a white gown from the open closet door. "I was hoping you could help me with my makeup and stuff since you are so amazing at it!"

"Oh, wow. I'm uh...honored... I guess. Is that what all this is about, though? Is that why you invited me over here? Where is your wife by the way?" I said, now questioning every motive and everything else going on.

"No, no that's not the only reason I invited you over. You're really beautiful and I am very attracted to you, for sure. And the fact that you would be able to help me with this makes you even more sexy!" he said as he slid the dress over his head.

In a weird sort of way, he looked sort of cute in the dress. So I figured that if I did like him, I might as well be open to helping him with this. I mean I expected all my boyfriends to be okay with Sarah Summers, so why shouldn't I be okay with someone I like doing drag, too? This was the first time I had actually been attracted to someone that did it so it would be a learning experience for me. If the relationship went anywhere.

So I kissed him again in the dress and helped him do his makeup. I showed him how to make his cleavage look real using blush and bronzer, which got him extremely excited. He had forgotten to tuck in the excitement following my being willing to help. He was so turned on I could see his good-sized erection popping up through the dress. I grasped it with my hand and stroked it as we kissed. He tightly grabbed my ass once again, making me tingle with pleasure. I felt a little naughty doing this with him in the dress he was going to be wearing while re-committing to his wife. But we were in the moment and who knew how long it would last?

His phone rang in the heat of the moment before anything else could happen. He had to take the call, so I went into the living room, still sweating slightly from all the hot action that had just occurred. He closed the bathroom door, but my supersonic hearing was in effect and I listened in on the private conversation. It was his wife. He was absolutely giddy as he told her how real his boobs looked and how glad he was to have met me. Of course, he left out the fact that he had just had his tongue down my throat and his hands all over me. He ended the call and motioned me back into the bedroom.

I helped him out of the dress and we kissed again, my body up against his now fully naked body. I guess his underwear must have 'slipped' off in the bathroom while on that call. I played with his cock a little more before he told me the bad news. His wife was on her way home from work so we would have to put any sexy plans on hold until later. Damn it! I was so ready for it too! My emotion-erasing sex would have to wait.

His wife arrived at the apartment about ten minutes later. She was not really what I expected. Shorter, plump (but not fat), mousy brown curly hair and glasses. Cute. But no Sarah Summers. I could see why he was attracted to her though. She loved all the same things he did. Video games, sci-fi, comics. But most importantly, she loved him. All of him. His fluid sexuality, his female illusion aspect and just everything he was. It was beautiful and it made me kind of regret wanting to break up this happy (albeit odd) home.

The three of us went out that evening to a local dive bar in Brooklyn. That's when things began to get weird. I tried to be nice to her and get to know her, but she was not making it easy. Every time we were seated together he was always next to me holding my hand or resting his hand on my thigh. She started throwing shady looks when she noticed. I thought they had an open relationship? When he and I stepped outside to the front patio area and he kissed me, she basically lost it and ran off. I guess an open relationship didn't stop jealousy from occurring, no matter how 'open' it was. He went to run after her, but stopped and looked back at me before he did. He grabbed my hand and said, "I had an amazing time today. Thank you for everything. We will talk soon."

He ran after her and, as beautiful as the sentiment of his words were, I knew that would be the last time we would be seeing each other. Another relationship thwarted by a woman! Just my luck.

So now I was some place in Brooklyn I had no clue about and it had gotten even colder outside. I found my way to the closest subway station and was able to make my way back to Canal Street through the tangled web of the NYC MTA system.

As I exited the train station by walking up the stairs, I was utterly shocked at the next thing I saw.

It was snowing! In the middle of April!

I hadn't seen snow since the last time I lived in New York and even then it was in December. So this was definitely a rare occurrence. As pretty as it was, it was also very, very cold. My LA leather jacket was no match for the freezing wind and the chill. I walked up Lafayette street with no clue where I was headed, but out of the blue (warm red glow technically) there it was, my saving grace.

The restaurant, with its orange awning and purple façade, was lit by sconces on the wall, looking like little balls of fire from the outside. With the snow outside coming down hard, that was exactly what I needed! Heat! Fire! Warmth! To my surprise, this little place would hold all of that within its welcoming door and my night got more interesting the second I walked in.

It was another lovely little place in SoHo, quaint like Paesano's, with its traditional paintings and trinkets, except this place was a French restaurant, Parigot, and everything in it was very French! Even the employees were French and they were both lovely. The two young girls invited me in out of the cold and immediately handed me a glass of red wine. I was in love already! The music was turned up and the vibe was happening. There was another table eating a late dinner and they seemed to be having a wonderful time as their laughter was infectious. The group consisted of two girls and an attractive guy and I immediately took notice of that cutie in the corner.

I was still in a little bit of a funk after the incident earlier with the bisexual couple, but after a few glasses of wine, I began to relax. They were playing some fun dance music so of course I put on a show for the employees and the table where the cute guy with the dark hair and dark eyes sat.

After a couple of dances (in a very 'Britney Spears style'), the gentleman held out a dollar for me to come collect. I thought it was very cute and definitely a come-on! I slinked over sexily and accepted the bill in my pants. Then I joined them at the table where we got to know each other a little better.

He was very cute, Latin, sexy eyes, chiseled jaw and I could tell he had muscles because they were popping through his tight shirt. We flirted up until the restaurant had to close and the girls he was with suggested he and I go back to my hotel. I was delighted when he said he thought it was a good suggestion.

We thanked the girls at Parigot as we left. I promised them I would be back soon. Rodrigo hailed a cab as we said goodbye to his girlfriends. We were soon on our way back to the 'hostel by the water' and making out heavily in the cab. He was definitely a sexy guy and I guess my body had been putting off some sort of pent up sexual vibes because he was all over me. He was not afraid to grab my crotch and lick my neck as the car drove us down the road. This was my kind of PDA! Didn't have to pretend we were 'just friends' in public with him like I did with Liam and there was definitely no handbag of a wife like Houston. As far I knew he was single, gay and all about me. That is all I needed to know.

Somewhere between the restaurant and the hostel (and deep breaths and passionate kisses) he told me this was his last day in the city on his vacation from wherever it was he came from. I was fine with that. I was just ready to give myself to him and have a little fun. And we did. Twice that night.

We got to the hostel around 1 a.m. and since I had moved my stuff to a private room, there was no problem with him staying over. Before we could even get into the bed our clothes were on the floor and we were getting hot and bothered. It felt so nice to have a man's hands appreciating my naked body again. With him I felt no reservation, he knew what he wanted. He was good at it too. We did just about everything one can do sexually that night and I was finally relieved of all my pent-up stress.

We woke up the next morning and I was snuggled into his under arm area where I wanted to stay all day, but I knew that he had to get to the airport and I had to find a new place to stay. He looked so sexy trying to put on his tight black boxer briefs over his light brown skin and his hard member. I couldn't resist and gave him one more goodbye blow job. Damn, it was hot.

We said our goodbyes and after he left I immediately got on my computer to start researching cheaper rooms around town. I found something in Chinatown online that definitely fit my budget of $20 a day, but it wasn't very clear on the description of the rooms. I was a little nervous, but what other option did I have? I wasn't exactly ready to go back to LA yet and I couldn't afford to stay at this hostel any longer. I figured I'd give this new place a try, so I packed my bags and prepared for my trip to China.

THE DAY I SAVED A LIFE

THE SUNNY DAY HOTEL. Wow.
The name was only accurate in the sense that when
the sun was out it could be seen shining directly
into the 5th floor windows all day. The name did
not relate to the room accommodations by any
means because it was a far stretch from reminding
its visitors of a happy, sunny day.

With the help of Tim, I had purchased a week-
long stay at The Sunny Day, in the heart of
Chinatown. Surprisingly, he said if I was not ready
to come back to LA yet, he would support me in
that decision to stay for a little bit longer. I figured
I had already been in Manhattan a few weeks, so
why not make it a full month? That's what all the
Europeans did when they went on vacay.

I arrived at the front desk and found myself stuck
waiting in line behind a group of Asian men who

were talking very fast in their native tongue. I didn't understand a word of it, naturally, but I was intrigued either way. They seemed to get louder and louder with each following syllable but they were smiling so I knew it wasn't an argument. Once they received their room keys and headed up the stairs, I made my way to the front desk to get mine. The guy behind the counter didn't speak much English but we were able to communicate enough for me to check in. He pointed me to the staircase that seemed to go up for miles. It was a walk-up building and I was on the fifth floor, so I figured I'd definitely be getting my exercise while staying here. I imagined how devastated I'd be if I were to forget my phone or something in my room after making it all the way down to the lobby!

I climbed the dirty, beige-painted stairs. When I passed the third floor, I was taken aback by what I saw. The third floor smelled pretty terrible and from what I could see, it looked like the rooms were awfully small. The guys walking through the hallway seemed like they were pretty destitute and did not look like the average paying traveler. I wondered what was going on there, but I hurried up the stairs to avoid any confrontation.

I finally reached the fifth floor, completely out of breath. I opened the large locked door that led into the hallway. When I walked in, I noticed that, like the third floor, the rooms were very tiny but this floor was much cleaner and didn't have the same obnoxious odor.

I walked down the narrow pathway to see rows and rows of what I can only describe as closet-sized rooms. There was literally a line of 12 doors down one side and 12 directly across, no more than an arm stretch apart. Three more 'hallways' like this took up the entire floor.

I walked down to the end of the last hallway to find my room at the end of the row. It was a corner room so I figured maybe it was a tad bigger. I opened the door to find a twin-size mattress on top of a wooden bed frame next to an open 'closet', which looked like it could hold maybe 3 outfits. When I looked above my head, I saw that the 'ceiling' of my room was nothing but chicken wire stretched across the top of the connecting wood support walls. What had I gotten myself into? If I thought rooming with a few strangers at the last hostel was bad, I was sure I was in for a real treat here.

As I put my bag down, exhausted from the journey up the stairs, I could overhear some guy complaining about his life to someone on the phone. His whiny attitude made me appreciate my life a little more. I was off on an adventure and feeling more alive than I had felt in ages. For the time being, I was grateful to be in this little closet because it was better than being on the streets in LA, pining over some drug-addicted rock star and looking like a complete waste of life myself.

Only two really mentionable stories occurred at this place. The rest of the time was spent sleeping or showering and then leaving for as long as I could. I ended up staying there two weeks, thanks to Tim and a mistake on my credit card, resetting my balance to zero a few times. Well, the credit card thing was not so much a mistake as a misunderstanding. I paid online through my bank and then the bank over-drafted me and paid the card off. The credit card company found out the bank payment was returned a few days later and then the circle of events repeated. I think both companies finally caught wind of what was happening and shut off my credit card and restricted my checking account for some time. The situation was good while it lasted, but resulted in major debt that I would eventually have to pay off.

One of the stories from this stay happened towards the end of my first week at the Sunny Day. It was one of those kismet sort of occurrences. Late one evening I was walking down the narrow stretch of street in Chinatown towards the 'hotel'. It was dimly lit and pretty empty. I had been out having a few drinks in the neighborhood and was headed up to bed when I saw a very sexy guy standing outside listening to his headphones and having a cigarette. When I say sexy, I mean like 'man I would marry' or 'man who could pick me up and carry me home' (if I got too drunk one night) and 'man I would make all the other girls jealous with' kind of man! He was tall, built like a brick, and his short dark hair and scruff put me over the edge.

I pulled out a cigarette and pretended to look for a lighter while I sat on the stoop close to where he was standing. I 'didn't find a lighter' of course (oldest trick in the book, I know), but before I got up to flirt and ask him for a light, I listened closely to see if I could hear what he had playing in his ear. To my surprise and delight, this big hunk of man was listening to the Will.i.am and Britney Spears song 'Scream & Shout.' It must be my lucky day.

I slinked up next to him and asked him for a light. He took a second to register what I said and then took his headphones off while he dug through the pockets of his form-fitting slacks. As he sparked then lifted the lighter up towards my cigarette, he spoke. It was like sex in my ears! "Here you are, mate! Nice night we're having eh?" he said in his manly Australian accent.

I had always dreamed of a lover with a body, attitude and style like his, but with the addition of the Australian accent it was almost too much! I stepped a little closer to him and decided to ask him about the song.

"I'm Kaleb. What was that song you were jamming out to?" I asked coyly, even though I already knew the answer.

"My name is Duke and that is Britney Spears and Will.i.am! It's my favorite song. You wanna take a listen?" he said, handing over his red Beats headphones.

I put the headphones on and started to dance a little for him. He must have thought this was cute or funny because he seemed to be enjoying it, flashing a big grin across his handsome face. Once again, Britney Spears was my in with a man. Go figure. She had been involved in a lot of the big moments of my life, some physically, but mostly in song. It is almost like Britney Spears was my spirit animal. Haha.

As the song finished, I handed him back the headphones and asked him what he had planned the rest of the night. He said he had none, so I suggested we go get two-for-one drinks in the Village and then sing karaoke. He seemed like he'd be up for anything and decided to tag along.

Walking around with this guy was like heaven. He made me feel like a damn princess. He was considerate and bought most of the drinks that night. I told him about my situation while we were on the train ride uptown. He, like most people, was flabbergasted when I told him the tale of the last few weeks and he was sympathetic towards my plight.

We ended up singing karaoke at this little place in the Village, that I love, called BoHo Karaoke. I had made friends with the female manger there who was a pretty but hard-assed Asian chick. She had kicked me out a few times when I had been a little drunk, but she had always let me back in the next time. I appreciated that. We had a great time and, around 4 a.m. when the bar closed, we stumbled out looking for somewhere to find food. I hadn't asked him right out if he was gay or straight, and honestly, I didn't want to know the answer. I was flirting with him and he was playing along. He even let me hold his hand for a minute when we were walking (being tipsy probably helped him loosen up to being open to that)!

We made it back to the hostel as the sun was coming up. As we walked up the stairs, he told me that he had a really fun night and would love to hang out again before he left. We did hang out one more time on his last day in New York and it was pretty nice. I met him in his room downstairs (the queen-sized bed rooms that cost more and were private) and laid on his bed while he got ready. We listened to 'Scream & Shout' a few times while discussing our personal plans for the future. He was off to Miami for his next stop in the States and I was still considering a good day to head back to LA. No date seemed right just yet.

We went out to dinner that night and to a few more clubs to drink and dance the night away. He was very sweet to me and I finally did find out he was straight, but he was happy to have me as a friend in the States. We traded Facebook info and have been in contact occasionally since he left, which he did the following day. Ahh, another one bites the dust! I guess I set my goals pretty high, but hey! A kid can dream, right?

The only other story of interest is from the end of my stay at the Sunny Day. Boy is it a kicker! It was the second week in May of 2014. I had just celebrated my month-long anniversary in New York. I still had not felt like I had found exactly what I was looking for in the city, so I decided to stretch my trip out for as long as possible. I had found a new 'home' bar down in the financial district I enjoyed going to called The Raccoon Lodge. I could be found there most nights in the booth in the back sipping on a Kaleb's Kool-Aid and working on my laptop (making use of the bar's free wifi) after scouring the city all day for work.

The Raccoon Lodge was a typical divey straight bar reminding me a bit of The Twisted Rainbow in LA. Dimly lit, a single bar with a cute big-boobed woman usually stationed behind it, a pool table, a digital jukebox and a punching bag game. The clientele was a mix of finance guys, frat boys and rocker types with a sprinkling of ladies thrown in.

One evening I made friends with a rather good looking (slightly intoxicated) gentleman who I proceeded to vigorously make out with at my booth/office in the back throughout the entirety of the evening. I didn't know if he was straight, gay, bi or whatever, but we had a good time drinking and kissing that night.

He had been falling asleep in my lap a few times and I kinda thought it was cute. The whole evening had been cute until I went to the bathroom. I left him at the table to watch our drinks and my belongings, then headed to the restroom to relieve myself. When I came out he, my computer and my phone were all gone! I immediately freaked the fuck out. I ran up to the bartender, who had seen me in there many times working at the back booth on my laptop, and asked him what happened to the random guy I had been making out with for the last two hours!?

He proceeded to tell me that the guy had passed out on the table and they had to ask him to leave. Apparently when he left, he grabbed all my stuff and took it with him! The bar staff assumed that I had known him for more than a few hours and let him leave with it. Can't totally blame them for that, we did look like a couple in love, and yes, I know I shouldn't have left my belongings unattended with some cute drunk guy I barely knew, but I trusted him. I mean his tongue was practically down my throat for the whole night and I thought we had something special going on! I was a love-sick fool, so desperate for a real connection to help me forget about Liam, that I was willing to put myself and my personal belongings at risk. Another reason I hated Liam. He turned me into this sad, needy version of myself, who was always struggling to get validation from a man to prove that I was lovable. I was never like that before him. I was confident. I was the one giving the validation!

I also forgot I was in New York City and maybe it WAS a little rougher than LA, like people had warned me. I was not New York tough yet, but this whole ordeal definitely taught me to be more aware of my surroundings and made me a little more cautious about the people I was making 'friends' with.

I left the bar and looked all over for that guy. I didn't know his name, his phone number or where he was from. I felt so stupid at that moment. I ran around the five-block radius of the bar multiple times, looking in every bar, shop and alleyway to see if I could find him ... I couldn't. Once again, I felt completely defeated. Why was stuff like this constantly happening to me?! Was this karma trying to kick my ass?! What did I do in the past to deserve ALL this shit happening in my life!?

The woe-is-me attitude and the complete and utter disgust with myself (and all human beings at that moment), gave me enough energy to survive the long walk back to the Sunny Day

Hotel. I ran upstairs and passed out in a stream of my own tears.

The next morning, I went to the corner drug store, bought a prepaid phone and immediately called Tim. He was not too surprised to hear this dramatic story as he had heard many like them before, stemming from my years of drug-fueled and drunken escapades. I had been through more phones in a year than most people go through in a lifetime, and had more things stolen from me than I'd like to admit.

Tim was always there to help me put the pieces of my broken life back together and I would always promise him I would do better. He truly was like a father to me in that sense. He was disappointed and upset at my childish behavior, but he didn't want to see me suffer too much. He would only help me out enough so I wasn't on the street. He wanted me to figure out solutions to my own problems. He told me, "You need to go to the police, Kaleb. I bet that bar has a camera system and you can get the footage from them to show to the cops. I'll help you out of this mess, but you have to promise you'll go to the police station this afternoon!"

I promised and then he said he would go down to the bank that afternoon to make a deposit.

It was noon in New York City, which meant it was 9 a.m. when he hung up the phone in LA, so I would have to wait until at least 3 p.m., my time, for him to deposit the money. I figured that would give me time to go to the police station to report the crime, and then get a few drinks with the money I had left before going to the bank. My day was all planned out in my head, but things in New York never seemed to go as I thought they would. This day was no exception.

I left the Sunny Day Hotel and headed down towards the financial district to The Raccoon Lodge, hoping that I could talk to the manager before going to the police. The manager was there and told me no one knew that guy or had seen him before, but to check back with him later in the week and he would try to get a picture from the surveillance camera. Well, at least that was a start. He also said I was no longer welcomed in the bar after the way I reacted to finding out all my stuff had been stolen the night before. Turns out, I may have yelled at people, thrown a drink and stormed out in a huff. I didn't exactly remember doing that though. Damn blackouts!

So at least they were still willing to help me out and that put my mind at ease a little as I headed to the police station. I was told I should go to the police precinct closest to the bar, which covered that area of the city. The one I went to first was not the right one and it was pretty weird going into a police station to ask for help instead of coming out of one after being arrested for public intoxication (which happened a few times in the 9 years I lived in LA and a bunch of times when I lived in Texas).

The officers told me I had to go down to the 2nd precinct, so I started walking in that direction. It was back up town a little way, closer to Canal Street, and on the path towards the station I saw a really divey bar that had $3 shots of whiskey for happy hour! I thought a couple of shots couldn't hurt. Maybe it would take the edge off of going into yet another police station.

I had a couple of shots, but not enough to get drunk and headed back towards the A train so I could get to the other police station quicker than walking. What happened next surprised the hell out of me and made me remember some very important things about myself that I had completely forgotten living in that fantasy rock star world of LA. It showed me who I really was.

I entered the subway station by walking down a flight of stairs that ran down to a lower floor where the police station I had just been at was located. It was like another world down in the subway system with offices, restaurants, shops and police stations almost creating their own little city. This was something I had never seen before. It took me a little while to even believe there was so much going on underneath the already crowded streets above.

I passed the police station and headed down another flight of stairs towards the train platform where I saw something horrifying. At the bottom of the stairs was an older white man (maybe in his 50s) laying in a large, spreading pool of his own blood. The sight was pretty disturbing and looked like something out of a scary movie. There was blood everywhere, especially on his ragged khakis, torn tan jacket and pair of worn out shoes. Blood splatter could be seen on each stair leading down towards his final resting place. I froze for a brief second to piece together what must have happened to this man. He must have tripped and fell down the entire flight of stairs and cracked his head open at some point during the fall. Why was no one doing anything? Where were the police?? Was this even real?

All those thoughts blinked quickly through my head, but before I knew it, I was leaping down the stairs towards his lifeless, bloody body. I guess the spirit of my mother (the award-winning Registered Nurse who I had volunteered with for years) took over my body and I knew that I was the only one who could save him right then.

I got to the bottom of the bloody stairs and kneeled down next to his head. I first noticed the giant gash on his forehead, but knew that the majority of the blood must be coming from a laceration on the back of his head. I looked around to see a crowd of people gathered around doing absolutely nothing. It shocked me that no one had done anything before I arrived. He appeared to be homeless and maybe that deterred some people from helping him, but that didn't matter to me because he was a human being and he was bleeding profusely. I had to do something.

I first put my ear up to his nose to see if I could hear his breath. It was faint, but he was indeed still breathing so I knew my next step would be to try and stop the bleeding. I took off my black-and-red Burberry looking flannel scarf and immediately made a tourniquet out of it by wrapping it under his head to cover the giant open wound I had spotted once I got closer. I held pressure on it, but the ripped skin on his forehead began to bleed even more once the pressure from the makeshift tourniquet was applied. I didn't have any other piece of spare fabric so while I was holding his bloody head in my hands I turned to the giant crowd behind me and screamed, "Someone come and fucking help me!" My eyes burned through the crowd of scared little sheep until I found a woman who had a 'I ❤ NY' t-shirt in her hand. I silently pleaded with her using my eyes. I was so happy that she had the courage to run over and ask me what she could do to help.

"Wrap your shirt around his head covering the wound on the top and apply continual pressure until the EMTs arrive!" I ordered, like a trained emergency professional. I guess I was a lot better under pressure than I thought, but at that moment all I could think about was keeping this stranger alive. I hadn't noticed that two cops had come down the stairs behind us and were now watching me as I tried to stop the hemorrhaging. They looked at us as they called for the EMTs on their radios. Instead of kneeling down to help us they offered us a pair of gloves. I looked at them with a look of confusion as I was already covered in this man's blood. Too little too late on the gloves, officers!

The wait for the EMTs seemed like hours. As I held the scarf around his head, I breathed into his ear and whispered, "Keep breathing.... just like this...keep breathing... help will be here soon."

I had this man's life literally in my hands and I just prayed that I was doing everything right.

The EMTs finally arrived and they came carefully down the stairs with their portable gurney. They looked at me and handed me a neck brace to help them situate it on him since my hands were already under his head. I then helped them move him from the ground onto the board and assisted them with strapping him down. I watched them put the air bag on him and start to pump it to ease his breathing and I felt like one of them for that moment. It wasn't until they started up the stairs and one of them patted me on the back that I jumped back into the present. What had I just done?

I stood up from the ground and looked down at myself to see that I was covered from head to toe in blood, but I was not for a second freaked-out or worried about anything. The lady cop who had been watching me asked if I wanted to go back to the station to clean up. I nodded yes as we walked up the stairs. The girl who had helped me declined to go to the station because she had not gotten too much blood on herself. I gave her a head tilt of thanks as she boarded the next train.

I entered the police station once again, but this time covered in blood and, according to the lady cop, a bit of a hero. She took me to the officer's locker room and handed me a towel and bar of soap. As I scrubbed the blood off of my hands, I looked in the mirror to see that there was a little blood on my face. I washed it off quite proudly as I started to realize that I had done something pretty amazing that day. If it hadn't been for me going into that subway, at exactly that time, that man might not still be alive. The female cop handed me a clean rag to wash what I could off my clothes and said, "You know what you just did today kid? You saved a life. You saved that man's life. You should feel very good about yourself. You showed bravery in the face of adversity and ran towards something that made other people turn and run away. You saved a life today. That's amazing."

And it was amazing. Here's this kid from Hollywood who loved to drink, do drugs, party and was basically written off by everyone for being a complete mess. Then he comes to New York City and in a month is saving a life?! Who would have thought? I definitely didn't see that one coming!

As big as that moment was in my story, it was but a catalyst that would lead to the events that occurred the next day when I saved another life. My own.

LET GO MY EGO

MY TIME at the Sunny Day was coming to an end as my credit card had been shut off and Tim was not too happy to be shelling out increased amounts of money every week. I wasn't ready to go back to Los Angeles yet. I couldn't. I couldn't face them all... especially Liam. I figured if I had literally saved a man's life the day before, why shouldn't I be able to save my own today?

I decided it was time to seek assistance and the first thing I thought of was the Gay and Lesbian Center. If the one in New York was anything like the one in LA, it would be full of resources and people willing to help. I was right.

When I walked into the Center that afternoon I went in open to receiving whatever help I could get. What I didn't realize was that my life was about to change pretty drastically. The lady at the front desk seemed very kind and open minded as she greeted me with a warm smile and a polite hello. The desk and walls were covered in pamphlets on everything from Safe Sex to Drug Abuse Assistance, but I didn't see anything on Homelessness.

Which was what I was. I finally had to admit that to myself. I mean, if it hadn't been for Tim, I would have been out on the streets this whole time. More than likely, I wouldn't have made it more than a few days before that dark voice came back and finally won. That's what I thought at the moment, but I honestly wasn't giving myself enough credit. I would soon find out how strong I really was and it all stemmed from this moment at the Center.

"May I help you?" said the middle-aged woman with her curly red hair and black-rimmed glasses, looking at me with curious eyes.

"I hope so. I'm ho...home...homeless...and I don't know where to go or what to do. Do you offer any assistance in that area?" I said, stuttering the words almost in disbelief that they were actually coming out of my mouth.

"We don't offer anything here, but let me refer you to an organization that is close by that does. Here's the address," she said, handing me the information on a yellow post-it note.

"Thank you, I'll go over there now," I responded with a smile. A small wave of relief washed over me for a second when I thought I might finally be getting some help. It felt like no one had wanted to help me in LA, but maybe I wasn't really looking for the real help I needed at that time either. Now I was ready to admit I needed assistance. So I exited the center with a sense of hopefulness and headed further into the West Village, down streets I had never seen before.

It was like The Organization was calling out to me because I got there quickly and without getting lost. I basically walked right into it after turning the corners into the unknown area of the city. The Organization was in a newly constructed, medium-sized building, so I immediately felt like it must be reputable. They welcomed me at this place as well, and I was grateful.

In the lobby, I looked around at the people seeking help. They looked pretty bad off. The types of people ranged from older men, whose clothes had seen better days, to women with their children, who looked beyond stressed out. What was I doing here? I wasn't like these people. I didn't look like these people and I wasn't helpless. I was just down on my luck at the moment, but I wasn't at the point that these people were at...was I?

Before I went to the front desk to ask for help, I ran to the bathroom to take a breath. It was there, in the mirror, that I saw the truth. The boy with the normally glistening eyes and clear skin was replaced by someone I didn't recognize any more. He was tired, skinny, had a broken-out face with wild long hair and a look of sadness that resembled the faces I had seen in the lobby. I was just like those people. I had to let go of my old way of thinking at that very moment. I no longer had a cushy job at a famous Hollywood cake shop. I no longer had a rock star love. I no longer had my own money and I no longer had a consistent place to rest my head. I WAS like those people and it was then that I realized I WANTED to be like them. They were brave enough to let go of their ego and ask for the help they so desperately needed, that I so desperately needed. Instantly my mind changed on the whole situation. I decided, right then and there, I was going to be brave too, let go of who I was before and ask for the help I needed.

I walked up to the front desk and met a guy who would become a face I would grow very fond of seeing as my time here went on. He was a tall, skinny, African American man who, even though he was missing a few teeth, gave me the biggest smile in the world. I felt no sense of judgment coming from this man, from this place, and I had a feeling that things would soon turn around for me.

Wayne, the guy at the front desk, asked me how he could help me and I told him about my situation. He directed me to the homeless counselor's office down the hallway. I thanked him and walked cautiously towards the door because I knew once I stepped through it, I would have to be completely honest with myself and other people.

I sat down in the room filled with black-and-white photos in frames of people appearing to be 'success stories.' Even though I didn't physically resemble the people shown, I felt comfort. I filled out the information packet that was on a clipboard sitting on the table covered in literature and contraceptives. This place seemed to have a vibe of safety, health and education, which made me think maybe I was in the right place. I hadn't even thought about my health in the last year while I was doing all those drugs and partying every night. It wasn't until I got to this place, The Organization, where the signs were literally everywhere, that I even thought about my physical well-being.

I finished the paper work as an attractive, heavy-set African American woman walked over and greeted me with another huge smile and lovely hello.

"Good afternoon, welcome. How can we help you today?" she asked with a sincere kindness to her voice.

"Well, I don't really know where to start. It's been a rough couple of months. I found myself here in New York with no plan and no place to call home. I just feel lost and honestly have no clue what to do," I said, letting a tear fall from my right eye down my cheek.

"You've come to the right place, darling. Let's go into my office and see what we can do for you. Would you like a coffee?" she said, giving me a warm reassuring pat on the back.

The Organization had resources I didn't even know existed and were able to help me in ways I never thought possible. They were able to get me on government assistance that very day, which included $188 every two weeks and $165 in food stamps. I NEVER in my life thought I would be using food stamps or taking 'handout' money from the government, but at this point in my life, I so desperately needed it. I let go of that 'I am better than that' mind set and graciously accepted it.

They also signed me up for Medicare and free health care at their office. They had a doctor's office in the building and said that if I wanted to continue to get help from them I would have to take all sorts of mental and physical tests to make sure I was trying to better my life. They also offered drug and alcohol classes and groups and said if I wanted to join one they would help me get involved. They didn't say I had to stop drinking, but advised it would be more productive if I quit doing that and drugs. I had only done 'kitty' one time since I had been in NYC and I really didn't see myself doing it again. Drinking, on the other hand, was my only solace in this lonely, scary world. I didn't know where I would be without it. It was my crutch, my motivator and my only true friend. For now, anyway.

I saw their doctor that afternoon and took all the tests they required. They said I was underweight and malnourished, which I already knew. They said I could get a hot lunch there every day during the week until I got back on my feet. The offer was great and I did in fact go there for lunch a few times when money got extra tight.

The last appointment that afternoon was with a housing counselor. I was surprised at how quickly they were able to work. They said they could find me emergency housing in a SRO (single-room occupancy) shelter. A 'homeless hotel' so to speak.

At that moment, anything would have been better than a closet-sized room with a chicken-wire ceiling where you could hear everyone's business at all times. I was ready for whatever was next... It had to be better... Right?

The lady, who became my case manager, typed some things into the computer and within minutes had a print out of the building and location of where I would be staying. I was kind of scared at this moment because I had only seen homeless shelters on TV and always heard awful things about them.

"Here you go, Kaleb. This place is on the Upper West Side close to Harlem and it is one of the nicer ones in the city. We were lucky that they had an open room today! I hope everything works out for you, dear, and the next time I see you I want to see a little more meat on those bones!" she said, playfully tugging at her own larger stomach.

"Thank you, Ms. Gena! I will make you proud!" I replied with a smile as I got up out of the seat and gave her a big hug. This was an emotional moment for me. I had let go of that person who thought he was too good for any of this and became the person who was beyond grateful to be receiving all this help from kind strangers. I left the office with a big grin and a wave to Wayne as I told him I'd be seeing him again soon.

My next step would be going back to The Sunny Day to collect my belongings before heading to the shelter. When I arrived back in Chinatown to my tiny room after climbing the 5 flights of dirty, beige stairs, I took a moment to call Tim and tell him what I had done. As the phone rang, I nervously anticipated his reaction. I wondered if he would think I was doing the right thing or if he would tell me to come back to Hollywood.

He was surprisingly impressed that I took the initiative to actually help myself. "I'm a little shocked to hear this, but I am very proud of you for taking this step to help yourself. It will be a lot better on my wallet, too. You know I am more than happy to help you when I can, Kaleb, but I am even more willing to help you when you are helping yourself and preferably when you are sober. How's that going?" he asked, always throwing that drinking thing in my face as if it was that easy to stop. I didn't blame him for trying though, that was the father figure in him coming out.

"I guess I'll be staying in New York a little bit longer," I replied.

We ended the call and I left the Sunny Day Hotel and didn't look back. I didn't know what the shelter system was going to be like, but I knew it was something I had to do if I wanted to survive in New York and make it on my own. I took the 1 train uptown and started making my way over to the address printed out on the paper in my hand. Another metaphorical ticket to my next adventure.

I walked up to the eight-story building located by Riverside Park and nervously approached the thick, metal door. I didn't know what lay behind the shelter door, but I knew I had to be strong and most importantly, I had to let go my ego.

A LITTLE BIT LIKE JESUS

I W A L K E D through the door to see a glass wall with a desk behind it, looking similar to what you would find at a bank. They needed that much security at this place? That had me slightly worried. The walls in the entry-way were beige and at the end of the hallway was a used-needle deposit box. I had never seen a secure trash can for used needles and I definitely started to feel extra queasy at that point. Maybe being in a closet-sized room listening to the obnoxious snoring and muffled solo orgasms of random strangers, was not so bad. I was already here though and this place was free. I couldn't afford the other place anymore, so this was where I was going to have to stay. Whether I liked it or not!

I approached the front desk to see a heavy-set, very dark-skinned woman with a military hair cut looking me up and down with a judgey sort of attitude. This was definitely not the welcome I had received at The Organization, but my case manager had warned me that it might be a little sketchy here, even though this was considered one of the 'better' ones.

"Yo! You checking in?" she barked at me, startling me with her militant and domineering tone.

"Uh, yes ma'am," I said, as politely as I could. Her butch attitude matched her army style haircut and looking at her I had a feeling she might be a lesbian. Maybe eventually I could connect with her on that level, but right then it was all about business.

"Aight, you in room 212. Here's yo key. You lose it, you gotta pay for another. There ain't no curfew here and you can't bring nobody in, understand? You gonna meet yo case manager in da mornin' so don't be late. We check yo room every mornin' at 9 a.m. to make sure you ain't dead. We had people die up in here before..." she went on and on with the rules. I basically tuned it out after the 'people dying' comment. Now I was absolutely frightened.

When she finished her rant, she pointed me to the elevator and told me to go to the second floor. I walked away a little shaken, but undeterred in my decision to stay at this place and get the help I needed.

The elevator was creaky and it was obvious it had been used a lot. An odd odor permeated the interior, the whole building really, and I hadn't quite figured out what it was yet. Maybe it smelled kind of like a mix of cigarettes, urine and depression.

I exited the elevator onto the second floor where I saw a bulletin board covered with notices about free haircuts, soup kitchens, food pantries and the required group meetings each person staying there had to attend. Group meetings? I must have missed that part of her rant.

I didn't have to walk far to the room and was pleasantly surprised to see that I had a bathroom next door. I thought it would be convenient having a restroom so close. It was definitely a step up from The Sunny Day's available facilities.

I put my key into the lock of room number 212 and was actually shocked when I saw what was behind it! The room was really big! There was a wooden table with 2 chairs, a mini fridge, a dresser with an old-style television on top and a bed with a pillow and sheet set. I couldn't believe that all this room was mine. I was so grateful for it after living in what was basically a closet for the last month.

I closed the door and sat down on the bed with a sense of relief. I took pride in the fact that I had actually done something good for myself. Finally.

I started to unpack the suitcase I had bought in Chinatown, which contained all my new worldly belongings. I had been buying a few new shirts and pants over the last month or so and I had also gathered some trinkets from my adventures including maps, business cards, strange Chinese herbs, random shot glasses and a journal I had started keeping. Once it was all unpacked and put away, I decided to go check out my new surroundings.

I walked down Broadway for a minute and found the laundromat and the Rite Aid. Down a little further was a liquor store and a couple of bars, one of which looked very interesting. I'd have to put that on my list of things to see after I got more acquainted with the area and my living situation.

I then headed over to Amsterdam Avenue where I found a Brazilian restaurant and a bar that would soon become my new 'home base' bar. I stopped in this place for a moment to get a drink and immediately fell in love with the vibe.

The Pour House reminded me a lot of The State Room with its wooden floors, dark wooden bar, wood-paneled walls, sports playing on every TV and a sexy, big-boobed girl behind the bar.

Kat was her name, and she was just as feisty as a feline, so of course we got along swimmingly from the very get go. She offered me a shot of fireball and I knew instantly that we were going to be great friends. We talked for an hour, in between her helping other customers, discussing my story and my current living situation.

"That's crazy! You've been through so much lately! You deserve another shot. By the way, have you talked to him since you left?" she asked, referring to Liam, whom I had just spilled the beans about.

"No. I tried a few times but he is such a mess that he can never keep a phone and the people I do still talk to have tried to stay away from him. I don't even know what I'd say, or if he even cares about me anymore. But I would love an apology or something! He really fucked me up," I replied, trying hard not to think about him. I had been so involved with the housing situation, making new friends and looking for work, that I hadn't thought about him very much in those last few weeks. Surprisingly, I was okay with that.

"You are in New York City now! Time to move on, I say. Good riddance," she said in a reassuring tone as we clinked our shot glasses together and swallowed the cinnamon-infused whiskey with a smile.

Oh, how I wished it was that easy to forget him, but we had been through a lot in that year we spent together. The whiskey helped though. After a few shots, I had forgotten about him and moved on to the cute guys sitting at the bar. Nothing happened with any of them (they were straight), but I did make some potential new friends and that was something I could definitely use.

I said goodbye to Kat and headed back to the "homeless hotel" to try and get some sleep before my meeting with the case manager in the morning. I called Cheri, Jackie, Annette and Lacy in Los Angeles and got them up-to-date on everything going on in my life. Like Tim, they were happy that I took the initiative to help myself. Cheri even asked if there was anything she could do. I said if she'd be so kind to send me some things from my storage unit, then maybe I could feel more like a regular person again. She said she would and I was grateful for her kindness, for the love from my bestie, my female husband, that I missed so much.

I slept pretty good that night on the new twin-sized bed with the fresh sheets and pillow. The room was pretty quiet, because it had an actual ceiling and not just chicken wire! That was until the morning came. At 9 a.m., on the dot, a loud, shrill voice with a funny accent, banged on my door and screamed, "ROOM CHECK!!" She blurted out some other things I couldn't quite understand, so I got up and opened the door. She was a cute little African American woman who had a sweet face and a kind aura around her. Vastly different from the army sergeant at the door the night before. She welcomed me to the "hotel" and introduced herself. Her name was Ms. Meyers and she had a speech impediment making her voice sound a little funny and hard to understand. As I got to know her though, I began to be able to understand her completely and she became someone there that I ended up really respecting.

She was also known for yelling out "HOUSING WORKSHOP!!," which usually followed her aforementioned daily call. Ms. Meyers was the housing specialist for the "hotel." She was assigned to help the clients/residents find a permanent place to live as this shelter had a six-month stay limit. I was hoping in less than six months I would be living in my own place with a good job and not relying on the government any more. Only time would tell.

I got dressed and went down to meet my case

manager and was rather surprised to see that he was a very attractive Spanish guy with lots of tattoos and big, bulging muscles. I thought if I had to report to him once a week, it wouldn't be so bad. At least I'd have some hunky Spanish eye candy to drool over.

Mr. Martinez was a looker and also an ex-con who got his case manager license while in rehab after completing his jail time for drug dealing. He was totally my type: dangerous, masculine, sexy and straight. Haha.

As we talked, he told me he had reformed from his drug dealing ways during his prison stint and rehab. He had been clean for over a year, which was pretty impressive. The longest I ever went without booze or drugs was 2 months, and I only did that because of a court order. So I respected him for his commitment to sobriety and listened as he made a plan for me to follow while staying at the "hotel." This plan, which included group meetings and supportive counseling, would conceivably set me on the path back to a "regular life" as soon as possible.

So after Rico-Suave, the Case-"big man"-ager finished his instructions, I was free to go and explore my new neighborhood once again. I headed back to my room but stopped short of the door when I saw two interesting African American guys chatting/yelling at each other. One was tall and a little chunky with a pretty face. The other was a short, skinny, older man who had a walker with wheels. I didn't know what they were discussing, but it seemed to be a lively conversation and I tried to sneak by without being noticed. I couldn't. The taller one looked at me and said, "Hey girl! Are you my new neighbor?"

Hey girl? He must play for my team. "Yea, it's my first official day here. I got in last night. I'm Kaleb and you are?" I responded with my hand outstretched towards him.

"I'm James but you can call me Jimmy...everybody does. This old geezer goes by Huggy Bear and he thinks he's the boss of this floor!" he said, shaking my hand and giving the side eye to the older man who was standing in his doorway.

"I AM the boss of this floor you fuckin bastard... yo' if you need some loosies come knock on my door. But not too fuckin' early and not too fuckin late... I like my fuckin' sleep!" said Huggy, as he too shook my hand and gave me the once over to make sure I was chill. "He seems aight Jimmy, but we'll see. Somebody goin' to get my damn beer for me?"

Jimmy and Huggy were just two of the outrageous characters I was destined to meet and befriend at the "hotel." The others came as the days went on.

The first week I often hung out with Jimmy because he was gay and he seemed to be a pretty good example for me. He, like many people in the "hotel," had a criminal record and had recently gotten out of jail. He said he used to have a problem with crack, but he was now clean and going back to school to get his social worker license. I told him about my past and we got along like two college girls living in an odd version of a dorm. We dished about all the latest "hotel" gossip, while enjoying bottles of cheap whiskey and eating whatever food we had received at the free church food pantry down the street.

Huggs (as we all called him for short) became a good friend too during the first few weeks. He and 'Mother Jimmy' (his new nickname from me) taught me how to play backgammon and we bonded over it many nights during my stay there. Huggs and I shared some good stories and I would listen to him sing sometimes. He was a hardcore, old-school gangster on the outside, but he was definitely a Huggy Bear on the inside. I was glad he felt comfortable to show me his softer side. He never really gave me a definitive answer on why he was called Huggy Bear but I assumed it was because he had to wear adult undergarments because of his age. I didn't try and push the subject because he did have quite the temper for an older man. He was cool with me and had my back which, in this place, was something to be thankful for.

There were other, not so nice, people in the building, too. There were a couple of meth heads who would come and knock on everyone's door at 3 o'clock just about every night and ask if the person in the room would fuck them. Then there were the straight up thugs who would snap and threaten you if they thought you were looking at them funny. There was an older black woman named Happy who dealt crack, as well a functional mentally disabled couple who did heroin with the only other white guy in the building. Then there were the working girls. Most of them lived on the 8th floor and seemed very snooty, but there was one that lived right across the hall from me who I actually became great friends with.

Her name was LaVonia and she was a tall, skinny, African American, transitioning - male to female - prostitute. We bonded over our love of wigs, dresses, makeup and men. She even got me to dress up as Sarah Summers a few times, show her some new makeup tricks and go out to some bars with her. NO, I did not let her talk me into selling my body for sex as much as she tried to persuade me. I was a little jealous though when she would come back to the room with $200 or $300 dollars some nights. Prostitution became almost considerable since I had stopped asking Tim for so much monetary help and, even though I was broke, and desperate for money, I was not THAT desperate.

That way of thinking, that "I am better than that" attitude, began to change as I became better friends with her, and the other people in the shelter, people I would never in my life have thought I would be associating with. No, I don't mean I changed my mind on prostituting.

I mean, I changed the way I looked at people entirely...on a soul level.

I didn't see LaVonia as a transsexual prostitute, I didn't see Jimmy as an ex-crack head and I didn't see Huggy as an ex-con, alcoholic cigarette pusher. I saw them as people, as equals and mostly, as my friends.

I started to become a person who saw the good in everyone and realized how true the old saying, "You can't judge a book by its cover," really was.

I decided to add a little more to that saying by finishing it with, "Because you may regret never reading the beautiful words within."

It was a different world for me in the "homeless hotel." After those first few weeks and making a good group of friends, I felt safer and ultimately humbled. As sacrilegious as it may sound, I started to feel a little bit like Jesus. Not the all-powerful only Son of God, but the man who saw everyone as equals, saw the good in all mankind, lived among the poor and was best friends with a prostitute.

I was never uber religious but I had become very spiritual as of late and I was noticing the signs from the Creator all around me more and more. A perfect example of this was when I noticed there was some paint chipped on my door under the room number. Upon closer inspection, I noticed something had been taped and painted over. Being curious, I decided to scrape the black paint off a little to see what was written underneath. I was surprised at what I found. I assumed that maybe it was some graffiti or that someone had scratched their name into the door. But it was something so much better, a sign from above.

Printed out on a strip of white paper was the Bible verse:

Psalm 121: "The Lord watches over you. The Lord is your shade at your right hand; the sun will not harm you by day, nor the moon by night. The Lord will keep you from all harm - He will watch over your life."

Wow! It was like the Universe was sending me a sign that I was being protected and maybe, now that I could see these signs, I was getting closer to my divine path. It was also on this day that my box from LA arrived filled with little pieces of Heaven that included clothes, underwear, my Nintendo Wii U, a carton of Camel Crush Bold cigarettes and a book that Cheri had thrown in that she thought I should read. I didn't read it then, but it would be a life changer, at the exact time I needed it, a few months down the road.

It was so nice to get that box from home because it made me feel a little bit more like myself again and not this homeless, struggling victim that I had started to think of myself as.

I put on my 'LA ❤'s ME' t-shirt that had made its way into the box and donned my favorite pair of white sunglasses and left the "homeless hotel" to head over to the Pour House feeling like my old Hollywood self!

On my way over to the bar, I saw an LA number flashing on my phone that I had never seen before. I decided to ignore it. I wasn't expecting any calls and didn't want to talk to any bill collectors. The only person I thought it could be who wasn't saved into my phone was Liam. Even if I had known it was him, I probably wouldn't have answered because I was still extremely angry and hurt. The number tried to call again and I ignored it once more.

By the time I arrived at the bar, I had put the phone call out of my mind and was hell-bent on having a good time. My other two bartender besties, Alyssa and Shira, were holding down the sports-themed fort that evening and it was karaoke night too! That evening was spent hanging with the bartender babes and my new friend Zak who was 'straight' and very attractive, but also seemed to have a lot of gayish tendencies and mannerisms. He was definitely my type and was one of those friends who was very hands on with the hugs and the closeness. This friendship started out as a bar thing, but he would soon come to my rescue and prove his real friendship about a month down the road. We sang, we drank and we carried on until about 3 a.m. before I headed back over to the "homeless hotel" and went to bed.

The next week was filled with more of the same things I would do with all the free time I seemed to have in New York City: job hunting, exploring the city, drinking and friend making. Mostly I was just going out into the world trying to figure out what I was supposed to be doing with my life and still not finding the answer. Then I would go back to the "hotel" and spend time with my new 'family' that I had grown really fond of during my stay there. I also found out Liam had somehow found a band that would work with him and went on a small tour. There was a report online that he had tried to call someone while onstage at a bar in Dallas (my hometown) and was kicked off stage for throwing the phone into the crowd when the person didn't pick up. I had an inkling that I was probably the cause of that outburst which secretly made me happy, because that meant he still cared, he was still thinking of me, and there was still love there.

Love.

Love, was something I tried not to think about

those first few months in NYC because of how terrible it had been to me in LA. I did make out with a beautiful girl named Natalia one night on one of my adventures out as Sarah Summers; and we even went on a date a few days later (she and Kaleb) but it wasn't a real love connection. It did make me think maybe this new Kaleb could be bicoastal and bisexual for a hot minute, but that idea quickly faded the day I met Alessio. The man who made me feel loved again.

BAD NEWS

I NOTICED HIM when I first walked into The Duplex in the West Village that afternoon. He was sitting alone at the bar, wearing a fedora, having a glass of red wine and looking very classy as he sat listening to the pianist play. He wasn't exactly the type I usually go for. He was skinny, shorter than me, with dark hair, scruff and he looked to be a foreigner. I couldn't exactly make out his heritage (maybe a mix of middle eastern and something) but I was interested and took the seat next to him.

I ordered my usual whiskey and Coke and pretended to listen intently to the piano player while I secretly observed him. It was hard to get a reading of his character just watching him, so I knew I would have to interact. I swallowed my first drink for a little liquid courage, then ordered a shot for myself and a glass of red wine for my soon to be new friend.

"Fireball and whatever this gentleman is having, please," I said to the bartender in my stateliest voice.

"Oh, thank you," he replied, revealing a pretty thick Italian accent. "I am Alessio. What is name?"

"I'm Kaleb. Nice to meet you! Are you visiting the city?" I asked, ready to become a tour guide if needed.

"Here for work. Off now. Time to have the fun!" he responded, his accent getting cuter by the second.

"Have the fun? Haha. I'm good at that! Hang out with me, I'll show you a good time," I said, raising my shot glass to his glass of wine. We then clinked glasses while looking deep into each other's eyes.

Most of that day was spent at The Duplex listening to the live music and communicating (to the best of our abilities) the stories of our past. I found out he was a computer guy from Crema, Italy who was in NYC for about a week because of business meetings. He was kinda secretive about the details of his job, something about internet security for big companies, which made him even more appealing. A mysterious man from another country, who also liked to buy me drinks and wasn't too hard on the eyes? Yes, please!

After a few cocktails (that he paid for) and an hour or so of getting to know each other, I decided

I was ready to get up and sing for him and the crowd.

I had to search the web for the sheet music to "Creep" (as it was not one of the commonly sung songs at this mostly Broadway musical-appreciating venue) and the pianist was able to pick it up in seconds. The song was quite beautiful accompanied by piano and it allowed me to emote in a different, more serene sort of way. Alessio seemed to be very impressed as he started to film it 1/4 of the way through and I took notice of that. As the song neared its end, I sang to him. I began to think that maybe he could be more than just a new friend after all.

We bonded that evening over drinks and our common appreciation of an eclectic mix of live music sung by strangers. We shared our first kiss that night outside of the bar, as he went to hail a cab. It was a sweet kiss, not a tongue thrusting, lust-fueled one, but it was sexy enough to make me want to see what else he could do, what else we could do together. We made a date to meet at The Duplex again the following day, after his business seminars. I went to the 1 train and headed back to the "homeless hotel" to tell Momma Jimmy about the cute boy I met!

The next day came and I got up a little early and went to one of Ms. Meyers "HOUSING WORKSHOP!" meetings so that I could start whittling down on my required count. The meeting was pretty informative as it detailed a lot of the permanent housing options available for chronically homeless. I didn't see myself as "chronically homeless" just yet. This was my first time truly being homeless and I was hoping that something magical would happen to take me out of the situation. It took time, but I learned a little further down the road that most of the time magical things don't just happen, they need a catalyst to start appearing.

I left the meeting full of ideas and plans of what my next steps should be to get out of that temporary "homeless hotel" as quickly as could be. I ran back up to my room to get ready for my date with Alessio and put the housing plans on the back burner for at least another few days. I mean there wasn't any particular rush because it wasn't like I was losing any money by staying there. I was only in my first month of the allotted refuge time anyway. Huggy had told me that he had even had his stay extended by his city case worker a few times and that he had been there for over a year. Made even more sense now why he thought he was King of the 2nd floor!

I perused through my clothes and finally left the building decked out in some more of my Hollywood apparel Cheri had sent to me. It was funny how just having a few things from home had made me feel like a real person again, like this whole thing was not just an extended dream/ nightmare but a new chapter of my life's journey.

When I arrived at The Duplex, Alessio was sitting at the bar waiting for me with a whiskey Coke and a glass of wine. A big smile appeared on his face as he saw me walk into the room and, for the first time in a long time, I felt wanted. I could feel his energy radiating towards me, his magnet of desire pulling me in, and I was gladly sucked into the gravitational pull.

That evening I took my Italian man to my favorite Italian restaurant, Paesano's, where we shared that expensive seafood pasta extravaganza I had dreamed of eating the day I went there with Maider. We then went to the roof-top bar of the Wydem Garden hotel just blocks away in Chinatown which, oddly enough, was situated directly across from the Sunny Day Hotel. As we had our glasses of wine overlooking the busy downtown streets, he kissed me and said, "Kaleb, I think I love you."

My heart stopped as I saw him pull from his finger the gold ring he had been wearing every day and place it around my right ring finger. I was pretty sure he wasn't proposing to me... or was he? It seemed a little too sudden for all of that, but it was magical none the less. I looked at the ring and looked at him and said, "I think I'm falling in love with you, too." We shared a passionate kiss with the moon shining brightly down on us. It was perfect. It felt like we were a real couple and, for those moments, I forgot the man from the past and the living situation of the present. He made me feel like myself again. I was happy.

He eventually told me that it was not a wedding proposal but a gift he wanted me to have so I would always remember the time we shared together. He said his mother had given him that ring and he felt like I was special enough to wear it and to keep it. That meant the world to me, especially because I knew if he was as close to his mother as I was to mine when she was alive, this was a big gift to be giving anyone.

That night he decided to ride with me back to the "hotel" to make sure that I got home safely. We had also gotten pretty sexually heated in the cab and the energy was so powerful that I decided I would try and sneak him in so we could have some fun that evening. We couldn't go back to his hotel because he was staying with co-workers, and even though I didn't want him to see where I was staying, I wanted to be with him that night.

Once we got to the "homeless hotel," it was clear we would not be able to get him into my room as the army sergeant security guard/desk woman was on shift that evening and she would have none of it! I suggested we go for a romantic walk in Riverside Park to end our awesome evening.

The walk was exactly that: romantic (and very, very sexy)! As we walked through the dimly lit paths holding hands, I could feel the energy rising between us. I had to do something about it. Being a little tipsy (and a little brave), I suggested we cross the Henry Hudson Parkway and sit on the rocks by the river. The highway was not super busy at that time of night but there was enough traffic to make it "sexy dangerous." We crossed quickly in between the various speeding cars holding hands and safely made it to the other side.

The adrenaline of the spontaneous street crossing turned into pure sexual energy once we had reached the other side. We could barely contain the lust burning up inside, so we grasped each other's bodies tightly and started kissing with an intensity I hadn't felt in years! The rain began to fall harder as we stood making out on the rocks next to the Hudson River. The sound of the rain hitting the water sounded like a staccato drum beat becoming the background track to our passion. I fell to my knees and unzipped his pants to reveal a surprisingly big package awaiting me. There in the rain, I performed an oral sexcapade like never before. He was beyond pleased. It was by far one of the sexiest, most romantic experiences I have ever had.

When we were finished, he walked me back to the "hotel" like a gentleman and told me he was excited to see me again the following day. I was excited too.

Liam who? He briefly popped into my mind and a smile crept onto my face as I thought about how he had never gotten anything that good from me. Now he never would. I was getting over him it seemed, but he was not quite erased completely yet. I still hated him for what he did to me, but now I had Alessio to keep my heart busy and he was very capable of that.

The next day I received my bi-weekly cash assistance payment from the government and decided I would budget half of it to spend that evening. I invited 'Mother Jimmy' to come out with me to the Village and meet the man I had been telling him about for the past few nights. Jimmy was more than happy to be asked to join as he rarely got to go out because of his parole-enforced curfew. This evening was one of his allotted 'late nights' and we planned to make the best of it on the town with my new Italian man.

Once we arrived to The Duplex, I introduced 'Mother Jimmy' to Alessio who introduced himself to Jimmy as my boyfriend (which I thought was very cute) and we began to drink. Funny stories were being told, songs being sung and Alessio and I were providing heavy PDA for the whole bar to see. Jimmy was hitting on the bartender, who thought Jimmy was very entertaining. The night was a pretty big success overall except for when my two companions decided it was time to leave. 'Drunk Kaleb' was not ready to go.

Anyone who knew me, knew that when I drank I became quite bullheaded and could hardly ever be told what to do. These two people were new to my life and I don't think they were quite prepared for what they would be dealing with. The blackout Kaleb was a force to be reckoned with, apparently, and was beyond difficult for most of my friends to handle. I didn't know this version of myself because I never remembered much from those occasions when this dark version of me would come out to play. He was out for blood this particular evening and soon he would find it.

Alessio and Jimmy later told me they pleaded with me to leave the bar with them that night, but said I fought them with all my might, determined to stay out and "have more fun."

The next thing I vaguely remember was standing in the middle of the street screaming, "You better fucking run, you pussies! I'll fucking kill you!" In flashes I remember being thrown to the ground and landing on broken glass, picking up a shattered bottle and, with blood spewing from my mouth, screaming as a group of three straight guys ran away from me.

When the ambulance arrived, I was sitting outside the Slaughtered Lamb bar on West 4th Street with a cut lip and a giant gash on the top part of my left hand's middle finger. I barely remember the EMT wrapping my finger with gauze before my next memory of the tall, attractive, Asian, female doctor at some hospital, sewing the sutures through the wide gash and warning me to keep it clean for the next few days while it healed. The next thing I remember after that, I was filling out the release paper work and exiting the hospital with a clearer mind. Luckily, I still had my gold ring that Alessio gave me and a $20 bill hidden in my wallet for emergencies. I was able to get a metro card and made my way back to the "homeless hotel" via the subway as the sun was coming out.

I had fucked myself over once again (with the help of excessive drinking) and I couldn't believe I had let myself get so crazy! I tried to blame Alessio and Jimmy for not trying hard enough to get me to go home with them and for leaving me alone, but I knew it wasn't their fault. 'Drunk Kaleb' would have to be tied down to actually listen to anyone and, obviously, it wasn't their job to do that. So I couldn't really be angry at them. I could only be mad at myself, really. And I was.

Jimmy told me to keep my chin up and go spend time with Alessio because, as he reminded me, "you only have a few days left together before Alessio leaves." I pulled myself together and made the call to meet up with my Italian boyfriend that afternoon.

That day was supposed to be our big final goodbye date as he was going to be leaving the following day. We started the day out by going to Central Park and walking through Strawberry Fields where we took pictures kissing by the water on the wooden bench under the gazebo. He didn't even seem to mind the single suture in my bottom lip. Magic! I wanted to have lunch at the boat house but he didn't want to. I wanted to go to the Central Park Zoo and he didn't want to. He kept fighting me on all the things I wanted to do and it really started to upset me.

I eventually ended up parting ways with him for a little while just to get some breathing room and a chance to calm down. We met up again later and went to a pub we had not been to before. We had a few drinks and ended up having a pretty good time. What I didn't realize at the time was that he was going to miss me and this was his strange way of showing it. He was trying to push me away a little to make it easier on himself, so that when he left, it wouldn't be as hard. We kissed goodbye as we left the bar that night, but I didn't think it was going to be our last time.

The next day came and I was going to meet up with him before his flight, but due to a plane rescheduling he had to be at the airport earlier than expected. So I wasn't going to get to see him one last time. He called me when he got to the airport as I was wandering around the streets of Harlem checking out the discount shops. I didn't think I had let myself fall for him that hard. But when he said that last, "I'm going to miss you much. I love you," I got all choked up and allowed a few tears to fall as I stood smoking a hand-rolled cigarette on some random street corner in the hood.

It wasn't the fairytale goodbye I had hoped for, but when those tears started to fall it made me realize something very important. I had feelings again. I was actually feeling something for someone and it hurt in the best way possible. This time I wasn't running away from anything and I was able to let it all hit me like the Universe intended. The spark inside, now slightly dampened by tears, was stronger than ever. I was growing again. I was becoming more and more alive every second, with every experience and it felt real.

Those tears, those emotions, were nothing compared to the ones that would follow next. I was about to receive a call from someone from my past and what they had to share was nothing but bad news.

WITHOUT YOU

A N E W M O N T H was upon us in New York and the weather was heating up. August, I had hoped, would be the month I would finally get out of the "homeless hotel" and back on my feet, living a little bit more like the person I used to be. In my defense, I am an uber optimistic person. In my mind, every month was going to be "the big month" where everything would change and somehow the planets would all align and I would make my way back into 'regular' civilization. This was not going to be 'that month' as I would soon find out when I received a disheartening call I was not expecting on August 2nd, 2014.

The phone rang around 11 p.m. as I was headed over to The Pour House to see Kat, Zak and the gang. The number was a Texas number and my heart immediately sank as I knew there could only be one reason my cousin Stephanie would call me so randomly. She and I were close when we were growing up, but after her father (and my other two uncles) disowned me following the passing of my mother, we had only spoken occasionally on Facebook and rarely on the phone. Stephanie was about a year older than me but we had been in the same grade as she was held back a year when she was younger. She now had a husband who loved her and a daughter who was struggling with autism. I had met the little girl a few times when she was very young and sent her a book one year for her birthday, but since my connection to my 'family' in Texas had been so limited since I left, it had been hard to keep up with all the news.

I really respected Stephanie though, she was dealing with a lot in her own small family while also going to see our Grandma Ellen as often as she could. My Grandma Ellen, my mother's mother, was like a second mother to me really and she was more than just a grandma. She drove me to and from school every day, until I was old enough to drive, because my mother was working all the time. She also became my sitter/house keeper after my mother won her settlement and my mother paid her for her work. My mother was really just letting her do the stuff she would normally do as a grandma but gave her money so she didn't have to work a 'real job' anymore.

Grandma Ellen was a strong woman with strong opinions and a no censorship kind of mouth. If she was thinking it, she would say it, and say it loudly with the vibrato of her thick German accent. She spent every day at the hospital with my mother as she underwent the pain and agony of battling leukemia. She showed me what it meant to be strong the day my mother died, every day leading up to it and every day after. She was devastated at the loss of my mother, her first child and her only daughter, but she tried very hard not to let others see her pain.

When I moved to LA, I told her I would come home to visit, but I never made it back to Fort Worth, Texas...not yet anyway. She was diagnosed with dementia and eventually put into assisted living as the disease grew stronger. The last phone call I remember having with her, she was in a nursing home and only spoke German, which I did not understand. It was hard to hear that my grandma was gone mentally and it made me respect my cousin so much for being there for her through all that, even when my Grandma had no clue who anyone was any more. I felt kind of selfish thinking that I had the better end of the deal because my memories of my Grandma Ellen would be of her, happy in her house, strong, able and mouthy as ever. Stephanie had to see the worst. I thank her for that.

So I knew when she called me it was the news of my Grandma Ellen's passing. I want to say that I handled it with grace, but that would be a lie. I was a fucking wreck. I felt powerless because I couldn't be there. I felt guilty because I never went back to see her. I felt ashamed and wondered if my mother was upset with me for not being there. The only thing I could do was drink. I drank for free that evening as my friends at the bar were there to take care of my bill and offer their condolences. That night, once completely liquored up, I made a number of bad decisions.

The first bad decision was punching a hole in the wall of my bedroom at the "homeless hotel." I broke every piece of glass I had laying around and sobbed uncontrollably. In my rage I reached for the electric clippers hidden in my dresser and decided to pull the ultimate Britney Spears move. Without even thinking about the consequences, I turned on the sheers and continued to cry as I shaved my head bald. Each strand of dark brown hair fell to the floor like another lost dream. But cutting off all my hair didn't make me feel any better. I needed something else to numb the pain. Something stronger. Something more dangerous.

When the tears dried up, I went and asked Happy to sell me some crack and bought some. I found the biggest, blackest thug who was down to smoke it and fuck me to come to my room. We smoked it and then we got naked and I let him be as rough as he wanted, and he was. I don't remember much but I remember waking up sore and with a few bruises on my body. I had lost it.

The complete loss of sanity continued the next morning when I bought the biggest bottle of vodka I could afford and decided to go on a four-hour Uber limo excursion through the city. How did I pay for this you must be wondering? The heart broken, soul shattered and DRUNK Kaleb had access to the Hollywood Cake bank account through a mutual PayPal account Tim had set up for the digital work I had done in the past. That's the thing about my evil, drunk self... I didn't care.

I didn't care about the repercussions of my actions (I don't think any addict ever did) and I didn't think about how those actions might affect others. I was hurting, I was alone, I was misunderstood, I was powerless, I, I, I, me, me, me... that's all I could think of at the time. Before I left that afternoon, I covered the hole in the wall with a poster. Then I put on my Kurt Cobain-style blonde wig with a black bandana wrapped around my head, black sunglasses and head-to-toe black, form fitting, mourning clothes. I ordered a black Lincoln SUV limo to come pick me up at the "homeless hotel" and after the driver opened the door to let me in, I looked into the rear view mirror and simply told the driver, "Drive."

The day played out like a scene from a movie. I had no clue where I was going. I just wanted to go. I synced my phone with the Bluetooth system in the vehicle and told him to turn it up as loud as he could. The attractive, young, tall and thin African American man was very accommodating to my requests and somewhere in midtown when we stopped to get some more liquor I told him my story. He joined the long list of people who were blown away by the harrowing tale and I could sense his sincere empathy as we continued the adventure.

I wasn't listening to sad, sappy music though, I had my pop mix playing on loop with Britney Spears and other pop divas contributing to the 'celebration of life' drive. I must of had a moment of clarity when I asked the driver to take me down to SoHo because it was then I remembered that there was one person I had to go see because this person had become a sort of 'rock' in my new, New York life.

Catherine was the owner of Parigot, the French restaurant I had stumbled upon on that random snowy day in April. We got to know each other pretty well over the last few months and she became someone I really respected and would ask for advice. Catherine was from Paris, France and about the age my mother would have been had she lived. She was an attractive woman, dark brown hair, about my height, thin, with eyes just as blue as mine and a great understanding of spirituality.

Catherine and I became very close through the late night glasses of wine and meaningful conversations. If Tim was my adoptive father, Catherine was on her way to becoming my adoptive mother. She was like a mother to me in the sense that she saw the best in me and always pushed me to do better. It showed a lot about this woman who grew to care for a random boy who somehow found himself at her proverbial doorstep. I knew she would be there to give me a big hug and some sort of advice on how to deal with all the pain. But I don't think she was ready for the show that was about to arrive that afternoon.

The SUV limo rolled up in front of Parigot on Grand Street in SoHo with the windows rolled down and the sounds of Britney Spears' 'Toxic' blaring to the heavens. The driver pulled over and attention was quickly drawn to the vehicle. The performer in me exited with pomp and circumstance to a street of onlookers prepared for a show! I delivered. I literally shut down the street for the duration of the song and danced while random people took pictures and danced along. It was just like me to do something like that. The bigger the show, the better. The alcohol helped alleviate any leftover inhibitions and I turned that street into my stage of release.

When I finished, I ran over to Catherine and embraced her for the longest hug I think I had given anyone in a long time. She knew immediately something was very wrong and just held me for those few minutes before I told her my heartbreaking news.

"It's going to be alright. You have to be strong, your mother and your grandmother would want you to be strong," she said, as she let a tear fall alongside my own. She then told me I should go back to where I was staying and rest because I had already had too much to drink. So I did.

I woke up the next morning with a pretty big hangover and something inside of me decided I had to go back to Texas for the funeral. This would not be any easy task to accomplish as I had no money and there was no way I was going to ask Tim. I knew he was going to be furious once he found out I had charged all that money for the Uber ride around the city so I figured my only choice was to sell my Nintendo Wii U (that I loved so much) and pawn anything else worth value. I figured I could get a bus ticket or a train ticket for $200 bucks (I obviously didn't know the cost of travel as of late) and so I sold my Wii U and a bunch of games at GameStop where I received about $100 for all of it. I went to the

Port Authority Station to see what my options were. There was no bus or train to Fort Worth, Texas for $100.

I knew I had to get out of the city though, I had to get away from the "homeless hotel" and all the people in it so that I could just grieve on my own terms. I found a one-way bus ticket to Boston for $60 and purchased it. I went out and bought another big bottle of cheap vodka and drank some of it while I waited for the departure time to come around. As I sat on the bench outside the station, drinking vodka from a paper bag covered bottle, it was apparent that I had no clue what I was doing nor did I care.

I boarded the green Peter Pan bus and found a seat in the very back where I could drink my vodka, cry and not be bothered. I fell asleep at some point and woke up when the bus was stopped in Connecticut for a food/restroom break. I bought another cheap bottle of vodka with cash and some chips using my Food Stamp Benefit card. I got back on the bus and fell asleep again before finally arriving in Boston.

Why Boston? It was close, it was within my budget and I had been there before on a high school choir trip when both my mother and grandmother were alive. I thought maybe a trip to Boston might take me back to that feeling I had in my youth when I was surrounded by friends and could call those two women I loved so much on the phone.

Boston was beautiful and the quiet moments by the harbor were cathartic. That night I drank the rest of my giant bottle of vodka and passed out in the grass in front of the bus station. When I woke up my phone was missing. Someone had come by and robbed me while I slept, it seemed, but left my computer bag because I was sleeping on top of it. I couldn't believe it had happened to me. Not now, not when I was all alone in this new city. All I could do was think more crazy thoughts!

Really?! What the fuck? Was my life not screwed up enough? Was I not already in so much pain and distress?

I ended up wandering around the city that day and selling my laptop to some black guy on the street who said he knew a guy that would give me $300 for it. He came back to me with $150 and said that's all he could get. I figured he had kept the rest of the money and I was in no mood (or brave enough) to question him. He looked like a hard-core drug addict, but I was so distraught and tipsy that I had trusted him anyway. I made a lot of bad decisions, but I continued to drink. It seemed like alcohol was the only thing that could stop me from thinking about all the negativity in my life. So I chose to drink...a lot.

After walking aimlessly around Boston for a while I finally got up the nerve to call Tim and beg him for help. I don't know how or why he hadn't given up on me at this point but I was sure glad he hadn't. I was relieved when I found a lovely girl working at the Boston Harbor gift shop who let me use her iPhone to call him.

Tim was BEYOND disappointed and this time he was pretty scared for my well-being because I was in an unfamiliar place with no friends and no place to stay. He told me I had to get back to NYC to the "homeless hotel" where at least I had a room and a bed. He helped me get a cheap bus ticket on the Lucky Star line which was scheduled to drop off passengers in Chinatown, NYC, a block away from The Sunny Day Hotel coincidentally. I was in no mind set to see it at the time but the name of the bus company was pretty right on in comparison to my life. I was definitely Lucky.

After a sobering 4-hour trip, the bus arrived back in NYC and dropped me off to familiar sights and sounds. I was relieved to see my good ole Chinatown once again, but knew I had to somehow make it back to the Upper West Side. I managed to borrow a couple of bucks from a girl I knew who worked at Duane Reade drug store close by and eventually made it back up to the "hotel" via the MTA.

Thinking I had finally caught a break, that things might be getting back to normal, I was surprised to see an envelope sitting on my bed when I walked into my room. I immediately got nervous. What if they had found the hole under the poster and had decided to kick me out while I was gone? All my stuff was still in the room the way I left it so I figured that I was safe. I opened the envelope and the letter inside stated that my room had passed inspection the day before and I immediately let out a sigh of relief. But the feelings of relief were to be short lived as the next day would soon turn out to be an even more disastrous than the ones before.

I got up early the next morning and decided that I should try and fix my wall before anyone else noticed. I figured since I had taught myself website coding, Photoshop, make-up skills and cake decorating, why not add handy man to the list? So I strolled over to the local hardware shop and asked the employee there for a quick wall patching tutorial. He assured me it was very easy and sold me a kit that included spackle, spackle knife, a wire mesh patch, a piece of sand paper and instructions. Looked easy enough!

When I got back to the "hotel," 'Mother Jimmy' came to my room to watch me work. It was pretty easy after all and I felt like a real man at that moment, spackling and smoothing until the hole was almost unnoticeable. I even had enough supplies left to cover up a few small holes in Jimmy's room that the previous tenant had left (hiding places for illegal drugs no doubt). I felt accomplished and Jimmy and I decided to celebrate.

We decided we were going to check out The West End Bar next to the laundromat since it was open at lunch time. As we were walking out of the building, my sexy, buff, Latin case manager stopped us to tell me that I needed to meet with the general manager of the building the next morning to discuss a couple of things concerning my behavior as of late and my room. I was pretty good at talking to people and had the power to usually get my way with a little charm and a promise to clean up my act. So naturally, I was not too worried about the meeting and Jimmy and I continued on our merry way.

We had a few drinks at The West End Bar and by the time night fell I was on my way to The Pour House to see my friends and sing karaoke. I knew that a couple of good songs and good company would get me in a better mood after all the drama of the past few days.

Kat and Alyssa were behind the bar and my friends Shira and Zak were sitting in the usual spot waiting for me to arrive. We all sang a couple of songs and I decided to keep the drinking to a minimum and leave early so that I would be fresh for the meeting with the general manager of the "homeless hotel" in the morning. I left the bar around 11 that night, which was very early for me, and headed back to my room. I walked in and up the stairs where I immediately got into bed after taking off my clothes. I slept pretty soundly until about 2 a.m. when I was awoken by the most disturbing sound ever.

The banging on my door was ear drum shattering and the voice outside sounded pretty irate. I slowly woke up in a bit of a haze and before I could even sit up I heard the sound of keys entering my lock. "SECURITY! SECURITY COMING IN!" said the voice of one of the night guardsmen who had a bad rap with most of the clients. He was a big, black guy, with a hardened but droopy face, who seemed a little slow. There was talk among the clients that he was a drunk who bought crack from the residents and would do it with them in their rooms for favors. This night he seemed particularly intoxicated as he burst into my room.

"Hey! You! What are you doing here? They

kicked yo ass out. You gotta get the fuck outta here!" he said as he grabbed me by the arm.

"Hey, don't touch me!" I said, finally waking up and feeling completely frightened. I put on my shirt and pants as I began my explanation of the situation, "Ummm... No, you are mistaken. I have a meeting with the general manager in the morning. They said I could stay in my room until after the meeting and we will see what happens then."

"Yo. They ain't told me shit. All I know is you can't stay here tonight. Get yo ass out!" he slurred, now aggravated and obviously wasted.

He grabbed my arm again as I grabbed my shoes and he began to drag me out of the room. What the fuck was going on? My case worker clearly told me that I could stay that night before the meeting. I was confused and visibly shaken. I hadn't felt so violated in a long time and it was such a shocking experience, especially since this was the place I was supposed to feel 'safe.'

So there I am, kicked out into the rain that had started to pour, at 2 a.m. with no jacket and nowhere to go. I started to cry as I put my shoes on outside of the thick metal door that had been slammed in my face. I didn't know where to go so I walked back over to The Pour House praying that maybe Zak and the crew were still there.

The girls were closing the bar and Zak was finishing his beer as I walked up to the door, rain and tear soaked. They let me in and I told them of the unthinkable drama that had just occurred. Zak was pretty upset and offered to let me stay at his place for the evening. I was grateful for his offer and after the girls closed the bar we went out for a few drinks at another bar close by. I was still in shock most of the night but tried to have fun anyway, but I couldn't really muster the energy because of all the thoughts running through my head.

What the hell just happened? What was going to happen now? Was I about to lose my room at the "homeless hotel?" I was scared. Even though I didn't love that living situation, it was all I had, and I made some good friends there. My world seemed to be crashing down even harder than before and as I looked out the window at the drenching rain I thought of the quote, "When it rains, it pours!" At that moment it was raining pain and pouring disaster. I hoped that dark voice wouldn't come back right then, because I didn't know if I would be able to fight it off again.

We finished our drinks, said goodbye to the girls and then Zak took me to his apartment which was a few blocks from The Pour House. His place was my ideal New York Apartment! Big living room, a kitchen with a dining table, two bathrooms and three bedrooms! The apartment overlooked a gorgeous church and an amazing statue of a giant stone angel that I had fallen in love with when I passed it the first time a month before.

I would often climb the fence after my nights of drinking at the Pour House, so I could sit beneath the statue and just pray. The statue drew me to it and I was obsessed. The statue was carved out of granite to look like a gorgeous, buff, male angel who was dressed in a loin cloth and a helmet to resemble a fighter at war. The stone angel had a snake in one hand and a sword in the other. Around its feet were many different animals and what looked to be the severed head of the devil. The statue gave me strength to keep fighting this particular evening and kept the dark voice at bay.

Zak was very sweet that night, too. He made the couch into a bed for me and asked if I wanted to take a shower...together. Maybe he was a little drunk when he suggested that, but it was a tempting idea. He was definitely my type, but we were becoming good friends and I was in no shape mentally or physically (I hadn't shaved my body in a while) so I pretended I didn't hear him say it. I didn't want to mess this blossoming friendship up, and I definitely didn't need another potential relationship with a 'straight' guy. The last one didn't work out very well.

We played a few rounds of the card game UNO and talked for a few hours before we both decided it was time for bed. He put the cover over me and said goodnight as he started to walk to his room. I didn't know what craziness the next day held for me, but for now I felt safe and cared for because of this man.

I sat up and reached across the couch to grab his muscular arm before he got too far. The world stopped for a moment when I looked him deep into his eyes and with the utmost sincerity said, "Thank you for tonight. Thank you for being my friend. I don't know what I would have done without you."

KALEB FROM THE BLOCK

THE MORNING came in Manhattan and the sun woke me as it began to shine through Zak's living room window. His couch had actually been pretty comfortable and, as bad as I wanted to just crawl back under the covers, I knew I had to face the day. I had no clue what would happen when I returned to the "homeless hotel," but I knew I had to be responsible and go meet with my case worker and the general manager.

I left Zak's apartment and headed back to the "hotel," walking past security without being noticed. I ran up to my room and furiously began to pack all my belongings into two suitcases (one I had found on the street a few weeks before). If the drunk, drugged-up security guard was right and I was being kicked out, I wanted to be able to pack my stuff myself and not have them throw everything into garbage bags like I had seen them do to others when they were kicked out.

Jimmy heard the commotion in my room and came over to investigate. I told him about the drama from the previous night and said that even if they let me stay there, I probably wouldn't after the way I was treated. Being physically thrown out into the rain was not something I took lightly. I told Jimmy to take whatever I couldn't pack. I figured he could get some use out of the television, and the dishes and other housewares I had acquired over those past few months. He was grateful for the gifts but saddened at the news that he would be losing his best friend at the "hotel."

Huggy came over too and we all said our goodbyes. It was kinda sad having to leave them because we had become so close and their friendship meant the world to me at a time when I was trying to deal with all the craziness of being homeless and poor for the first time.

I made my way downstairs to the manager's office and found her, my caseworker, and the butch security gal talking... about me. The manager was apologetic about the way I was treated the night before and said my case worker had forgotten to leave a note for the evening security guard letting him know that I was indeed allowed to stay there that night. She also informed me that my room had been 'closed,' aka they were kicking me out.

Obviously, I wasn't too shocked at the news but I was a little nervous about what would happen next. Where was I going to go?!

My case manager told me I should go back to The Organization and see if they could get me into another shelter that day. He told me they would put my belongings in storage and when I had secured a new place, I could come and retrieve them.

So I made my way back to the Village to the office of The Organization where Ms. Gena was there with a smile and a shoulder to cry on. I didn't really cry, but inside I felt like I was bawling. I told her what had happened to me and she was pretty upset. She told me she would make a call to report the shelter for their mistreatment of me and immediately began searching her computer for another shelter with an open room.

She was able to find a space for me and told me it was in the Bronx. The Bronx?! I had only heard bad things about that area from movies and the news, making it sound like it was the East Coast's version of Compton (the "bad" neighborhood in LA). I asked her if she could keep looking and try to find something in Manhattan, but she said the way the system works was when she put a name into the computer it automatically put the client in the next available room. She assumed that someone had been kicked out of this place in the Bronx the day before and that's why it was open. Made me wonder who would be getting my room in the "homeless hotel" I had called my home for the last 4 months and would they be nice to 'Mother Jimmy' and Huggy?

My only other choice would have been to sleep on the street that night or ask Tim for money to stay at a real hotel and then come back to The Organization the following day to try again. I had made a promise to myself that I was not going to ask Tim for any more money for a while and, honestly, I doubt he would have given me any. He was pretty fed up with the sob stories at this point and was playing the fatherly card again by trying to make me learn my own lessons.

I accepted the room and Ms. Gena printed a map of the Bronx for me. It showed the shelter was around 150th street in a part of the city I had definitely never been to before. She gave me a 2-trip metro card and wished me luck, once again, on the latest leg of my journey.

Getting to this new shelter would not be an easy feat. I ended up getting off the train at the wrong stop and walking around for hours in this "scary" part of town. It wasn't exactly as scary as one might think, but because of all the bad press this borough had gotten, I felt a little on edge.

The culture was not as ethnically diverse as Manhattan though, as this area was mostly concentrated with Latinos and African Americans. The Texas conservative babble I grew up hearing all around me sometimes reared its ugly head and allowed certain thoughts to come into my mind. Those thoughts didn't last long though, because I was the kid who was raised not to see color and have always had friends of different races. It was pretty strange being the only white boy in the area. Even though I had gotten used to being the minority at the "homeless hotel," at least when I stepped outside my door I would see a more diverse variety of people. People who looked like me. In the two hours I spent trying to find the shelter, I honestly don't think I saw another white person.

When I finally found the place, I was a little tickled inside when I realized that the street it was on intersected with Melrose Ave. It was like I had left LA, where my first job was at that clothing store on Melrose Ave., and had gone full circle to starting my life over yet again on a street of the same name. A coincidence? Or a sign from the Universe?

The security guard at this place was also a lady but unlike the butch, drill sergeant at the last shelter, this woman was friendly and greeted me with a smile. Ivette was a larger, light-skinned Spanish girl, with brown eyes, a kind face and her brown hair in a ponytail. She wore an official security guard uniform complete with an embroidered silver badge on her cop-style, button-up shirt.

Ivette, the security guard, introduced herself and checked me in to what I ended up calling "The Melrose House." This place was a three-story walk up with only 5 rooms per floor. It was definitely a step up from the "homeless hotel" which had 30 rooms and only 2 bathrooms per floor that filled the building's 8 levels!

She walked me up the wooden stairs to the third floor where I had been assigned the room at the back end of the hall. The walls were painted beige and some African-style paintings hung on most of them. As she led me through the hallway, I was happy to see that outside my door was a nice kitchen with a 2-chair dining table and a clean bathroom next to that. She unlocked my door and I was pleasantly surprised to find that the room was pretty big and came furnished with a twin-size bed, sheets, one pillow, a TV dinner style table, a folding chair and a dresser. There was no television in this room, like there had been in the last shelter, but I was told that there was a big screen in the basement that the residents could watch.

Ivette also informed me there was a weekday curfew of midnight and failing to comply with the curfew more than three times would result in removal from the shelter. I was definitely going to follow all the rules at this place because I didn't want to have to go through the whole ordeal of moving again. I thought of this place as a step up from the "homeless hotel" and decided I was going to try and really focus on getting a job, getting my own apartment again and getting all my stuff from the storage unit in LA! It was time to get my new, New York life in order or at least that was the initial plan.

It was mid-August now and that meant my little get away vacation had turned into an almost 6-month adventure and I still hadn't really found what I was looking for. I was thinking about going back to LA less and less, but never took it off the table. I would go back there eventually, but I didn't even know what I was looking for at this point in my life. I knew I had to keep searching. There must be a reason I was in New York at this very moment.

"There will be daily room checks around 9 a.m. and you will be meeting your case manager tomorrow morning. Sleep well," said my new friend the security guard.

I thanked Ivette for being so kind and locked the door before I laid down on my bed. I had gotten so stressed out and tired just trying to find 'The Melrose House' that when my head hit the pillow I instantly fell asleep.

The next morning came and so did the screeching loud, high-pitched voice of another Latin woman. "Room check!!!!!!"

I managed to get out of bed and open the door to find a short, thin, average looking, badly dyed blonde, youngish Spanish lady standing outside. Mari was her name and she seemed almost shocked when she saw me open the door. "Good Morning, Kaleb. I see you are our newest resident. Come down and see me this morning after you get ready. Lots of paperwork and stuff to fill out."

"Okay," I said, wiping the sleep from my eyes. She seemed pretty harmless at the time and, even though she was not as exciting to look at as Mr. Martinez, she struck me as a pretty chill person. I hoped that maybe she would have some more knowledge about the homeless system in New York and could help me fast track my way into some of the programs I had been hearing about.

Using some soap and water, I freshened up my clothes in the bathroom sink. I hadn't been able to get much from my room at the last place before I left. Everything I owned was currently in two suitcases at the "homeless hotel" waiting to be collected. I walked down the 3 flights of wooden steps, then down another flight into the basement where the office and the television room were located.

I walked in and sat on the folding chair in Ms. Mari's office as she began to hand me a few stacks of papers with rules and agreements. Midnight curfew on weekdays, no guests allowed, no hanging out in other client's rooms, no access to other floors unless going out to smoke on the first floor patio, no outside furniture. The rules went on and on. Even though the rules seemed a little over the top, I guess having more rules than none at all meant I would be a little safer here and maybe this place was a little more professionally managed than the last place I called 'home.'

I walked out of her office and back up the stairs to the first floor where I entered and made my way to the back patio. An older African American man gave me a funny look as I walked by and then spoke, "Yo! Welcome kid." He wore a navy-colored army veterans hat and, even though he was a little shorter than me, you could tell he had a fire inside of him. He looked like someone who had seen a lot in his lifetime and he actually reminded me a bit of Huggy Bear in the face and in stature (minus the adult diapers and frailty). He didn't say his name that day but this man and I would soon become very good friends.

Labor Day was the first real day that anything particularly interesting happened at "The Melrose." The last few weeks had been spent handing out resumes and working at the library on some digital projects for the cake shop in Hollywood. Tim and I were talking again and this time he agreed to only give me money if I did some work for it. I was happy to do the work as I needed the money. It gave me a reason to get out of the Bronx and do something productive with all the free time being jobless, and in a shelter, provided me.

The sun was shining on Labor Day and the first weekend of September when "The Melrose House" decided to throw a BBQ for its clients. The men of the shelter got together outside on the back patio and set up a few tables and a little red grill. I helped out by sweeping the patio clean of all the cigarette butts and leaves that were littered across ground. I also helped set the tables and set out the plates and cups. It was pretty cool to see this rag-tag group of ex-cons and druggies coming together to share a meal. "The Melrose" was a men's only shelter and the guys here were mostly African American with a few Latinos and only one other white guy besides me. This day was a pretty good day where everyone seemed to get along without any drunken or drug-fueled instances.

Once everything was in place and the burgers were on the grill, the men started to play card games under the tent they had set up. The older, black veteran motioned for me to come sit and be his partner for the game. The guys were playing spades and I was pretty clueless about how it worked. Clarke, the veteran (who introduced himself as I sat down), showed me the rules. By the third game we were kicking the asses of all the other teams. We bonded over the game and later that evening bonded over our mutual love of vodka.

Clarke and I walked down to the liquor store that was a few blocks beyond The Projects, the city-funded apartments that were notorious for gang violence and drug trafficking. As we walked into the store, he told me of his previous life in Carolina and the stories of his time in the Army. We both bought a few airline-sized bottles of vodka (Clarke later told me the urban nickname for the bottles was 'nips') and headed back to the shelter. As we walked back by The Projects he warned me, "Don't ever go in those projects kid. That's no place for you. It's dangerous. All sorts of crazy shit goes on in there!"

I told him not to worry. I never planned to step foot in those buildings because I appreciated being alive far too much! We went back into "The Melrose" and since it was the weekend, and there was no security guard, we went into Clarke's room to drink our vodka, watch sports and chat about life. I liked talking with Clarke and even though we were both poor, homeless and in a shelter, we became close friends who enjoyed the company of each other. Yea, we liked to drink, but we were a lot better off than most of the people in the building who were constantly high on heroin or smoking K2 and wasting away as each day went on.

The next morning, I woke up from an unbelievably vivid dream, stirring some creative vibes inside I had never experienced before. Something at that moment told me I needed to start writing down my thoughts and dreams so that maybe one day, when life was more stable, I could write a book or maybe a memoir about my time in the shelter. I thought that the story of a privileged white boy making it through the trials and tribulations of the New York City shelter system would be pretty inspiring. I didn't know then that the story would grow to be much more than that, but I started writing down thoughts and moments, just in case.

Clarke and I started going to the Catholic Charities food pantry down the street on Wednesdays and the Salvation Army food pantry once a month. Having my buddy there with me made me feel more comfortable standing in line waiting for the free handouts we would receive. I became so humbled in those first few months of friendship with Clarke because he showed me how to live on basically nothing, using the resources we were given and letting go of my ego completely. We would always get canned food at the pantries and occasionally we would get fresh chicken or beef. Clarke started teaching me how to cook in his southern style. We spent many nights cooking food and sharing it with two of the other housemates who we became pretty close with too. Feliz and Miguel were a couple of Latin guys, who as the time went on, actually became a couple. The four of us looked out for one another and kept each other company on the days when we were stuck in the Bronx.

As the months at "The Melrose House" went on, I found myself busy with many different ways of trying to make money and assimilate back into the real world.

The end of September had me working on a website for a local chiropractor, allowing me the money to get a new laptop that I so desperately needed.

In October, I briefly worked as a fundraiser on the streets of New York for a Grassroots organization, but that job ended after missing a few shifts because of hangovers. October was also the month I got my first New York State ID card, which was such an amazing feeling! Unlike my expired California ID (which I had lost months prior), this ID had the correct spelling of my name and, even though the address on the card was that of the shelter, I was still proud to officially be a New Yorker! I also studied for and passed the exam for my New York Food Safety License, which Catherine at Parigot inspired me to get by saying how helpful it would be when applying for restaurant jobs.

November was another slow month of drinking and cooking with Clarke, job hunting and continually looking for opportunities to get out of the shelter system. I did find a job at the Hallmark Store at Rockefeller Center, but lost that to drinking too. Coming into work still drinking on Black Friday was a sure fire way to lose a job. The night before, on the holiday, was a bust too. I actually had the chance to spend Thanksgiving evening with my 2nd boyfriend ever... Tristan.

Tristan was a guy I met when I was attending TCU and he was an absolute dream boat. Tall, dark and handsome didn't even describe him thoroughly. He was tall and had an amazing body. His chiseled face and his dark brown hair made this man handsome enough to be a model, and back in those days (2001), he was. He was there for the beginning of Sarah Summers and was my first real relationship outside of high school. He had moved to NYC many years before I came back on this adventure and was doing quite well for himself. He was now an activist and a business man who had his own place in Brooklyn. We had been talking over Facebook for many years and I think he had always been hesitant to invite me over because of all the crazy, drunk posts I would make on the social media site.

For some reason, he felt bad for me this year and decided to invite me over for Thanksgiving. Maybe it was because he read online that I was in a shelter and had nowhere to go for the holiday or maybe he felt bad because he hadn't reached out to help me before that moment, but either way, the invitation was extended.

I had a few drinks with Clarke before I headed to Brooklyn to celebrate the holiday with my ex. I picked up a few 'nips' of vodka for the long ride from the Bronx to his borough. Basically, I had been drinking all day and when I showed up I was just tipsy enough to have the courage to ring the bell and see my handsome ex for the first time in over 13 years. That was not a good idea. Drinking for me never really was a good idea, but it always seemed like the right thing to do at the time.

He opened the door to his brownstone apartment after I rang the bell. From what I remember, he looked just as handsome as ever. He invited me in and introduced me to his friends. The apartment was immaculate and his friends seemed very adult and classy. I was definitely the odd man out, as my life had changed dramatically since the last time I had seen him. I felt like I was a charity case. Even though I didn't know if his friends had heard my story, I felt as if I was being looked down on. I had lots more to drink that night and the next thing I remember was waking up naked in his giant bed...alone.

I looked around his room to see if I could locate my clothes. I spotted a pair of his boxer briefs and a half empty bottle of Jack Daniels by the window. I slid on his underwear, took a swig of whiskey and then quietly made my way to the bedroom door. I opened it slowly and peered out into the living room to see if any of his guests were still there. The place was silent, but I did see his muscular legs peeking out from under a comfy looking blue blanket laying on his couch. I tip-toed over and watched him as he slept for a minute. He was as handsome as I remembered and with the ray of light from the window hitting his face perfectly, he looked like an angel. The devil in me, still a little tipsy, straddled his shirtless body and began to kiss him awake. He kissed me for a minute, but then slowly guided me off of him. I was hoping for a little 'been a long time lets re-make some magic' morning sex, but it was not meant to be. He got up and helped me find my clothes. I remembered that I was supposed to work at Hallmark that day for Black Friday. The busiest shopping day of them all! I knew I would be in big trouble if I showed up late, but I decided it would be better to show up and ask for the day off instead of not showing up at all.

I got dressed, put the bottle of whiskey in my bag when he wasn't looking, said my goodbyes sealed with a sweet kiss and headed to the train station. I wouldn't talk to Tristan again for a long time and I don't really blame him because of the state I was in. I probably would have turned myself down and stayed away from me for a while, too.

I got fired from Hallmark that day and throughout the rest of the year I was unable to land a new job either. I got close at a couple of places a few times, but they all ended up never hiring me. I spent a lot of time drinking and bonding with my friend Clarke, who had started to call me his "white son," and we tried to make our time at the shelter as enjoyable as we could. We saw many a heroin addict, crack head and ex-con come in and out of that place before Christmas. It made us glad we had each other.

Christmas at the shelter was pretty uneventful, but I spent what little money I had to help buy some extra lights and a star for the Christmas tree in the community room. The owner of the property bought us a scarf/hat combo that couldn't have cost more than $3, but it was really the thought that counted. A couple of people from high school, who had been seeing my updates on Facebook, were kind enough to send me gift cards for food and clothes, which were such thoughtful and meaningful gifts from people I had not seen in years. I didn't ever truly see myself as a charity case, because even with all my problems and needs, I was still the most put together and well off person in that shelter. This reality sort of skewed my view on what my life really looked like on the outside.

I was grateful to get those gifts, from the few people who sent them, and it made me feel like someone still cared when I had all but lost hope. New Year's came and so did my old friend, Maider. We didn't see each other that night, but I had been seeing the bottle for sure. I must have had a lot to drink that night because the next morning I remember waking up to the security guard opening my door and it hitting my head. Yes, I had fallen asleep on the floor and woken up in a mess all around me. A little bit of vomit and whatever drink I had been working on before I passed out were in little pools covering various parts of the bedroom. I cleaned up quickly hoping no one would notice, but unfortunately the story had made its way to the to the people in charge.

My case worker and the owner were pretty worried about me when they heard the news of my latest drunken scene and decided to have a meeting with me. The owner, Mrs. Zana, was a well-educated, tall, voluptuous and quite attractive, African American woman. When she told me I needed to straighten up or she would be forced to kick me out, I took notice. I didn't want to lose this place because I had gotten very attached to my friendship with Clarke and knew that the next place they would put me in could be far worse than this. I wasn't going to let that happen and I knew

I had to change, at least until I got out of this place.

So I decided I would clean up my act and try and go sober for a while. Start really focusing on my goals and dreams again. Maybe, just maybe, with the clarity of sobriety I could be like J.Lo and make my way out of the Bronx. Become famous like I had always dreamed. And maybe one day, the world would call me: 'Kaleb from the Block.'

IT WASN'T ALL A LIE

JANUARY 1ST, 2015 was the day I decided I would quit drinking, for the first time, in New York City.

I had quit a few times in Los Angeles and had gone to AA because of a court requirement and at the wishes of Tim, but it just never seemed to work for me. I was clean for a few months in LA, but I felt like I had really just swapped one addiction for another. Don't get me wrong, AA is awesome and I am so glad it works for a lot of people, but for me it didn't work. It became my new addiction.

Once I really got into the depths of AA and saw how it worked, I became obsessed. I wanted to go to every meeting, have the best stories and volunteer for every position available. I looked at it like a show and I had to be the star, like I did with most things in my life. Maybe that need to be the best or 'popular' stemmed from all those years in school feeling like the outcast or maybe it was the need just to be loved because deep down I always felt so alone. Either way, the program simply didn't work for me. I did like some of the steps; taking responsibility for your actions and making amends to those you had hurt in the past. I figured even if I worked my own kind of 'program' it would be good to work those ideas in.

So that first day of the new year I quit. Maider, my bestie from Spain, and I met up for her last day in the city and an early celebration of my birthday. We went to Times Square to the bowling alley and as we played a few games she was drinking cocktails and I was having Shirley Temples in a martini glass. We strolled through Times Square, went to the M&Ms store and took pictures all over the place! We even went back to Paesano's where we finally shared that amazing seafood plate we had wanted to share the first time we met. The servers were quite surprised when I turned down their offer for free wine but, for that day at least, I was committed to giving the sobriety thing the old college try. Maider told me it was the most fun she had with me in New York and, even though she missed her drinking buddy, this version of me was even better.

She wasn't the first person to tell me that and she wouldn't be the last. In that first week of sobriety, I found support in some of the most unlikely of places. Tim, of course, was very supportive via phone and reiterated how much better my life would be if I continued on my path of sobriety and how he was much more willing to help me when I was sober. I knew I would have his support, but it was Clarke and the people at the shelter who really surprised me with a hopeful amount of backing.

Clarke, my old drinking buddy, was proud that first week I made it through without a drink. I think he knew how hard it was for me. When we would hang out cooking or watching television, he would drink his vodka when I wasn't looking. He told me he was proud of me every day I went without a drink and that meant the world to me. Clarke was my best friend and I was his 'white son' so his support was pretty imperative in those first few weeks. Even Mrs. Zana, the owner of the shelter, became a fan of the sober Kaleb and was constantly giving me encouragement and words of wisdom. She was pretty impressed that I was turning my life around while still living there and being around all those men who were doing drugs and drinking heavily.

The first week of sobriety turned into weeks. By the second week my mind had become more clear. The time I had wasted drinking became open and I needed to find new purposes to fill it. I had always dreamed of going to NYU, so I decided I would look at my options for applying. I went down to the school and learned of an under graduate program for people like me (over the usual college starting age) and decided I would give it a go. The new, sober Kaleb figured now was the best time to start living and maybe rekindle some of those flickering dreams that had seemed to have all but disappeared.

I met with an enrollment counselor and got all the needed materials to apply. A funny thing happened that day when I went back to the Bronx. I had decided to stop in the Goodwill store to see if I could find a couple of new things to wear. When I first entered the giant store, I saw a shelf with some stuffed animals and was shocked to see a little brown teddy bear wearing an NYU sweater! I thought it was so random that all the way up in the Bronx, at a random Goodwill store, there was an NYU bear sitting all by itself. It's like that little bear was placed there for me, for inspiration, and I took it as a sign from the Universe that I was on the right path. But that wasn't all! When I went over to the clothing section, the first black T-shirt I pulled out to look at was an NYU shirt, in my size!! This was starting to get a little creepy! I took that as sign number 2 and bought both of them immediately. When I got back to "The Melrose" shelter, I showed Clarke what I had found and he was pretty tickled and approved of my decision to apply.

I asked Tim and one of my choir teachers from high school, Ms. Laura, to write letters of recommendation and they agreed. I was so ready to go to NYU but was NYU ready for me? The approval process took a while, so I had to find other things to fill my new copious amounts of free, sober, time.

I had been talking to my friend Lacy about getting into the acting world like she was. She suggested I should register with Company Casting. Company Casting was a huge company with headquarters in LA and New York. Its main purpose was to cast background actors for television shows and movies. Lacy had been with them for years and worked on tons of awesome projects with them in LA. I had always wanted to join them, but when I was in LA, I guess the cake world and the nightlife world kinda distracted me from most everything. I had dreamed of becoming a famous entertainer since I was a child. I missed expressing myself in that creative way. I decided now was the right time to finally take that step and see where it would lead me. I had all the free time in the world. I had no bills to pay because I was living in a shelter, so I had no reason to be worried about looking for a 'regular' job anyway.

I put on my nicest outfit one Thursday morning in that fourth week of January and headed into Manhattan to register with Company Casting where I would hopefully get my big break! I didn't know how all this stuff really worked and the only time I had been in a movie was back in 2004 when I played a Britney Spears lookalike in 'Miss Congeniality 2.' I thought if I got on a set a director would see something in me and then be inspired to give me a line or a part. (I dream big!) I registered that day and then headed down to see my enrollment counselor at NYU. While I was in her office, I received a call that I was selected to play a club goer in a show called 'Power' later that week and it was filming at a studio in Brooklyn. Wow! I already got my first call!! I definitely took that as a sign from the Higher Power and was thrilled. My enrollment counselor thought it was pretty cool, too.

I rushed back to the Bronx to tell Clarke. He was very excited for me and told me how proud he was of me for everything I was able to accomplish in such a short amount of time. I was pretty proud of myself too.

That Sunday, February 1st, was my birthday and it was also the Super Bowl, two events I usually would drink tons of booze during. This year was different though. I had a pretty strong commitment to my sobriety and made it through the day drink free. I received tons of posts from people on Facebook wishing me a Happy Birthday and messages of congratulations and pride for my ability to stick to sobriety for that length of time.

I was about a month into my latest go at being sober when I stepped foot on my first TV show set in Brooklyn. After a long train ride and a following bus ride, I made it to the studio. It was jaw dropping! The facility itself was huge and there were many different sound stages bustling with energy. I found the correct one and made my way into the background actor holding area where I signed in and received my first non-union waiver. It was a piece of paper I had to fill out to receive my paycheck for work, but to me it was another 'ticket to freedom,' much like that airplane ticket I held in my hand almost one year before when I decided to leave Los Angeles on a whim.

I filled out the waiver with excitement, and simultaneously began making friends with the people around me. My fellow background actors and I had a blast that day. While sitting for long periods of time in between filming, we shared stories of our past and our hopes for the future. Most of my new friends (like everyone else I had ever told) were shocked when they heard my story. It was nice to hear the words of encouragement from them about how the acting world had made their lives better. I truly enjoyed my first day on set and, when lunch came, I was pretty happy too! I even posted on Facebook that day,

"Did we just get paid to eat good food, make new friends and dance on camera? Awesome! I could get used to this!"

The month of February had me on the set of 'Law and Order: SVU' and a miniseries called 'The Slap.' Although I was just doing background acting roles with no lines, I was happy to be working in the field I loved and learning so much about the business. I was even asked to play a waiter in 'The Slap.' I was certain I had gotten a pretty good shot during one of the scenes but would not find out for months until the show came out! I also met a girl on set named Adrienne who became a good friend and someone who would be very helpful to me down the road.

The beginning of March started off with the crushing of one dream, but also the celebration of my official 60-day marker in sobriety and an offer to finally work at Parigot.

March 4th, I received an email from NYU that I wholeheartedly expected to be my acceptance letter, but it was not. It was a rejection letter. My heart sank. I knew that if I had still been drinking, this would have been one of those days where I would have had a massive melt down followed by a disastrous bender. Something inside of me though didn't let it get to me. It didn't let that dark voice of temptation win and I stayed sober that day. I figured that maybe NYU wasn't part of 'The Plan' the Universe had for me at the time. I was very proud of myself for giving it a shot. So I refocused my attention on getting out of that shelter and finding a job other than the sparsely available acting gigs. I was inspired after Clarke had been given the opportunity to get his own place and figured if he could do it, so could I!

It was a sad and happy day for me, the day Clarke moved out. The shelter had already changed so much. Ivette had left because she got a promotion and Ms. Mari had gotten fired for inappropriate relations with clients. Clarke was my best friend and my rock, my encouragement through my journey of sobriety. It was nice getting back to the shelter after sober days on set and telling him of my adventures. I didn't know how my life would be once I was alone at that shelter, without my buddy for constant support. I helped him move into his new studio apartment and told him how happy I was for him. I was happy for him, but I was also a little nervous for me. Would I be able to continue to be sober without him there? I needed to find a job to keep me busy. So I did.

It was later in that month when Catherine, my 'French Mother,' who I had still often been going to see, told me she was very proud of the headway I was making in my sobriety and in the entertainment business. She had agreed that if I made it to 60 days of sobriety, she would give me a shot at serving tables at the restaurant. On day

66 she gave me that chance and I started working there.

I kept a total of the number of days I was sober on each daily Facebook post, but working at Parigot and bar tending had made me get a little too comfortable again with alcohol. I was tasting drinks here and there to make sure they were correct and eventually started having one or two drinks myself to see if I could handle drinking like a 'regular' person. I lasted for a while. Every night I made it home without blacking out, I marked as another day of 'sobriety.' I figured drinking wasn't my problem, it was the blacking out that was really my issue. If I could keep that under control, then I would be fine. Boy was I wrong.

I wasn't the kind of person who just did something a little. I was always a go big or go home kind of kid and sometimes I let myself forget that. I had been working at Parigot for about a month and was touting to Facebook that I had finally made it to 90 days sober when my world would collapsed again. This time in a more dramatic way than ever before.

Day 90 of my so-called sobriety, I decided to celebrate by drinking over at Clarke's new apartment. I bought a huge bottle of vodka and my new friend Adrienne met me there with a big bottle of wine. Adrienne was a tall, very pretty, modelesque African American girl with curly black hair, a spunky attitude and a penchant for drinking like me. Clarke and Adrienne got along quite well and both were a little nervous that I was drinking that day, but I assured them I had it all under control. We had a great time, from what I remember, but by day 91 I was drinking in the morning on my way to work at Parigot to try and kill a massive hangover.

I thought I was being pretty slick, but Catherine could see through my facade and called me on it. She waited until the shift was over and fired me on the spot. Just like everyone else, Catherine had been under the impression that I was sober. When she found out the truth, she was appalled, and rightly so. How long did I think I could keep it up? I gathered my stuff and left in tears.

That evening the dark voice came back, stronger than ever and this time he was out for vengeance.

I asked one of the guys at the shelter for some crack and he sold it to me. Swank was a newer client at the shelter and had been showing signs of heavy drug use. He was a nice guy, but a little strange and I figured he would be a good hook-up for the stuff. He was another African American ex-con who told me of his past gang involvement, but said he was trying to get away from all that drama on the streets. He was a shorter, stick-thin guy with a shaved head who was tough but had a sweetness to his face. You could tell he had a rough time growing up on the streets, but deep down inside there was still a person who just longed for friendship and the want to be respected and treated like a real person. I think I felt the same way in certain respects and that's why we got along. It wasn't long before I started doing crack with him just about every day and we became close friends, but really we were more like drug buddies.

I spent the last bit of money I made from Parigot on booze and crack and spent my days playing games on my Wii U and smoking and drinking with Swank. He became like my body guard and I was happy to have protection in that place now that Clarke was gone.

The month of April had come and gone and some new guys had moved into the building. One in particular moved in next door to me and he kind of caught my eye. He was a sexy, ripped-bodied, Latin guy who seemed like he was interested in me. He always walked around the floor shirtless and would come and ask me for food sometimes. Maybe it was the booze or the crack, but I started to take a liking to this guy and eventually asked him if he wanted to sleep in my room with me one night.

My god! It felt so good laying in a sexy guy's arms and feeling his tight body next to mine as he held me in the bed. I sucked him off a few times and I seriously thought we had something going. What I didn't stop to think about, while I was in my drug-fueled lust, was that maybe he was just using me to get what he wanted. I had given him money many times during the week. What I didn't realize was that maybe those few nights I let him stay in my room he was secretly casing the place to see what he could steal. I would soon find out things were not as they appeared and the shelter was not as safe as I thought.

May 7th was when the shit really hit the fan and I was too blacked out to really know what had happened. I remember waking up with a throbbing headache, a towel around my face and a massive pain in my swollen right hand. There was blood on my floor and when I went into the bathroom and looked into the mirror I saw that under the towel was a giant gash on my chin that had barely stopped bleeding. I shook my head as I looked at the mess in the mirror looking back at me and tried to put the pieces of the previous night together.

Swank ran into my room and asked me if I was okay. He said we had gotten separated the night before and the last time he saw me I was talking to some thug and walking towards The Projects. I thought I must have made a deal for crack with someone who lived there and who ended up stealing my drug money and beating me up. I couldn't believe this had happened to me. Why did all this drama seem to constantly follow me?

Clarke had warned me about going into The Projects and I'm sure the sober me would have listened, but the blacked-out, crackhead Kaleb must have thought he was unstoppable and maybe immortal. I could have gotten fucking shot in there. I could have ended up dead. I was lucky to have made it out with only a sprained left pinky finger and a giant bloody gash on my chin that would no doubt become a noticeable scar.

I stayed in bed for a few days until the wound scabbed over. Swank would go out and bring me back some vodka so I had something to kill the pain. I probably should have gone to the hospital to get my injuries taken care of, but I was so ashamed of the fact I had been smoking crack and had been attacked, that I didn't even feel safe to leave my room. Swank said he told his old gang members on the street to try and find whoever did that to me but without a description it was next to impossible.

It was a Sunday night in May when my $188 bi-weekly budget from the city came in and I was feeling a little better. I had decided I would take Swank into Manhattan for dinner that evening for taking good care of me while I was on bed rest. We had a fun time at dinner that night in the city but when we got back to my room was when I lost it.

Someone had broken into my room and stolen my Wii U, my DVD player and my big flat-screen television Tim had gotten me as a birthday gift! How the hell could someone walk out with a fucking TV and no one know it?! Swank and I confronted all the guys in the building and no one would fess up to the crime. I was distraught. I had been beaten to a pulp the week before and now this?! I knew I had to get out of that place and the next morning I would.

That night, fearing for my safety, I put my bed against the door and barely slept through the night. The second the clock struck 8 a.m. and I knew the security guard and the case manager were there, I bolted downstairs to report the theft. I knew there were cameras in the building so they should be able to catch the guy who did it and throw him out.

The new security guard told me the cameras did not actually record footage so there was no way to prove who did it. With that announcement, I was done. I threw my hands into the air and started screaming at the top of my lungs!

"Fuck this, Fuck that, Fuck you - I'm through!"

I raced back up the creaky wooden stairs, past the cheap wall art and into my room where I began to pack. I was not going to stay there another minute. I was not going to be a victim any more. I packed my suitcase with as much would fit, including a few changes of clothes, all my important documents and my laptop. I told them to put all my stuff in garbage bags and put it in storage because I was leaving right then.

I stormed out of "The Melrose" in such disgust and rage that you could almost see the cloud of hate following me as I rolled that suitcase down the densely populated Bronx street. I'm sure all the Latin and African American onlookers got quite a kick watching the angry little white boy storming down Melrose Avenue in a huff towards the 2 train entrance.

I made it to The Organization around 2 p.m. and the look on Ms. Gena's face was pure shock. I was visibly upset but she was quick to try and comfort me. When I told her of what had happened in the past few months and how the last few weeks had been hell, I could see the disappointment written all over her face.

"You were doing so good, Kaleb. This makes me very sad," she said. Makes her sad? Fuck, it made me sad.

As she searched the computer for a new open room somewhere in the city, the depression mounted heavily on my heart. I had come so far those first few months of sobriety and knew if I could just get back on track I might be okay. I had done so much in those 90 days (even though only a little over 60 of them were actually alcohol and drug free), there was some real progress and it wasn't all a lie.

I CAN'T LIVE LIKE
THIS ANYMORE...

M S .   G E N A   was quick to find me an open room and told me it would be in a shelter on Staten Island. I looked at her with disbelief and told her that there was no way I was going to live on an island outside of the island I was already on... Manhattan. I had lived in the Bronx and I was dead set on not going back there, but I was definitely not going to Staten Island! I felt like the shelters were jail enough and now she wanted to put me on an island? Might as well be Alcatraz! I begged her to try and find me something else but she reminded me that the system would only offer a client one room per day. If I wanted to try again, I would have to wait until after the weekend. I decided I would wait and find somewhere else to stay for the next couple of days.

I couldn't stay with Clarke because his real son was already living with him at the time and he didn't think there was enough room for another person in his small studio apartment. I thought maybe I would have to beg Tim for more money, but I knew he was once again very disappointed with me and would more than likely say no, if he answered my call at all. I thought I might have to resort to sleeping on the street, but before that happened, I got a text message from a friend I had forgotten to ask for help.

Adrienne sent me a message asking how I was and I quickly asked if she would be willing to let me crash with her. She said she had room at her apartment and I could stay a few days, if I could make my way to New Jersey. New Jersey?! I had only been to Jersey once and that was only because I landed there after I left LA. I figured it might be fun to explore New Jersey with my actress friend and it might be a nice little vacation from the drama of the city.

I made my way to Port Authority where I got a ticket for a New Jersey-bound bus. With my suitcase rolling behind me, I was on my way to a new state and hopefully a new state of mind.

I made friends with a woman on the bus who said she lived in the same area as Adrienne and that her husband would give me a ride with them once we reached the bus stop in Hoboken. I said thank you and accepted her offer as we continued on the trip. When we reached the city, her husband was there as she said and we both got into his SUV. I asked him to stop by a liquor store so I would have something to take to Adrienne's house that we could share. I bought a huge bottle of vodka and we proceeded down the road.

The streets of Hoboken reminded me a little bit of my hometown in Texas. It was very small-town suburbia looking and the area she lived in had only one big 'main street.' The little shops and even the people there all seemed like they enjoyed the distance from the big city and were happily going about their lives unaware of the mental turmoil I was struggling with. The nice couple dropped me off a few blocks away from Adrienne's house and the brisk walk in the cool air and the greenery of the trees had a calming effect on me.

I reached the door of her one-bedroom apartment around 4 p.m. and it was so nice to see a familiar face of someone outside the shelter world. A 'normal' person who wasn't forced to check in with some case manager every morning or be woken up at 9 a.m. for a room check. Adrienne's apartment was pretty big and nicely decorated, too. It was nice to see some other artwork besides the dollar store pictures lining the walls of "The Melrose House."

Adrienne welcomed me in and I sat on the couch as she fixed us a couple glasses of vodka and orange juice. We ended up having a really fun weekend of bonding over Netflix and our troubles with the world. It turned out she was having some financial issues as well and we were actually more alike than I had thought. This realization reminded me that you really can't judge a book by its cover, you have to read through the story to see the truth.

As the weekend drew to a close, we decided we would go get a couple of bottles of wine to share before I headed back to Manhattan to face the 'real world' again. Before we left her apartment, I noticed that my wallet was not in my back pocket or in my jacket like it usually was. I immediately got nervous. I rummaged through my suitcase at an alarming rate and was enraged when I couldn't find it. I figured I must have left it at the liquor store I went to when I first arrived in Jersey or maybe I had left it in the couple's car. Whatever the situation, I had no way of getting it back. I had no clue who those people were and they had no clue where I was staying. If I had left it at the liquor store, I couldn't get it back, because I had no idea where that store was. Fuck! It's like one bad thing after another just seemed to keep happening to me.

Adrienne calmed me down and told me that there was a Wells Fargo bank at the end of the 'main street' that would be open in the morning. I found it pretty crazy that of all places my bank would be here, so close to her house. Maybe it was the Universe giving me one more little helping hand. I had opened an account with Wells Fargo in Fort Worth right after my mother died back in 2001. I had some ups and downs with that company but could always rely on them. When I moved back to New York, I was surprised to find that there were very few of their bank branches randomly placed around the city so finding one in Jersey seemed almost magical to me. I planned on going there in the morning but first we were going to cook dinner and drink lots of wine.

That evening was great and Adrienne's friendship cemented itself in my life for good after the way she so kindly took me in. Where had all my "friends" in LA been when I was evicted and homeless? Made me think for a minute about all my past friendships and question their validity. I even briefly thought about Liam for a moment, but quickly changed my thinking to what would happen once I got back to Manhattan.

The next morning, I went to Wells Fargo and after many identity confirming questions I was able to secure a withdrawal from my account. I withdrew enough money to get back to the city and have a few bucks left over to get a metro card so I could once again go see Ms. Gena at The Organization. I prayed that this time she would have the perfect place for me because I didn't know if I could take any more stress. I was beyond depressed and I was just praying and wishing that something good would finally happen for me.

An hour or so later after a Jersey bus and NYC subway train, I made it back to The Organization office where Ms. Gena was expecting me. She put my name into the computer system and the first listing that came up was in the Bronx. I was pretty leery of going back to the Bronx after everything that happened to me the weeks before, but she assured me that this shelter was on the opposite side of the city and it was very close to Fordham University. That sounded promising, as I had heard good things about that college and figured the surrounding area would be a little nicer and maybe a little more diversely populated than the last hood I lived in. I agreed to take the room because it was really the only option I had and I needed to have someplace to call 'home' while I tried to recoup and figure out what the hell I was doing with my life.

She printed out the directions and wished me good luck again. I could see the look of pity pointed in my direction as she handed me yet another piece of paper, another ticket to a chance at getting my life back together. I was hoping this next place would be the place where I would finally settle down for a while and feel safe, but that, unfortunately, would not be the case.

I found my way to this new shelter quite easily compared to the hours of searching I did to find "The Melrose House." I was surprised to see it was very different from the other two shelters I had lived in. I walked up to the building number listed on the paper in my hand and was surprised to see that it looked like a rundown apartment building. I tried to find a call button for the office, but did not see one so I rang the bell for the room number I was supposed to be staying in. No one answered. I got pretty frustrated and tried to call Ms. Gena, but she had already left for the day. My only other option was to press the buzzer for the other rooms and hope someone would let me in. After pressing each one for a few minutes, someone finally let me in. When I got into the entrance, I realized these were all apartments and not rooms.

I walked up the dirty concrete stairs to the 2nd floor where I saw a metal door with a brown sticker that read, "2B." I knocked on the door and was kinda shocked when it came open by itself.

Was a case worker supposed to be meeting me here? Were my keys somewhere inside? How the hell did this place work?

I opened the door to find a very run down and completely trashed two-bedroom apartment. The walls were grease-stained beige and there was trash and broken glass strewn across the floor. There was an old futon couch, a table and one chair up against the window. The window was the only thing that gave that place any sense of life. It was huge and overlooked the 'backyard' of the building, which was covered in tall green grass and weeds. The bathroom had trash all over it but it was obvious someone lived there. I suddenly wondered if I was even in the right place?

I opened one of the bedroom doors and saw a bed with sheets covered with tons of various types of clothes stacked on top. I figured the person who owned all this must be my roommate. I walked over to the other bedroom door and was a little put off when I saw just a mattress on a frame and a dresser in the otherwise empty room. I figured that whoever was living here would come back at some point in the evening and we could discuss cleaning it up and the key situation. Whoever it was didn't come back though. In fact, I was stuck alone in that apartment for 3 days, only leaving during the day when I knew there would be a neighbor around to buzz me back into the building.

I hadn't loved the security and the rules of the other two shelters, but the complete lack of structure at this shelter was almost unbearable.

I got very frustrated at the whole situation and angered that I couldn't seem to get the building management on the phone either. It was like I was in the freaking homeless shelter twilight zone. I kept myself busy by trying to clean up the place and trying to get a wifi connection for my laptop so I wasn't completely bored.

Finally, the evening of the third day, the roommate returned and introduced himself. He was a queeny little African American gay guy who seemed like someone I would actually get along with... at first. We talked about doing drag and what we liked to do for fun while I encouraged him to help me clean the place up. After the place looked a little better, we decided to go out and get some drinks and, after cashing my $188 bi-weekly state benefit, we went to the local liquor store. I grabbed a bunch of vodka 'nips' and we drank them as we walked along the streets of this new area in the Bronx towards a bar that was near the apartment building.

I remember us dancing and talking to some girls, but that is the last thing I remember before waking up in the hospital where apparently I had been escorted by police that evening. Turns out I couldn't find my phone and I had gone back to the apartment to try and get in. The little bitch of a roommate called the cops saying that I was 'scaring' him. I was probably accusing him of stealing my phone or something along those lines. I had to stay in the hospital for a few hours to be monitored because they had to pump my stomach due to alcohol poisoning. This was another low moment in my life, but I was grateful that at least I didn't get arrested.

Later that day, when I went back to the apartment to get my belongings, the roommate said that management had come to pick up my stuff and had said I needed to find a new room. I called the management via payphone and was finally able to get ahold of them. They said they hadn't sent anyone in. That little bastard had lied to me. He had made up this story so he could steal my computer and anything else I had of value in my suitcase. What the fuck?! I didn't want to get the cops involved again, so I left. I called the management company again, as I walked down the littered street, to find out they could do nothing about it. Once again I was left with nothing and at my complete wits end. How could I let this bullshit continue to keep happening to me? What was wrong with me?

Completely defeated for the umpteenth time, I relinquished any amount of pride I had left and painfully made my way back to The Organization yet again. Ms. Gena was not happy.

"Kaleb, what is going on with you kid? You can't keep moving from place to place. Pretty soon they might not take you in anywhere and we would have to remove you from the program all together. You wouldn't want that would you?" she questioned, looking very serious.

I stopped for a minute and thought that maybe getting kicked out of the program was what I needed. Maybe then I could find my way back to LA and try and start over there. Maybe now Cheri or Jackie or someone would be willing to take me in and help me out. That was doubtful though. Everyone in LA was still living their same lives and had their plates full of their own problems. Maybe I could try and get ahold of Liam and see if.... No. I was never going to talk to him again, so that option was ruled out. The only thing left to do was to just stick it out with this program and pray that maybe I would be able to figure out what the hell I was supposed to be doing with my life once and for all.

"Find me another room, Ms. Gena. I've come this far... I've survived this much... let's just see it out til the end. I'm going to make it damn it, or I'm gonna die trying to figure it out," I said to her with a tiny glimmer of hope appearing in my eye. The tiny voice, the little spark, even though quiet and dim, was still there telling me not to give up yet. I could hear the vague sounds of the soft spoken words it was speaking and the muffled sounds of that crackling flame. I realized then that I could not and would not give up. I would take this next room, wherever it was, and I would make the best out of it because I wasn't ready to call it quits. I looked over at Ms. Gena who was holding a new piece of paper that had the address of the available room and said, "Tell me where I am going. This has to be the right place, Ms. Gena. I don't know how much more I can take."

The room was located in Jamaica, Queens at the YMCA and I was kind of put off by the idea of living at a place that was known for kid's activities and cheap gym rates, but figured maybe it would be good for me. Hell, if I decided to clean up my act, maybe I could get a free gym membership and start working out. Haha! Always dreaming big this kid. I took the piece of paper and, with much trepidation, left The Organization once again with high hopes that something better was on the horizon.

I had to take the E train all the way to the last stop in Queens. It seemed like that ride went on forever. With no phone and no laptop, the ride was very, very boring, but it gave me plenty of time to think. Why on Earth had God, or whatever was in charge, let all this shit happen to me? Was I a bad person? Did I do something awful in a past life or was I just a worthless human being with no real future? The dark thoughts over took my mind and all I could think about was getting off that train, getting a drink and then going to see what the YMCA had in store for me.

When the train stopped, I got out and took in the view of my new hood. This place was much like the Bronx in its not so diverse populous. Once again it appeared I was the only little white boy in town. I made my way through the sea of people, walking down three crowded blocks from the station, before I spotted the Y. I figured I might as well check in first before I went to get drunk. So I made my way in and up to the front desk. The kindly looking, older, African American gentleman at the front pointed me to the elevator and told me to go to the second floor to meet my newest case manager for the Y's program. Oh god, another damn case worker? Hopefully, this one would be the one who could actually work my case the way the others had not been able to and fix my life! That was a lot to expect of someone who was dealing with the problems of many other poor, unfortunate souls, but I hoped this person would get the job done.

Ms. Janene was a younger woman from Africa who had sweet features on her kind face. She was of average build and height and her office was decorated with pictures of President Obama and Bible quotes she had printed out. She was a nice woman who had recently graduated and seemed very eager to help. She mentioned some various programs I had not heard of and said that we should start working on them immediately so I could get out of there as soon as possible. I liked her from the get go! Her positive attitude made me almost believe that she knew what she was talking about and that maybe she would be the case manager that got through to me! She showed me to my room and we made an appointment for later in the week.

The first couple of weeks were pretty good. We had our meeting and she introduced me to another organization that helped people like me transition into more permanent housing situations. I had an interview with that group and, even though I drank the night before, I was not hung over and the meeting went well. We didn't hear anything back from them though and I figured maybe they thought I wasn't right for their program or ready to get my own place just yet. So I put that dream on the back burner yet again and decided to look for a job.

I actually found a job working at a patio bar over by the United Nations. While it lasted it was pretty good. Unfortunately, I was not able to bar tend and refrain from drinking while I was working and was quickly fired from my position. I guess I was like most alcoholics and didn't realize I had a problem. Drinking was a way of life for me and booze was my best friend. I figured all the shit that was going wrong in my life was because of fate or the fault of everyone else around me. I wasn't the one with the problem.

When I would get fired, in my alcoholic mind, it was because everyone else couldn't handle my big personality, not because I was drinking. When I got attacked it wasn't because I was drunk, it was just because they thought I was an easy target because I was white or gay. None of the issues were my fault or the alcohol's fault. I couldn't see why no one would help me. I was just the victim in all this. Right?

Wrong. But it took me just a little longer to come to that realization and it all happened the weekend of Gay Pride in NYC when my thought process changed and I had the eye opening revelation that "I can't live like this anymore..."

THE SIGNS

GAY PRIDE IN NYC was a big deal! There was always a huge parade and a bunch of parties all over the city where you could drink for free. I told myself I was going to slow down on the booze and I even made it a couple of days without drinking before the weekend of the event.

I had been at the YMCA in Queens for a few weeks and had been going to the library to use the computer so I could check my emails and update my Facebook. It was nice to see messages of encouragement that people from my high school days would send me or inspirational quotes they posted to my wall. I spent part of my bi-weekly government assistance buying another burner phone and used that number for the new batch of resumes I had printed out. I also got my trash bags full of belongings moved over from

"The Melrose House" and was quite disappointed when I noticed a few things were missing. The suit I had bought at the Goodwill store for background acting gigs was gone and that really stung. It was like the Universe was making me start over from scratch once again to see if maybe I would get it right this time. If there was a God, or whatever, I would tell it that I was tired of all the fucking tests. I had fought to live more times than I'd like to admit and I was starting to feel like there wasn't much of a reason to keep fighting anymore.

The day of the Gay Pride parade I walked out of my room towards the bathroom I shared with the 40 other guys living on that floor, and was pretty shocked to see a pile of human feces just laying against the wall in the hallway. What a piece of shit my life had become. Literally. I was living a life surrounded by shit and I couldn't wait to get out of there for the day. I went down to the cafeteria where they served three meals a day and got lunch. The food was not anything to write home about but I was grateful for it on the days when I literally only had pennies to my name.

After lunch, I made my way into Manhattan and used the other half of my bi-weekly government assistance money to buy a giant bottle of vodka and some snacks at the parade festivities. I ran across a private party in a random park where I pretended to know the host and was allowed entry. I ended up drinking for free the rest of the day and don't remember much except for the gay couple that I saw sitting on the bench just holding each other.

Even in my drunken haze, I could remember thinking how sweet it was and how badly I wished I had someone to love me like that. Somebody to hold me while I was going through some of the worst emotions I had ever felt in my life. I thought about how different my life would be at that moment if Liam had been different, if he had let go his ego and really let our relationship have a chance. Fuck him and fuck everybody else for not being there for me and letting me end up like this. Maybe they would all be happier if I was dead. Maybe if the people in LA got a call from some random case manager in New York telling them that Kaleb was dead, they could all live a better life without me. Drink, drink, drink. Drink the pain and the thoughts away and maybe I can finally be free of all of this shit that was my world.

I drank a lot that day and somehow I made it back to the Y in Queens and woke up in my twin-size bed sick as a dog. I threw up and then threw up some more. I tried to eat some food but I couldn't keep anything down. Not even water could rest in my stomach at this point. I must have had alcohol poisoning again and it was complete agony. The vomiting lasted through the next day. I think I maybe got two hours sleep during those 48 hours. The chills and then sweats, the head pain and the hunger I couldn't satiate, were driving me insane. I honestly felt like I was going to die and at that moment I didn't care. I didn't call for help and I just let myself suffer through it. Self-punishment, I guess, for the life I was living. I didn't want to go on anymore. I looked around the room at the plastic grocery bags filled with vomit and the empty vodka bottles littering the room and said to myself, "If you make it through this, you have to quit drinking for real... you have to give it your all."

I finally fell asleep. My body was exhausted from the lack of sleep and the constant fits of vomiting. I woke up the next day feeling much better and decided I would give sobriety one more chance. I would give myself one more chance. I got out of bed and noticed a letter had been placed under my door and immediately got kind of nervous. I could only hope this letter wouldn't be a warning or even worse a pending eviction letter. I didn't think I could handle something like that.

I opened the envelope with a slight hesitation, but was pleasantly surprised with its contents. It was a letter from Ms. Janene saying the Housing Group I had interviewed with before had selected me as a candidate to receive a one-bedroom apartment.

Wow! It was like a gift from the Universe. It made me think that maybe it was a proverbial reward for managing to stay sober for those few days and possibly a sign that if I kept it up, more good things might come. I immediately rushed to her office and we called the group to set up another meeting. She was just as excited as I was. The good energy in the room gave me a sense of hope I hadn't felt since I had landed in NYC a little over a year ago. Was this the real ticket out of the homeless hotel hell I had been living in for the last year and a half? I could barely contain my excitement, but soon realized it wasn't going to happen overnight. A few more interviews to attend and multiple forms to fill out awaited me, but I decided right then and there I would be ready for them. I made a commitment to myself that I would stop drinking and turn my life around or at least give it my hardest try.

Around this time, I started to see signs from the Universe. The little spark inside of me that had almost burned out was now growing with each new realization that came to me. As I sat on my bed at the Y thinking about what my new apartment would be like, I saw a commercial, on my YMCA provided TV, for a car company using dynamite to blow car shapes into a mountain like Mt. Rushmore. For a brief moment, I wondered how the real monument was made. I thought maybe the next time I was in the library I would look it up and then sort of forgot about it. Low and behold, a few hours later PBS was doing a special on Mt. Rushmore and the man who didn't let anyone tell him his dream to create something that extreme would not work. I watched the whole show and felt very inspired by the pure determination and commitment of that man. I also thought it was so strange how that show was just randomly on television. Had God been listening to me? Was the Universe trying to tell me something?

I wrote in my journal that evening about this strange coincidence and then prayed for more inspiration. If the Powers that Be were listening, maybe it was time to start asking for what I really wanted: a better life. The answers started coming at a pretty rapid pace and I was thrilled and in awe.

Two days later on my 5th day of sobriety, in which I had basically secluded myself in my room at the Y in Queens, another sign came to me and it was by far the most profound one ever. I didn't expect the blueprint for the rest of my life to come in the way it did and where it did. But I am so grateful it did.

It was around 3:30 a.m. and I was getting ready to sleep by flipping the channels to find something I could use for background noise. Sometimes having something play in the background helped lull me to sleep. I came across a channel with some evangelical guy speaking about who knows what. I figured that would make good background noise so I went to turn it down a little, but something inside me told me to turn up the volume and listen for a minute.

I am not a Christian, Jew, Muslim, Buddhist or any religion really, but I do respect them all. I have been known to go into a random synagogue, church, or other place of worship, and take a moment to be inspired. Many faiths have rules or guidelines to follow, the Ten Commandments being the most prominent. Buddhists have their Precepts and Hindus Sanatana Dharma. On this particular evening it was a Christian Pastor from Texas, Mike Murdock, that inspired me. This gentleman may have been a Christian Pastor but his words could be molded to any way of life. A simple changing of words could make this list fit any religion or non-religion. It's more of a guide, less like commandments, and if followed, promised a better life. So, I listened closely, and what he had to say woke me up inside and shaped the way I looked at my own world from then on.

His whole show that evening was about finding your divine path, your universal assignment and what you can do to find it and stick to it. He gave a list of 7 things and a few of them hit me like a ton of spiritual bricks. I wrote them down in my journal and they were:

1. *Your assignment is any problem you are designed to solve.* (I didn't quite know what that meant but I hoped I would figure it out.)

2. *What you love is a clue to the gifts and wisdom you contain to complete your assignment.* (Well I love acting and performing and I really loved helping people. Maybe those were part of my assignment?)

3. *What you hate is a clue to something you are assigned to correct.* (I hate injustice and I hate seeing people who aren't getting the help they really need. But what could I do about it?)

4. *What grieves you is a clue to something you are supposed to heal.* (What grieves me? My downtrodden life riddled with pain and addiction was what grieved me. How was I supposed to fix that?)

5. *If you rebel against your assignment God may permit painful experiences to correct you.* (DING! DING! DING! This one was the one that hit the major chord with me! My life wasn't in shambles because the Universe hated me or was trying to punish me. It was trying to direct me back onto my destined path. More on this later.)

6. Your assignment will require seasons of preparation. The greater the assignment the longer, more difficult the training. (BAM! PUNCH! KICK TO THE SOUL! If this was true, then my life assignment, my purpose must be pretty grand because I had been through some very, very long and difficult seasons of training.)

7. You will only succeed when your assignment becomes your obsession. (Okay, so I just have to figure out what that is and start doing it. Sounded a lot easier than it actually was.)

He also said, "You are where the Universe has divinely placed you - where you have no rivals." That quote made me think that maybe that's why all that craziness happened in LA, all at the same time, so that I would end up in New York at that very moment, in that very place to hear all this stuff on television and change my life for the better. Oooh, I hoped so.

He ended his time by saying, "The price of your future is your life." I didn't quite get what that meant at the moment, but I wrote it down in hopes I would understand one day. I turned off the TV and slept like a dream that night. I had a feeling something different was coming and I was ready for it.

The July 4th holiday came and went and I was so proud of myself for making it through the weekend without a drink. The temptation was there. The money was there. The liquor store was screaming my name, but I resisted. On the day America celebrates its independence, all I could think about as I watched the fireworks in the distance from my tiny window, in my tiny room at the Y, was how badly I wanted my own independence again and how I wasn't going to let anything stop me this time. The evangelical's list kept popping into my head and number 5 was flashing in bold! I didn't want to give the Universe any more reasons to let bad things happen to me to try and get me back on my path, so I stayed sober. I felt proud. I was doing it on my own and I knew if I kept fighting the rewards would come. And then they started to.

The next day I got up and got out of the shelter and printed more resumes at the library. When I got back to the Y, I saw an envelope containing the replacement ID I had sent off for a few weeks prior. I was so happy it arrived. I knew I wanted to get back into the acting world and would need my ID for the paychecks when I got them. I'd also need my ID to sign for the apartment Ms. Janene and I were still waiting to hear about.

The following day, my tenth consecutive day of sobriety, I woke up from a fantastical dream where I was the prince in a Disney Channel movie and kept singing the line, "Things are about to change in a big way!" I took that as a sign from the Universe that I was definitely on the right path and that helped me commit even more to my plan to live a clean life. I took my ID and went and re-registered at Company Casting hoping I could get back to the acting biz and start doing what I loved again. Maybe that was part of my assignment?

The next week was full of mind-opening walks

by the Hudson River, applying for jobs and finally reading the book Cheri had sent me. It was called 'Outrageous Openness' by Tosha Silver and it was exactly what I needed at exactly the right time. It's like the Universe knew I wasn't ready to read it when I received it, but now, with a clear mind, I could take in all the divine resources the book provided and it opened my eyes to the world even more.

I was growing up at a rate I couldn't even express. I could tell I was changing when I got a call from a job I had interviewed for saying they went with another candidate. This time, I didn't break down. I didn't go off on a drunken bender or find a crack head to get high with. I realized maybe that job was not part of my path and whatever was meant for me would come in due time. I had to get used to the fact that there would be a lot of NO's before the perfect YES, and I did. I was proud of myself and so was my good friend Tim.

When I told him I had made it to 13 days sober and that I was waiting on the news of a move-in date for my own apartment, he was beyond thrilled! He was so happy he offered to get me a replacement iPhone so I could throw away the burner phone and feel more like myself again. I was beyond grateful and he reminded me, "Kaleb, I know you are going to do great things with your life. I have always supported you and I want you to know I will always have your back...especially when you are sober. This is the kid I like talking to, let's hope he sticks around."

It was nice having Tim in my corner and I

wanted to make him proud this time. I wanted to be someone else besides that drunk, waste-of-a-life I had let myself become. I wanted to find my divine purpose and live it! I was on my way.

That 13th day, the signs led me to a random restaurant in Hell's Kitchen where I dropped off my resume and was asked to come back the following week for a secondary interview. The manager really took a liking to me and I had a good feeling about that place! After the preliminary interview, I went to 7-11 to grab a soda. What I found really shook me to the core.

The Coca-Cola company was doing a promotion where they had people's names on the bottles to 'share a Coke with' and for some reason I could never find my names. This day I found two bottles of coke with my First and Middle names on them at the front of the case as if it was a sign from the Universe letting me know I was on the right path. Once my mind was clear and completely open it was as if I could see the Universe guiding me along my path and it felt magical.

Day 17 of sobriety and I was on the bus to Steiner Studios in Brooklyn for a costume fitting for a TV-show filming I would be doing later in the week. My first gig back in the entertainment business and my first job back on the sober train. Things were looking up, and even though I figured it was all too good to be true, and the next dramatic turn of events was just around the corner...it wasn't. The bad stuff didn't happen and in fact the good started coming more frequently and I couldn't have been more grateful.

335

Day 63 of my sobriety was when I finally picked up my pen and wrote in my journal once again and this is what I wrote:

44 days have passed since I have physically written an update to my story in this book. I have been posting daily updates on my Facebook page with photos which has been my journal as of late. Facebook is good for me to be able to record my thoughts and share them with others in hopes that maybe people can get some inspiration from my life as it goes along. I've also unfortunately lost so many written journals in the past – moving, stolen, etc. that Facebook seems to be the safest place to record my journey as I know it will be there forever... Or at least until the world ends. LOL.

I read somewhere that keeping a physical journal helps keep you closer to the Creator and if that's true, then that's where I want to be. Closer. I can't tell you how grateful and appreciative I am for this life I am leading right now. It's full of opportunities, possibilities, connections and visions of a rich and fulfilled future.

Since my last entry 44 days ago, I moved into my own apartment in the University Heights area of the Bronx. It is a huge one bedroom in the safe part of town. It's close to the Bronx zoo and a community college. There's lots of shopping, grocery stores and parks close by.

Thanks to the awesome Housing Group, the apartment came furnished with a few simple things I needed. A couch, coffee table, small TV, dresser, bedside table, queen-size bed and kitchen table, chairs, pots and pans. I am beyond grateful and more appreciative of having my own apartment again after the most trying year and a half of my life. It is thanks to the Universe for allowing me to find my path, remain clearheaded and be more determined than ever to make my dreams my reality.

I got that job at the restaurant in Hell's kitchen and I absolutely loved it and the people I worked with. Unfortunately, I was only there a week before they decided to close up shop and start remodeling a new place a few doors down. But the owner really liked me and said, "you are the best server I have, I knew it from the second day of your training." He says once the new place opens up I have a position waiting for me.

Like everything else, that was part of the Universe's plan. The week of work allowed me to get a brand-new laptop with money I earned on my own and that made me proud. Taking a hiatus from being a server has allowed me to focus all my attention on my acting career. Which is going amazing! I have been working 3 to 4 times a week, most weeks, which is fantastic for a background actor, I've heard.

I am still waiting to get my SAG waivers but I know the Universe has a plan for that too and they are just around the corner. Maybe I'll get my first one tomorrow on 'The Blacklist.'

I love working on that show. I have made some fun friends and I'm officially a CORE background actor on the show playing an FBI technical analyst in the war room. CORE means that every time a scene is shot in the war room, I will be in that episode. Tomorrow will be my fourth episode.

I'm sure I'm leaving out some of the other amazing... OH YEAH!!! I auditioned for my first off-Broadway play and got cast!! I went in with a funny little monologue I found online. I guess the director liked me because she gave me two roles!! I will be the lead in a twisted version of sleeping beauty playing a necrophiliac Prince and in a separate BDSM short based on the Picasso painting 'Guernica.' Rehearsals start next Tuesday, September 1st and I pretty much have all my lines memorized. This is so exciting for me. This is something I've always dreamed of doing and now here's my chance. I can't wait to meet all my costars and get to work! This is going to be a life-changing experience for the better. Great things will come from this I know it!!

Looking back on that journal entry, I can still feel the joy and the magic that was unfolding in my life. I still remember the feeling of waking up in my own queen-size bed for the first time in over a year and a half. Being in my own apartment with my own bathroom, my own kitchen and my own couch made me realize how extremely far I had come. Remembering the kid that landed in New York City not so long ago and was living in homeless shelters. Just using my own bathroom, buying my own toilet paper, stocking my own fridge, became blessings to me. I didn't take anything I had for granted and respected everything and everyone in my life in a brand new way.

Getting up in the morning and getting out of my own bed to go to rehearsals for my first off-Broadway play felt like a dream. Being on that stage dressed like a prince reminded me of that dream I had in the shelter a few months prior. Maybe that dream was a prophetic sign, because "things had changed in a really big way" like I was singing about. Now in real life I was going to be playing the Prince that I had been in my sleep. The show was going to be amazing and it even rekindled a very important relationship from my past.

I hadn't talked to my friend Michael in a long time. In fact, after the whole eviction debacle in Los Angeles, I had kind of written him out of my life. One night I was on Facebook and I got a random message from one of the girls from my high school. She said she was reading my daily Facebook posts and had been inspired by them. She said she was going through the whole homeless process like I had done and asked me for advice.

While we were talking, she mentioned our mutual friend Michael and asked if I knew how to get ahold of him because she really wanted to reconnect with him. I still had his phone number so I sent him a text to see if he was comfortable with me giving her his number. He called me instead of texting me back.

We ended up having a two-hour conversation about our lives since we last saw each other in Hollywood. He was brought to tears when he heard the story of how I had turned my life around and all the success I was having. Our friendship seemed to be back to the amazing closeness it was when we were young. After those few hours of reconciliation and over the next few weeks, he became my over-the-phone scene partner, helping me memorize all my lines. I was so glad to have him back in my life and gave a big amount of thanks to the Universe for letting it happen when it did.

Life was beyond amazing at this time and I really felt like maybe I had found my path. Now I just needed to keep searching for my purpose. The next few months of my life were filled with more amazing ups but there were some pretty difficult downs too. I was pretty sure I could get through whatever came next if I stayed on my path and kept looking for the signs.

IS THIS REALLY
HAPPENING?

MY FIRST off-Broadway show came to a close on my 90th day of true sobriety and the performance was a smashing success. Thanks to my rekindled friendship with Michael, I was always prepared with my lines and put on a great show because of it. I really got into my roles and being on stage made me feel alive once again. Acting and performing, it seemed, were exactly what my soul... my spark... needed to thrive on my newly found path. Sobriety came easier as the months went on and when the cast went out for a celebratory closing night wrap party, I was completely fine having non-alcoholic beers and Shirley Temples as the rest of my cast mates drank.

The night was filled with laughter and, of course, there was some drama. Two of the actors made out! It was my first New York City off-Broadway wrap party and it was amazing. It was even better to wake up the next day in my own apartment with no hangover and a clear mind. Sobriety was treating me right!

I had to go back to the set of 'The Blacklist' the next day and, on what should have been a regular work day, had another one of those ah-ha moments of clarity and another sign I was definitely on the right path.

The day started out like any other, my fellow background actors and I got there super early and checked in, then got our wardrobe, makeup and hair approved for the day. Then our production assistant, who was the epitome of a laid back, cool, hippie kinda guy with dreads, told us what scenes we would be in and what we had to do while the lead actors were performing their lines. Usually it involved walking around with files or typing on computers to make it look like we were working hard on whatever assignment the lead actors were discussing. The day went great and Chris, the PA, who was in charge of placing the background, had been using me for more featured shots in the scenes than usual. It was nice when I got to actually act (albeit with no words) and feel like I was a necessary part of the production.

During lunch, sitting with my 'Blacklist' Background BFFs, we were talking about the business and how being in the Screen Actors Guild was such a big deal. This was my most committed battle against drinking and this time I was super focused on my acting career. I knew I wanted to join SAG more than anything, but found out it was a little harder to get into than I expected. One of the guys in the group, who played a security guard, was in SAG. He told me how he had seen some people doing background acting for years and never getting the required number of waivers to join the union. I figured I wouldn't have that problem because I was special, I was focused and I wanted it more than anyone! Right?

Turns out, he was right, they were not easy to get and there was no real surefire way to get those SAG waivers. Sometimes you just had to be in the right place at the right time or have some sort of special talent requiring the production to give you one. I mentioned to my coworker on set that I had been in 'Miss Congeniality 2' as Sarah Summers all the way back in 2004. He suggested maybe I should look into it. Being a female illusionist in a movie usually required the production company to give the actor a special rate and waivers for each day they worked. If that was true, then I should already have done all the required work to be eligible to join the union. Now I just had to do some research. I put it on the back burner for the time being but told myself to look into it when I had some free time.

My life had gotten so busy and I tried to keep up relationships with people from my past as much as I could. I still spoke to Tim nearly every day and it was so encouraging to hear how proud of me he was. He would often tell me people would come in to the cake shop, people who knew me when I was close to my rock bottom, and ask about me. He told me he would beam with pride as he told of my harrowing tale from homeless, alcoholic wreck to drink-free, big-apartment-living, full-time acting, inspiration of a person. He said people were happy for me and they asked when I planned on returning to LA. Ha! It made me stop and think for a moment how this "little mind clearing vacation" had turned into such a life-changing, year and a half long, adventure. An adventure that showed no signs of slowing down anytime soon.

I spoke with Cheri, Annette, Jackie, Lacy and the rest of my LA friends via Facebook and occasionally via phone on special occasions. I still had heard nothing from or about Liam and, honestly, I was okay with that. I had stopped thinking about him daily, in fact it was rare if he ever crossed my mind at all. My attention was focused on finding my divine assignment and sticking to the path that was being so graciously laid out before me with each new day. I was on my way to doing some really great things and I could finally feel the good coming!

I came out of my daydream as the PA yelled, "That's a wrap!" We all began to change back into our street clothes. I handed in my fake FBI badge and headed to the checkout table where Chris was sitting. I had been working with this guy for months and he had become someone I respected. I guess you could say a friend. So I was a little surprised to hear the words coming out of his mouth that day.

"Hey, Kaleb, I just want to tell you I think it is really amazing how far you've come buddy. I don't know if you remember this, but I saw you this summer, before you started working here, when I was assisting on another project downtown. You were completely wasted and trying to get into the scenes. I just remember thinking how sad that guy was. I've overheard you guys talking these past few weeks and I just want to say I am proud of you buddy. For not drinking and for really shaping up to be a great guy. Good job!" he said, as he signed me out for the day.

Woah. I didn't remember that at all. It must have been on one of Blackout Kaleb's drunken afternoon adventures. I was a little perplexed that he had not said anything before this moment, but was glad he didn't hold that one intoxicated instance against me.

"Thanks, Chris. That means the world to me coming from you. I really respect you and thank you for everything you teach me here on set. It's been a pleasure getting to know you," I said, feeling a moment of great pride. He was right: I had come such a long way in the past 3 months of sobriety and I couldn't wait to see what was next.

A few days later I got booked for my first national commercial for E! Network and Absolut Vodka. I thought it was a little funny that my first commercial would be for a liquor brand when I was still battling alcoholism on a daily basis. The battle had gotten easier after 3 months though; I wasn't craving it or fiending for it. I could be around it now without being tempted (like I had been in the first few weeks). It was like the Universe had a funny sense of humor making me promote a product I couldn't have and had been so destructive to my life. Or maybe it was a test?

Maybe the Powers that Be were trying to see if I'd be persuaded by the glamorization of booze the commercial presented. Either way, I had to say yes to the project! It was my first national commercial!

The day of the commercial, I had to be up at 2 a.m. in order to be on set in SoHo for the 4:30 a.m. call time. Talk about early! I made it to set with a few minutes to spare and began looking for a familiar face to connect with. I didn't want to have to spend the whole day trying to make new friends or just sitting in a corner, alone. I scanned the crowd and was happily surprised to see a beautiful Asian girl I had worked with on another show just weeks before. Sitting by herself in a booth, the tall, thin, model-looking girl with the luxurious long black hair and sweet brown eyes was so happy see me when I walked in. She jumped up and gave me a big hug! I thought that was very sweet. We had only talked for a few hours on the other set and hadn't even exchanged phone numbers. But after bonding over our many similar interests this day on the commercial, we were destined to become great friends.

Amanda was from New Jersey and had just gotten into the background acting world. She told me stories about her family and we connected when we both shared about losing our mothers. A terrible thing to be bonded over, but it was nice for us to know we had both been through it. We also talked about boys, of course, and she even convinced me to flirt with one. Nothing came out of it, but it was fun to flirt anyway, and the scene I made had us laughing and enjoying our time together even more.

The day on set was very, very long and I was so glad she was there to keep me company the whole 14 hours! We traded phone numbers and promised to keep up with each other from then on out. I had hoped we would, because I didn't have a lot of close friends at the time. In fact, Clarke was the only person I really hung out with any more and even that was rare. I guess I had become a homebody since I decided to quit drinking.

It wasn't that I didn't want to go out or was scared that I might drink, I just wasn't feeling the bar scene anymore. There didn't seem to be anything there for me and I really started to dislike being around drunk people because I started to feel bad for them. I also saw people acting ridiculous or sometimes like zombies. It scared me to think that my inebriated self had been just like that and much worse. I realized in those moments why people couldn't be around me when I was drunk. Highly intoxicated people are tough to handle.

It wasn't like I was on some sort of high horse; I just couldn't enjoy myself the way I had previously. If I saw someone who looked like they had a problem, I wanted to help. That wasn't my place though. I didn't know these people and honestly, there was still a daily inner struggle continuing to win my own battle. I wasn't quite ready to help others just yet, but hoped the day would eventually come.

In the next week, I continued to work on television projects and had been asked to do my second off-Broadway show with the same theater company. Yes, I said asked. The director of the first production had a new project she would be doing for the holiday season and said I was perfect for a role. She said she had auditioned people for the part but had not given it to anyone because I was perfect for it. While I didn't really want to do another non-paying theater gig, I took the offer as such a high compliment and gladly accepted the role. I figured more stage time meant more practice and that was key now that I was making my acting career my top priority. My obsession.

It seemed to be there was truth to that evangelical's words I had heard on late night TV four months prior. When my passion became my obsession, coupled with the strongest go at sobriety, my life seemed to be full of blessings. The good that was promised seemed to be coming every day and I was grateful. I was on set of another NBC cop show one day in October when another one of those magical epiphanal moments happened.

I was sitting in background actor holding on stage with two female actors and we were discussing the world. They asked about my story and were shocked and inspired as I told them. We actually had a moment where we prayed together by giving thanks for the many different gifts the Universe had given us. When it came my time to speak, I looked around and realized that the three of us were sitting in the jail cell set of the show. I gave thanks for being able to have seen the signs leading me to this path today. Instead of being in a real jail cell because of drugs or alcohol, I was on a TV set, sharing stories of light and doing the job I loved so much. The blessings were apparent and felt by all that day.

A few days later I decided to make that call about my role in 'Miss Congeniality 2' to see if in fact I had earned the required amount of waivers to join the Screen Actors Guild. The first call forwarded me to another phone number where the woman on the other end said she would have to do some research to see if the records still existed. I waited another few days for her to get back to me. The wait was annoying, but when she did finally call, it was all good news!

Maura was the faceless lady on the other end of the phone, in an office somewhere in Hollywood. Though I didn't know what her face looked like, I assumed it must be that of an angel with the information she had for me! She said I had worked enough days as a special character role to earn enough waivers to become SAG eligible. She said the information would be emailed over that afternoon and that the next step would be to show the documents to the SAG rep in NYC to validate and confirm it. Awesome!

I immediately called the office in NYC and spoke with a representative about how I should get the documents to her. She initially said the files would have to be faxed to them, but who the heck has a fax machine anymore?! I asked her if there was any way I could just forward the email from the payroll company in LA. She finally agreed saying, "We don't usually do this but you sound like a good kid, so I'll do it. I'm going out of town for a week so you might not hear anything until then. We will see what the admission department says."

Ooooh! It was so close I could taste it! I guess I would have to be patient, which was not one of my strong points. Luckily, another amazing side effect of sobriety was learning: learning how to be patient, budgeting money, managing all the free time not spent drinking, actually feeling emotions and most of all, learning how to love myself again. It had been so easy to pretend I loved myself when I was drinking and doing drugs. In my messed up mind I was perfect and graceful while reality seemed to see someone very different.

On my 100th day of sobriety, I was feeling more grateful and proud than ever before and knew it was a huge deal to have made it that far all on my own. There were no AA meetings this time, no sponsor to call and no steps to follow, or so I thought. Even though I was not in AA, I was naturally doing some of the things the program suggested.

I was calling Tim just about every day, like calling a parent when you are far away, but it was also like he was a sponsor because he was very encouraging and his obvious pride in my changes made a big difference. I started trying to rebuild relationships I had messed up because of drugs and booze and had made great strides with that. In some of those instances, making amends were very necessary and in most cases the friendships were mended, like with Michael.

On this day, while on the set of another FBI-type show, two phone calls came in that were polar opposites in the feelings they produced. The first was a call from my SAG rep in NYC officially confirming I was SAG eligible and could now join the prestigious actor's Union. I had no idea how I was going to pay the $3100 initiation fee, but was determined to figure it out because it was such an important step to take in a professional acting career.

The second call was quite scary. When I picked up the phone, while on lunch break on set, I was surprised to hear Clarke on the other end. He asked me if I was seated and then told me, "Hey son, I don't want to scare you or anything, but I just got back from the doctor and they told me I have prostate cancer..."

I wanted to drop the phone and cry, but I knew I had to be strong for my army veteran best friend. I could tell he was noticeably shaken over the phone by the trembling in his voice. It scared me because I had never heard him sound so vulnerable. He explained to me that the doctors thought they caught it early enough that he wouldn't need chemo, but there would be more tests needed quickly.

"Whatever you need me to do, wherever you need me to go, I'll be there, Clarke. Just let me know," I said, still fighting back tears. I realized no matter how tough this was going to be, I would be able to handle it if I stayed sober and allowed myself to feel all the emotions. I hadn't been able to be there for my mother the way I would have liked to because of my youth and high school. I was determined to be there for Clarke in every aspect possible and maybe my mother, if she was watching, would be happy. He told me he had another appointment for testing the following week and asked if I would go with him.

"Of course I'll be there, Clarke. Of course," I said.

We hung up the phone and I headed back to set to film some more scenes for the show. The rest of the day was clouded with worry about my friend, but with random bursts of excitement about the news of my Union eligibility. It was an odd day for sure. If I had still been drinking, it could have ended in a blackout, trying to deal with all the emotions, but that was not going happen. I would not let it happen.

The next day I got another random call but this time it was something normal, not overly happy and not uber depressing. Amanda, from the Absolut Commercial, called and asked if I was free to meet her for lunch in the city. I was a little surprised to hear from her because we had only texted a few times since we had last seen each other, but I am so glad she did. It was perfect timing, kismet, because as I would soon find out, we both needed a friend badly at that moment.

We met up for dinner that evening and she told me of the troubles she was having with her ex-fiancé. They had decided to call it quits after much debate and she was still currently living in the apartment they once shared. She was in a lot of emotional pain and I was there for her with a shoulder to cry on. When I told her about Clarke and the cancer she comforted me too. We also talked about our dreams and the future.

The next month would bring rehearsals for my second off-Broadway play, finding some way to save enough money to join SAG, continuing to work towards furthering my acting career and maintaining my strongest commitment to sobriety ever. I couldn't believe the blessings I had received in the last 100 days being sober. I often had to stop and smile while I pinched myself and thought, "I am finally living my dreams. Is this really happening?"

WHAT I AM
THANKFUL FOR

OCTOBER was under way and with it came new and exciting opportunities and blessings. I still couldn't believe the life I was living and how much had changed in such a relatively short amount of time. Rehearsals for my second off-Broadway show were progressing and I was thrilled to be meeting new people with common goals and interests. 'The Gayest Christmas Pageant Ever!' was a holiday play offending just about every race, religion and sexuality. It was hysterical, but not for the ultra-politically correct.

The character I had been selected to portray was the flamboyant costume designer of the play within the play and the director told me at one point I needed to "gay it up!" Haha. I guess after years of hanging out on the Sunset Strip and not going out to gay clubs in the past few years, had made me lose a little bit of my feminine ways. I picked it back up pretty quickly and by the end of the show would become the crowd favorite with my snarky one liners and fiery red wig.

Day 102 of sobriety, I had my first real depressing day in a long time and it hit pretty hard. It seemed like the last 100 days had been a dream. The time was filled with nothing but blessings, positive energy and light-hearted thoughts! It's like I had been living in a type of sober bubble and didn't realize there was anything that could bring me down.

Since becoming SAG eligible, I had started looking for Union roles during the 30 day "trial" period (the span of time after receiving your eligibility where you can take on higher paying Union roles before joining) and had finally gotten the chance at one! My casting director at 'Blacklist' told me he was going to try and book my first Union role that Friday. I was beyond excited. I could already see it in my mind: walking on to my favorite set, surrounded by my favorite people, and picking up my first SAG pay waiver. I envisioned my fellow actors and PAs being so excited for me and how proud my 'security guard' friend Sheldon would be that I took the initiative to look into and receive my SAG eligibility.

That dream was crushed when late Thursday evening I got a call from my casting director saying he could not make it happen and they had to move me to another show on Friday. I was heartbroken and distraught. I was so depressed when I realized my perfect plan would not come to fruition. The news was so devastating it made me seriously consider having a drink (or twenty) that night.

I didn't.

I had come too far to let something like this bring me down. I resisted the screaming temptation to drink and just dealt with all the emotions of disappointment I had not felt in months. I went to sleep that evening and prayed for continued strength and understanding of why the Powers that Be were letting all this happen.

When I arrived at the set of the other show the following morning, I had a sober moment of clarity and realized I may have overreacted a tad. Yes, it was depressing that I didn't get to work my first Union job on 'Blacklist' that day, but I forgot to look at the situation from another perspective. This wasn't a personal attack on me, maybe it was just a smaller scene than originally thought, or perhaps there were people with more seniority that were chosen first. The casting team also took the time to make sure I was booked on another job, which they didn't have to do, and was something I overlooked during the initial bout of anger.

So, the day didn't turn out the way I pictured it, but it was a good day and I figured out the lesson that the Universe was trying to teach me. Patience. I was able to overcome the dark voice once again and realized that if this was my biggest problem at the moment, then I was truly at a wonderful place in my life. Just three months ago I was wondering where the money for my next meal and next drink would come from and now I'm getting upset about not getting a certain kind of acting job? I laughed when the realization hit at just how silly it was to get so upset over it and I was instantly 100 times more grateful for my life. These were much better problems to be having.

Day 108 was a pretty eye-opening day as well. My dear friend Amanda called me with some troubling news and asked for my help. She needed a place to stay for a couple of days because she had finally decided it was time to move out of her place. I immediately said yes and was so glad to now be in the position to help someone in their time of need. I told her to come to the Bronx and stay at my apartment for as long as she needed. She accepted the offer and made her way over from Jersey.

When she arrived with her big red suitcase I took her into my arms and gave her the biggest hug I could. We talked for hours as we ate boxed cake and cheese dip. For the first time in the longest time I felt like a true friend. Being able to provide a place for Amanda in her time of need made me feel good because I was getting to finally be a friend for someone the way I had so desperately needed back in Hollywood.

We told each other everything about our lives and on this night we cemented our best friend status for sure. I even read her the couple of chapters of the book I had started to write back when I lived in "The Melrose." She was so intrigued that when I got to the end of the last chapter she looked at me and said, "and then what? Oh my God, Kaleb! You have to finish this book!"

And with that friendly bit of inspiration, I started to work on my novel once again. Picking it up where I had left off, but instead of writing a semi-factual/semi-fictional novel where my character and the rock star end up together, I decided to tell the truth. I edited the first four chapters and wrote two new ones the next morning while she slept. I started writing daily since then and it became easier with a renewed sense of purpose.

Another odd thing happened early that same morning when she woke up. We had been talking about the adventures of Sarah Summers the night before and Amanda was very interested in seeing Sarah in person. I hadn't dressed up in months and I figured since there was time, I would give it a shot.

Sarah Summers made her debut about 45 minutes later and the two girls got along swimmingly! It was nice to know I could still put 'her' on in record time and was glad to see she looked just as good as ever (even with a big scar on her chin).

Going through boxes and realizing I still had all the makeup and outfits necessary, I thought if I ever had to do a Sarah Summers show again that I was definitely prepared. A Sarah show was pretty unlikely though, as no one in New York knew about my alter ego anymore and I wasn't going out to the gay clubs either.

Another surprise blessing happened when I got a call for my first Union role that same day! I was amazed at how being creative and expressing shared good energy affected the world around us. Was there truth to the old saying that "what you put out, is what you get back?" Maybe there was, because we were putting out a ton of positive energy and we were both about to get a ton of it back.

In the next couple of days, I worked my first SAG role and booked another featured Union background part for later in the week. Amanda was working new acting roles and also got word that she would be able to get an awesome apartment in SoHo in a relatively short amount of time. A few days later, I was able to use some hard-earned (and dutifully saved) acting money to pay off some debts at Wells Fargo that had been looming like a dark cloud over my head for years. I then made a payment plan, with monthly due dates, for the rest. I was determined to live my life better each day through sobriety and made a surefire plan to become a fiscally responsible adult within a few months.

The same day that started the journey of financial recovery was the day I did my first featured background role on 'Unbreakable Kimmy Schmidt.' This was the instance where my divine assignment became clear. Acting was in fact my true path. I was booked to portray a florist (typecasting much?) and the role was initially meant to be a bit part. The director ended up making it a big feature. By the time we were done he was calling me by name and giving me a high five for my acting skills. Even though there were no lines, it was one of those moments when I felt like the part I played really meant something to the show. In between takes I chatted with Jane Krakowski for a few minutes and her words of wisdom inspired me to be the best I could be. The scene went amazing and I left feeling my spark turn into a roaring fire!

A day later, I was back on the set of 'Blacklist' where I was bumped up to Union status and even got my first shot at being a stand-in. I learned even more about how the whole film world worked and again left feeling more blessed than ever before. It was as if the Universe was finally giving me the gifts it had promised and it didn't seem to stop.

Even on day 120 of sobriety, my four-month marker, I was blessed in a different way. I received a call from Clarke saying he had decided to move his prostate cancer surgery up and he had gone into the hospital that morning to get the procedure done. I was scared and shocked at the suddenness of the whole thing. He said he didn't want me to worry and I could come see him the following day once he was in recovery. I prayed extra hard that night that he would make it through with flying colors and not end up like my mother and father who had both lost their battles with cancer. He was that special to me. I didn't think I'd be able to stay sober if he didn't make it.

Luckily, the Powers that Be decided to give my friend a miracle. The doctors were surprised at how well the surgery went and said they were able to completely remove the tumor without much stress. The day after his surgery, I spent it with Clarke at the VA hospital. I wasn't too shocked he made it through so successfully. He was one of the strongest people I knew and he proved it the way he kicked cancer's ass. I thought about how blessed he was to have won his battle with cancer and how grateful I was to be winning my battle with alcoholism and addiction. If I had been drinking or using drugs, there would have been no way I could have been there for him the way I was. For that I was thankful.

By the time Clarke got home from the hospital a few days later, I was off to my first leading role audition for a national commercial. Instead of completely stressing out on whether or not I would get the part, I listened to the Universe and learned another valuable lesson: not setting high expectations. If something is meant for you, it will happen. If it doesn't, don't fret, there is something better coming along when the time is right.

I didn't get the role but it didn't bother me. This time I didn't get depressed or want to go on a massive bender because of it. I was growing again and it felt amazing. I continued to grow that same day as my finances had aligned where my savings could afford to pay off the rest of the debts with Wells Fargo. I had finally paid all of them off and was officially debt free! Fiscally responsible Kaleb celebrated with a Shirley Temple in a martini glass and a call to Tim.

Tim was shocked to say the least. He was so proud of me he made an offer that would change my life. "Listen Kaleb, I just want to let you know how amazing I think you are doing. I knew you had it in you kid! I've told all those naysayers, who told me to fire you many times over the years, that you are finally living your life right! I know you've been trying to save up enough money to join the Screen Actors Guild and I know how much it means to you," he said as he paused for a minute to catch his breath.

"Kaleb, I'm going to invest in your future. I'm going to pay for your initiation fee."

Wow. Tim had done some amazing things for me in the past. He had gotten me out of trouble more times than I could count... but this... this was huge!

"I expect you to keep pursuing your dreams and continuing to maintain your sobriety. When you make it big, you can pay me back for all the money I've loaned you over the years! Haha! Good luck, kid. By the way, how's that book coming you were telling me about?" he said, his smile radiating through the phone.

"The book is coming along. I'll send you what I have so far....and thank you, Tim. This is the greatest gift anyone has ever given me. I will not let you down. Thank you, thank you, thank you!" I replied, letting a tear of joy slide down my cheek.

The next day I went down to the SAG office in midtown and became an official member. Another check mark on my divine path's list. It was time to start adding new goals to that list and remembering to be grateful for each new one that came to life. I made a commitment to not let Tim down, but more importantly, I renewed the commitment I made to myself a little over four months before. Nothing would stand in my way of fulfilling my dreams this time around. Nothing.

As the excitement about my future bubbled over and the month of November was coming to a close, I was thrilled to be sharing Thanksgiving with my friend Clarke. Just one year prior he and I were making turkey legs and ambrosia salad in a homeless shelter and now we were together cooking at my apartment, sharing gratitude for our friendship and his health. This day I was happier than I had been in years, more alive, more committed and more present in my own skin. This year, we were blessed, and it was so easy to see what I am thankful for.

ON THE RIGHT PATH

MY SECOND off-Broadway show, the Christmas-themed one, came to a close before December had even begun. I was still getting rave reviews every night from the audience about how much they loved my spunky character. I had made some good friends with the cast, especially a certain long-haired, buff, blonde, straight boy (don't even get me started about the comparisons and my type and all that). As the show was ending, I realized how much I would miss them. We had created a little dysfunctional family over the month and a half of rehearsals/shows and I valued their friendships individually.

The evening of the last show I got the surprise request of a lifetime. When I walked into the theater at The Times Square Arts Center that day, pre-show, the owner of the theater company was talking with my director and one of my cast mates. They all turned to me when they noticed I had arrived. I guess they had been talking about me and so I was surprised when the owner approached me and asked, "Kaleb, I've been hearing that you do drag, is that true?"

"Well, I was quite the prominent female illusionist for a while...on stage, television and film...but I haven't really done it professionally in a while," I replied, wondering why he was asking me this out of the blue.

"I have a proposal for you. I was thinking about trying out a new style of show, maybe once a month. A drag show. I have some time slots available on the weekends in the evenings and would like to maybe compete with some of the local shows of its kind. What do you think? Would you be interested in putting something together?" he said nonchalantly, as if what he was asking wasn't a huge deal to me.

"Wow... Are you asking me to put on my own off-Broadway show? I'd have all the creative rights to do whatever kind of show I wanted?" I asked.

He nodded and I began to think really hard about the offer. I had not done a Sarah Summers performance or show in about ten years, but I had just randomly tested out my makeup skills with Amanda a month prior and knew I still had the look and the skills to pull it off. (The alignment of those two things did not pass me by. Had the Universe been secretly preparing me for this next leg of my journey?) I hadn't danced on stage in years and I had never in my life taken on the reigns of creating and producing a whole show. I had been a part of other people's productions many times, but being at the head of the entire process seemed rather daunting. I didn't know if I could do it, so I had no choice but to....

Accept the offer.

"Sure, I'd love to put something together! So when would this show be happening?" I asked, pretending to be uber confident when in fact I thought I might be getting in over my head.

"How about January 9th at 10:00 p.m.? I'll email you all the details and the contract later this week. Have a good show tonight!" he stated, rather matter of factly. We shook hands before he left.

So that was that. I had just agreed to writing, directing, producing and starring in my very own off-Broadway show! I called Tim immediately and he was almost as excited as I was, if not more. "Kaleb, this is a big deal! Some people work for years and never get the chance to do their own off-Broadway show. I'm talking people with degrees and years in the business! This is amazing!! I'm so proud of you! I know you are going to do a fantastic job," he said.

He was right. It was almost unbelievable the way amazing things seemed to magically fall into my lap those past few months of sobriety. I think finding (and sticking to) my divine path was the key to unlocking all this good the Universe was providing. I wondered if maybe all of this had been meant for me before now. If I had never started drinking would I be further along in my career at this point? Probably not.

Number 7 on my list came to mind: *"Your assignment will require seasons of preparation. The greater the assignment, the longer, more difficult the training."* It seemed like I had to go through all these struggles to become exactly the person I was at this moment, so that my story would be able to touch people's lives and really make a difference. That's what I hoped it all meant anyway.

Day 159 of sobriety was the day I had my first pre-production meeting for "The Sarah Summers Experiment!" The show was aptly titled because the production I was planning combined many different elements, hopefully resulting in a successful and entertaining outcome. I called upon my co-stars from the past two productions and a few of my fellow background actor friends to meet me that afternoon to brainstorm ideas for this hopefully amazing variety show. I wanted to emulate old-time variety shows like 'The Ed Sullivan Show' with special guests, musical and dance numbers, magicians and comedy skits! I knew from the get go it was going to be a huge undertaking, but I felt like I had a talented cast of friends behind me who would help me blow this out of the water.

It was not as easy as I had hoped, nothing ever was for me.

By day 165 of sobriety, I was starting to get a little depressed once again. Trying to come up with all the scripts (most from scratch and also re-working a Britney Spears 'SNL' skit) was a lot of work. Add on top of that trying to find days where everyone could make it to rehearsal. I also needed to fill a very important role: my character's love interest. I had written the part for someone special. The blonde guy from the Christmas play. He initially agreed to take part in the show, but because of conflicts had to back out pretty early on. The role was that of a character who resembled Kevin Federline, named EFed, to complement my version of Britney Spears. As hard as I was trying, it seemed like I couldn't find anyone to play him. Frustration number 1.

Trying to get a group of creative people together all at the same time seemed to be another almost non-workable idea. Everyone had jobs, so I settled on just meeting with as many people as we could at a time and hoped by the show date it would all come together. My faith played a big part in this process. My personal faith and my faith in the people I had selected to help make one of my life-long dreams a reality. My faith in people was tested very much when people would flake on rehearsals or call out at the last minute. Frustration number 2.

This show was exactly that: a lifelong dream. I could remember watching Johnny Carson, Jay Leno and 'SNL' when I was younger and thinking how much I wanted to do exactly that when I was older. This was my first shot at doing something similar and I wanted it to be perfect.

Then there was trying to come up with a budget for the show. I wanted it to look super professional...I mean this was Sarah Summers' big return to the New York City stage. The pressure was high!

I think I had started to let the stress build a little

too much and I posted online how badly I wanted a drink that day. I wasn't going to have one, but it had been a continual thought throughout the production process. Amanda saw my depressed Facebook post and seemed to take it pretty seriously. She showed up at my apartment in the Bronx just an hour later.

Amanda had moved into her new apartment in SoHo and loved living in New York for the first time. She was excited she could get on the train close to her place and be at my door in less than an hour. I was glad she could, too. I didn't really think I needed anyone that day, but I guess the Powers that Be thought differently because when she arrived the magic started happening again.

She knocked on my door and looking through the peep hole I saw her standing there holding a boxed chocolate cake and cheese dip. She was definitely my best friend! She knew exactly how to cheer me up. We spent the evening talking and discussing plans for the show. We were even able to get the opening number completely choreographed! (I didn't know my bestie was such an amazing and trained dancer!)

By the end of the night, we were worn out from all the fun and progress we had made on the show. Before she left she got a random friend request on Facebook and asked me if I knew who the guy was. I didn't recognize him, but it turned out he and I were Facebook friends and he must have found her profile through mine. I told her to click on his picture so we could get a better look.

When the photo zoomed in I said, "ooh, he's

kinda cute! I bet he is a background actor I met on set one day or something! Should I ask him if he wants to play EFed? (my show's parody of KFed). Couldn't hurt, right?"

"Yea, why not?! Maybe he can be your real life love interest too! Haha!" Amanda said in her playful tone.

I messaged Joshua from my account a few minutes later. We were shocked to get a response so quickly. He didn't quite remember where we had met either, but said he was very interested in doing the show. Awesome. I told him to come to the next rehearsal and we would let him give it a shot. I needed a butch guy to play this part and the boys in my cast weren't going to cut it! Haha.

He agreed to meet us that weekend and I sent him the scripts. My interest was definitely heightened when I viewed a couple more of his pictures. He had a bad boy look to him: dark hair, dark broody eyes, muscles and scruff. He looked like he was about my height and he definitely had a KFed vibe to him. I just hoped he was a good actor and that he would be okay with getting close to me. I had written in a kiss for the other boy who was supposed to play the role, but now it was going to be all on him. Wonder if he's a good kisser?

During that following week, with my spirits once again lifted, I continued to work on the show as well as other creative projects. I was working on my novel with a serious sense of purpose; a side effect of all the creative juices flowing around me.

I turned the long, daily train rides from the upper part of the Bronx to the lower part of Manhattan into my creative writing lab. Using my iPhone, and my fingers, I took the back and forth 45-minute rides to work on new chapters. I started sharing those chapters over the phone with Michael. He would tell me how much it meant to him that I was sharing my work, my life, with him on a nightly basis. He gave me some good pointers and helped edit some grammar mistakes along the way too. Years later and he was still the Giles to my Buffy.

On sobriety day 169, the positive energy flowed over to my television world when I was asked to play a featured role on 'The Good Wife.' I was selected from 100's if not 1000's of faces to portray a new hire junior associate at one of the star's law firms. I was a tad nervous when I walked into the room and it was just me, four other chosen background actors and two of the leads. In the scene I was seated next to one of the female leads and was asked to give her "actions of acknowledgment" as we listened to Christine Baranaski's character introducing us to the firm. We only had to do a few takes and we were done! It was so thrilling to be in that big board room set knowing I had been handpicked by the director to play a part in such a big scene. My inner flame was now a raging inferno of hope, pride and joy! I was on my divine path and it was fantastic.

Later that week, in between TV work, "Sarah Summers Experiment" rehearsals and helping Amanda move into her new apartment, I made another very important relationship right. It had been months since I had been to Parigot, but now that Amanda was living so close I figured I should go and talk to Catherine and try to make amends so I could take Amanda there. I wanted her to experience the French restaurant the way I had when I found it a little over a year ago.

I didn't know how Catherine would react to seeing me again, but I hoped the 'spiritually adopted mother' side of her would come out and be proud of how far I had come. Luckily, she had been reading my Facebook updates. When she saw me she gave me a big hug and told me how proud of me she was. It was like her cold shoulder had been warmed by the good news and she was back in my life like no time had passed. I sat with her at the bar that night and told her about all the things I had done in just the few short months since she had fired me. She was genuinely happy for me and glad I had turned my life around.

I told her I was putting on my own off-Broadway show and that tv/film work was starting to slow down for the holidays so I wouldn't have a source of income to allow a show budget. She looked me up and down with her skeptical motherly eyes and said, "If you think you are ready to come back, I think I can work you into a few shifts to help you out. You better not let me down!" She gave me a maternal double handed hug-slap on the face as she smiled wide. The good energy that sobriety had brought to my life seemed to be contagious and I loved the way it was spreading.

Later that week, I worked my first shift back in the restaurant as the bartender. I got asked often by customers if I was nervous about working with booze so closely now that I was sober. My answer was matter of fact.

"I made a choice to quit drinking. I made a commitment to myself. I know now that my life is better without alcohol and so it doesn't tempt me a bit."

It was true. I didn't crave it or even consider drinking it. To me it was just another product that I served to my customers, but now I served it with a bit more conservativeness.

I recognized now that being a bartender was a huge responsibility because people's lives were literally in my hands. I learned when to cut people off when needed and was quick to tell my story when people asked. I helped a lot of people that way. I even had a few customers come back and tell me they quit drinking because of my story and were inspired by all the progress I had made in such a short amount of time being sober. I felt honored and blessed to hear this from them, because it meant I was making a difference... and I was definitely on the right path.

THE BIG SHOW

DECEMBER was turning out to be an interesting month filled with Sarah Summers rehearsals, bartending at Parigot, background acting work, novel writing and even a few "dates."

My new cast member, Joshua, turned out to be a great fit for the role of EFed and was also a very interesting guy. When we met in person, I was instantly attracted to him and thought maybe Amanda's joke a few weeks back could become real: maybe he could be my real life love interest. I thought I'd give this potential romance a shot and invited him on a "date" to attend a Screen Actors Guild screening of 'The Danish Girl.' This would be my first date with anyone since my relationship with Alessio over a year ago. (He and I still talked via Facebook messenger and occasionally had some naughty web time chats but he had met someone and seemed happy now.)

The evening of the movie date, I was actually a little nervous. I wore my best looking, body hugging, black suit with a black button-up shirt underneath and an electric blue tie making the color of my eyes pop. I had never gone to a SAG screening as a member of the Union and was looking forward to experiencing the event with Joshua.

We met up by the fountain in front of the Metropolitan Opera House and he was also wearing a suit. He looked very handsome and it was clear he took some time to get ready. It wasn't officially a date but it felt like one as the night went on.

We went to a bar close by and he got a beer while I drank a non-alcoholic one. We discussed the Sarah show, our dreams for the future and our back stories. He was very intrigued by my life story, especially when I told him of my rock star relationship and my sobriety. It seemed he was also troubled when it came to drinking and doing drugs. I didn't judge him or look at him any differently, but offered to listen and advise. We got to know each other very well at the bar that evening before heading to the theater. Turned out he was also a very talented guitarist. When I mentioned possibly ending the show with a live version of 'Creep,' he was ecstatic. He told me that was one of his favorite songs and knew how to play it. What a nice coincidence, or a perfect gift from the Universe. We decided the song would be the closing number and headed to the theater.

Once inside, it was pretty cool to check in as a SAG member and see the look of admiration on Joshua's face when I did. As an actor, his goal was to ultimately join the Union as well. I think he saw there were things he could learn from me. That was one of the benefits of our relationship. Being cast in my show was another pretty good perk.

The movie was fantastic and I connected with the main character on so many levels. I could remember the first time I put on my first blonde wig and the way I felt when I looked in the mirror. Just like the character, I too had to learn how to dress, talk and act like a woman. Those moments on screen were acted so brilliantly that I was touched and inspired, but the real character that got to me was his wife. This woman loved him so much that she was able to stick with 'him' as he became 'her' and dealt with all the emotions in a beautiful way. I wished...prayed...that I could one day find someone like that who could love every part of me, inside and out.

I looked over at Joshua towards the end of the film to see him crying streams of tears, so I grabbed his hand and leaned in closer to him. It was so beautiful the way he was affected by the story and it made me like him even more. I held his hand until the end of the film with my head rested on his shoulder and, for that moment, felt a little spark between us.

Once the final credits rolled, the actress who had played the wife came out for a Q&A and she was so gracious and intelligent. The way she spoke of taking on the part and creating the character to be her own was completely inspiring. I learned a lot from listening to her speak and was even more motivated to continue on my divine path once we left the theater.

Joshua and I rode the train together for a little while and we were sitting body to body holding hands. I told him I didn't care if he was straight, gay or bi but from that point on he was going to be my 'fake boyfriend.' I said, "Whenever we are together I want you to act like the man in my life. Hold my hand, cuddle me at the movies, take me to dinner. All that stuff! Think you can handle it?"

He agreed playfully and I was happy. Secretly I was hoping that maybe, through faux relationship osmosis, it would turn into a real emotional connection and hopefully this plan would not set me up for another heartbreak. We had a huge show to put on! Was I crazy for trying to get involved right now? Probably. But I did it anyway.

We took the last week in December off from rehearsing for the show so that my cast could go visit family and enjoy Christmas vacation. I had made plans with Clarke for Christmas Day, but had nothing planned for Christmas Eve, the day that use to mean so much to me when my mother was alive. I kind of figured I would feel lonely that day and I might be tempted to drink. But I wasn't, because something really magical happened.

Christmas Eve I worked the brunch shift at Parigot and to my surprise it was actually a pretty busy shift. The Solita Hotel next door seemed to be extra full with holiday travelers and since I had made friends with all the desk clerks, they were happy to send the guests over for meals. I made some pretty good tips that day and decided I would treat myself to dinner at Paesano's and spend the evening with the boys of my 'Italian family' who worked there.

They sat me at a table in the front that looked out onto Mulberry Street and were quick to help me get settled in. One of the guys sat a table of four French people next to me and made my whole day when he said, "Oh, you guys are getting a great table tonight! See that guy sitting right there? He's on TV every week! He's a big time actor and he's writing a novel! Keep your eye out for him! He's a big deal!"

The table of French people started to ooh and aah and it took everything in my body not to start cracking up. I mean, he wasn't lying but he may have over exaggerated the situation a tad. Either way, the table of tourists were eating it up! We talked, I told them about 'Blacklist,' stories from a few movies I had done recently and indulged a little about my novel. By the end of dinner, they were asking for my autograph and taking pictures with me. I felt like a star for that hour on Christmas Eve and I couldn't have asked for a better gift.

It was nice feeling those emotions and having a taste of what being a famous actor could be like. I thanked the guys at Paesano's for an amazing dinner and ran off to meet up with my bestie Amanda for a quick dessert. She knew how much Christmas Eve had meant to me in the past and made time for us to spend together that night. We shared an amazing ice cream cake in SoHo, exchanged small gifts and gave thanks for our friendship. We ended the night with a big hug and then I headed home to the Bronx.

While I prepared for bed, I watched the 'Tonight Show' while laying on my couch and thought about how blessed my life had become. I felt so loved and so content that I didn't feel lonely at all that night. I felt like the spirits of my loved ones were with me and I knew I would be seeing my best buddy Clarke the next day. Couldn't ask for a better Christmas Eve.

Christmas Day arrived and Clarke came over in the early afternoon. We cooked and ate while we exchanged gifts. I got him set up with a Facebook page and spent hours teaching him how to use it. It was like spending the holiday with family because that's what he was to me. He left before it got dark and I spent the rest of the evening finalizing all the different elements of "The Sarah Summers Experiment!"

Two days later, I celebrated 180 days of sobriety and at the six-month marker I posted this to my Facebook wall:

180 = 6 MONTHS!

Wow! Look at that. I did it!

I knew there was a reason I feel extra good today.

180 as defined by dictionary.com: hundred and eighty degree turn or 180° turn
noun
1. a reversal of direction.

2. a complete reversal in thinking or behavior

And yes... That is exactly what has happened in my life in the last 180 days. It's hard to believe that 180 days ago I was in a homeless shelter in Queens waking up to a room full of empty liquor bottles and broken dreams. Something happened that day that changed it all like never before. Something inside was tired of being a screw up and feeling sorry for all the misery in my life. One hundred eighty days ago I turned the other way and started heading in the opposite direction and I am so glad I did.

I'm not saying it is easy because it is not. I'm not saying that fantastic things will immediately happen to you if you take this path, but good things will come in time. These last six months have been a challenge, but the rewards have been amazing. If you are reading this right now and think, oh I drink too much but I never got as bad as him... Or you are someone still struggling with staying on the path... maybe it's time for a change. A 180.

I am not perfect by any means, but I have come a long way in one hundred and eighty days and I owe it all to sobriety, faith and drive. Thanks to all my friends who have supported me along the way!

So blessed to be sitting at one of my favorite places in NYC eating lunch around my favorite people while writing my novel and preparing to go to another one of my favorite places to work!

Happy 180 to all!

Stay Strong, Committed and Dream Big!

It was a miracle I had made it that far and it was unbelievable to recount the many blessings I had experienced in 6 months. Just 3 days later, I received news about Liam from an unexpected source.

Joshua called me and said he had been looking online and came across an article published on a celebrity gossip site discussing Liam's latest arrest on the streets of Hollywood. He was locked up for DUI once again and it broke my heart to hear it.

It hurt my heart because we were so close once, not because I still had feelings for him. I just didn't wish ill will towards him. I hated to see talent wasted because of addiction. I had fallen victim to the evil ways of drugs and I now realized what people were trying to tell me, how they were trying to help me, when they said I should stop. I was wasting my talent but it wasn't until I WAS READY that I was able to commit to sobriety and let my talents shine again.

I tried to help Liam when we were together, but I was under the spell of drugs and alcohol too. I may not like him after what he did to me, but there is still love there and my wish for him is that he will one day see the man I once saw in him ... and be ready. Ready to see the beauty sobriety can lead to. Ready to take a chance on himself again. I thought about reaching out and simply saying, "Good luck to you...dude," but I figured it would just be a waste of time at this moment in my life. I didn't know if I would ever see him again and I was okay with that.

I turned my attention back to my upcoming show and working at Parigot on New Year's Eve.

The party at the restaurant that night was pretty great and I had brought a bottle of sparkling cider to work so I could toast with the guests. The tips were great that evening and helped pad my bank account for the show's budget which I would be spending very soon.

January was upon us and it was 9 days to the premiere of my off-Broadway show! We were all working feverishly that week to perfect our varied roles in the production. That week my cast showed up and put up! Some of the actors I had worried about in the beginning because of flakiness became integral to the running of the show. I was grateful for their willingness to help out and make my job a little easier.

Thursday night rehearsal went well and there was a pretty magical moment that occurred at the end of the day. We all had our lines down, our dances, the live version of "Creep" and knew exactly how the show would play out, but the one thing that hadn't been tried was the big kiss that would happen at the end of the show.

Everyone but Amanda, Joshua and I had already left for the day when the subject was brought up. So we decided we should practice it. I was nervous. He was nervous. I even think Amanda was nervous to see if our connection was real and if the kiss would come off naturally. The first kiss was crap. Felt nothing. We were both holding back. The second kiss was better, but It seemed as though I was holding back because he looked at me and said, "Kiss me like you mean it!"

The third time was a charm. Literally. I was charmed by the way our mouths met in the heat of passion, the way he held me close as he kissed me and the electricity rushing through our bodies was insane. It was one of the hottest kisses I had experienced in a long time... ever maybe. He agreed when he sent me a random text that evening telling me how much it meant to him.

So with the kiss out of the way and a dress rehearsal under our belts it was almost time for the big event! I had procured a wine sponsor for the show, thanks to one of my cast members who worked for an alcohol company, and the ticket sales were through the roof. In fact, we were SOLD OUT!!

I couldn't believe it! I had tested myself to do something I never thought I could do and the results were beyond amazing. My inner spark was now a burning star flying high in the universe!

The day before the show, Tim called to congratulate me, wish me luck and give me one last surprise gift to let me know how proud of me he was. When I answered the phone he said, "I know you are going to be amazing tomorrow! I know you had mentioned you wished you could get ready in a hotel close to the theater so you wouldn't have to ride the train from the Bronx to the theater as Sarah. I think that's a fine idea! It's Sarah Summers' big return to the showbiz world and your first off-Broadway show... so I think it deserves a little class! I booked you a room at The Solita Hotel next to Parigot for the weekend, starting tonight, so that you can get ready in a space made for a diva. Enjoy it...because you deserve it. Break a leg tomorrow kid!"

Tim had done it again! He gave me a gift that the words "thank you" we're not appropriate enough for (even though I did say it 100 times). The Universe had done good when it chose Tim to be my replacement father figure and I was beyond grateful.

The morning of the show I got ready in the mirror of my hotel room and Sarah looked better than she had in years. I took extra time to perfect each eye, each contour and each layer of lip gloss applied. I felt the cosmic energy rising as the doorman hailed a cab for me standing in front of the hotel. I knew it was going to be a fabulous show.

When I got to the theater my cast surprised me with a card and flowers before we started our last dress rehearsal. The emotions were so high I had a brief moment of weakness. I didn't cry but I took Amanda aside and said, "I think I want a drink. I'm so nervous and I have never performed as Sarah sober before. Maybe if I have a drink as Sarah it wouldn't count... right?"

She gave me a discerning look and then I stopped and thought about what I was saying.

"No. I don't need a drink. I can do this. I've come way too far to mess it all up now. I know if I had a drink I'd feel immediately guilty and let down not only myself but everyone who reads my daily updates on Facebook and the people closest to me who put so much belief in me.

Forget I even said it!" I stated, coming to my senses.

Once again that evil little voice tried to get inside and knock me off my path. The struggle was real. But I was stronger. I was always stronger. I just had to remember to keep the faith in myself, my future and my commitment.

The show was amazing! Catherine and the Parigot people came, my background actor friends showed up and the cast's friends too. The room was packed and everyone (except me) enjoyed the free wine throughout the show. The magician was magical, the comedian was hilarious, the Broadway singer sang beautifully, the skits brought uproarious laughter, the kiss was passionate and "Creep" brought tears to people's eyes.

Ending that show with the song that meant so much to me, a song that had played such a big part in the last few years of my life, was the best decision I ever made. Sitting on that barstool, across from a man I adored, I sang my heart out and brought emotions out of myself I didn't think were there anymore. When I saw the tears rolling down the cheeks of the audience I knew it was all a success. The song, the show... my life. I had successfully navigated from rock bottom all the way to the top and I couldn't have been more proud.

When the show was over, I met with the audience and heard nothing but great reviews. My sold out off-Broadway show was a hit and all the work we had done paid off. I said my goodbyes and thank-yous to my cast, gave my 'fake boyfriend' a kiss and hugged my best friend before catching a cab back to the hotel.

As I washed the makeup off my face, in that fancy looking hotel mirror, I was so glad to once again see the clear-faced kid who had made the journey of a lifetime into a success story. I laid down on the fluffy bed, completely exhausted from the day... from the last year and a half... and wrote down the beginning of the final chapter in my book. The chapter in which I would recap the trials, tribulations and blessings of my craziest adventure yet. But before I could complete it, I fell asleep and dreamed of the next big show.

EPILOGUE: THE NEXT CHAPTERS OF MY LIFE

THE SUN ROSE over lower Manhattan and peered through the silk curtains of the fancy hotel room window. I awoke in the king-sized bed, wrapped in the encompassing warmth of the down feather comforter, not wanting to even move. When I finally opened my eyes I saw the reflection of the light in the mirrored wall and the mahogany desk where a copy of my off-Broadway program laid. The show had come to an end and all the hours of hard work had paid off.

I sat up to see the remnants of Sarah lying all over the floor and I smiled. The first call I made that morning was to Tim and the conversation centered on how we still couldn't believe all the amazing things I had done in the past few months. After the call, I noticed at the foot of the bed was my journal open to an incomplete page. I decided to finish writing before I started to get ready to check out of the swanky hotel.

I later posted the entry to my daily Facebook blog and it read:

194

The day after.

Wow! I can't believe I did it!

I woke up this morning at the Solita Hotel with a sense of accomplishment and pride that I haven't felt in a long time...

I was just on the phone with my friend/mentor Tim in Hollywood and he put it all into prospective for me. "You wrote, produced, directed and starred in your own off-Broadway show. Some people work their whole lives and never get that opportunity. I am very proud and you should be so proud of yourself and everything you have accomplished in the last 6 months. I know this is only the beginning."

This is just the beginning! I feel so honored that the theater owner asked me to do this and I seriously cherished every moment of this experience. My friends who became my cast turned out for me and made me proud. I thank them for that.

Yesterday I did something that I didn't really think I would have the chance to do again...and really, I wouldn't have been able to do it if I hadn't given up drinking.

That was the best decision I have ever made.

Some people have asked me why I count my days... Why I am so open about my struggle with alcohol ... and what do I hope to do with these daily posts?

The answer is simple. It's about inspiration.

But to explain a little further... I count to keep myself accountable for every day that I have won the battle and continue to fight. I am honest because I want people to know that it takes courage and will power to take a stand for yourself. And I do these daily posts to not only inspire others to find their true paths but to be able to have a daily diary of my own to inspire myself when I look back and see how far I've come since I put that bottle down.

If you are still struggling... Take a chance on yourself. It's so much easier to see your path with clear eyes and a clear mind. Feeling all the emotions of life can be scary but it can also be so very rewarding. I am proof of that. You can do it. You can become the true YOU.

I love you all for being my support and I hope I continue to be there for those who need a little bit of daily inspiration!

On to the next chapter! Thanks for going on this journey with me!

Stay Strong and Dream Big!

Those last five words had become my tag line... my mantra... and now I practiced them every day. My alcohol and drug fueled life in LA and the struggles of the NYC shelters made me forget all the strength my soul possessed. It also made me forget to dream those big dreams I had as a child. Through the last year and a half my inner strength returned and with sobriety, the dreams that seemed lost were now within my reach...some had already come true.

I got another call that morning from my 'fake boyfriend,' Joshua, wishing me congratulations and telling me how amazing he felt after our performance. He also called to find out how I was feeling and asked when I was free to get together. I had started to have feelings for this guy and was interested to see what would come of it. He did tell me he was straight but that he was also having feelings for me and felt a little confused.

Oh boy! Just what I needed! Another confused straight boy in my life! I guess the idea of a relationship of its kind potentially working out this time, the way it hadn't with Liam, gave me enough courage to keep talking to him and nurturing the relationship. After the phone call ended it had me thinking about Liam and reassessing the way I thought about him. I tried to imagine what I would say to him if I ever saw him again.

Sure there would still be anger, disgust and questions about why he did what he did to me, but I think the first thing I would say to him is, "Thank you."

"Thank you for turning me away in my hour of need. Thank you for choosing her over me. Thank you for never reaching out to me and thank you for breaking my heart. It saved my life."

Maybe I will get the chance to say it to him one day, but until then I continue to wish him the best. I heard that he lost his beautiful house up on Sunset Plaza Drive and it made me feel sorry for him. I hope that maybe one day he will read my words and the spark inside of him will start to flicker again.

Back in the hotel, I packed my suitcase full of the memories from the night before and let out the biggest sigh of relief and gratitude. I had come so far. Just months prior I had been living in a homeless shelter in Queens surrounded by empty bottles and broken dreams and now here I was at a beautiful hotel surrounded by testaments of my accomplishments and dreams fulfilled. I realized what an amazing feat it was... a miracle of strength and commitment...and then, inspired, I wrote the last paragraph of my book:

I hope that you have enjoyed my story so far and I pray that my words have inspired you in some way. Whether the words helped you quit drinking, follow some forgotten dream, love yourself again or just entertained you... I say thank you. Sharing this story has helped me, too. Releasing those thoughts and those emotions have cleared the emotional blockage and assisted me in taking the next steps to living an even more fulfilled life. I leave you with this. No matter how old you are or how low that rock bottom seems... now is the time to take a chance on yourself. Find your divine path and make your dreams your obsession. You will be amazed at the magic that will happen when you are free of those dark voices that try and stop you. Stay Strong, my friends, and Dream Big! This book may be finished but this is not the end for me... I guess now it's time to put the pen down and go live the next chapters of my life.

ACKNOWLEDGEMENTS

I would like to acknowledge one thing before I begin my list of many thank yous and gratitude: my name change in the book. I had originally planned for this book to be a half fiction, half reality story where the lead character would end up with the rock star. As I started to write it, I decided it would be much more impactful to just tell the truth.

Kaleb was a name my friends and I would call the person I was when I was blacked out, the person who rarely remembered what he did. I always liked the name until we gave it to my dark side. I thought this might be a good way to change that. I also decided to keep that name because as I was writing my story, it was easier to use the name Kaleb, so I could sort of take myself out of those emotional situations when remembering them to write down. I became my own character and it just kinda stuck. I could just have easily replaced Kaleb with Kody, but I decided to leave it.

Sarah Summers was actually my first drag name before Britney Valentine. Really it is my true female name. If I had decided to transition or live my life as a woman, it always would have been Sarah Summers. Britney Valentine sounded good when my whole career was focused on impersonating Britney Spears, but now, with this book, I had the opportunity to use my true inner female name. It also made sense because I mention Britney Spears' name so many times, I didn't want the reader to get confused. Now, on to the thanks I owe to so many amazing people.

First and foremost, I want to thank Tom Rosa, aka "Tim," for being a friend, a mentor, and the best father figure a kid could ask for. Thank you for always believing in me no matter what. I'm glad we could work on this project together and so happy you were able to put your degree in writing to good use by helping me edit the book. It was nice to help you reignite your passion while working on mine. I love you!

"Cheri" for being one of the truest friends a person could ever have. I meant every amazing thing I said about you and honestly I could write a whole book of compliments about you. Thanks for being my "husband." Love you.

"Jackie" I am so proud of you for everything you have done since I left LA. You made a music video! A beautiful one at that! It makes my heart happy to know you have not given up on your dreams either. Can't wait to hear about your next big thing. Love you!

Amanda. I couldn't ask for a better best friend. You are always there to listen to my problems and take care of me when I'm feeling low. You have been one of my biggest supporters and for that I am grateful. I know we haven't known each other for that long but every time we are together, it feels like I've know you forever. Thank you for inspiring me to finish this book! Let's make a hair prayer! Love you Amanda Panda! Xoxo Kody Bear

"Michael" My Giles. What can I say here that we haven't expressed over the phone during this whole process. You are my lifelong friend. We have been through the ups and downs over the years and I am so happy we are in each other's lives. I don't know what I would have done without you running lines for my plays with me and letting me read all the unedited chapters of this book to you. Thanks for always being there. I Love you. Now and forever.

Lisa. My sister from another mister! Love you so much. Thank you for inspiring me, even when you didn't know you were. I always looked up to your drive and passion when it came to the acting world. I'm so happy I can now share those common experiences with you. Can't wait to work on a tv show or film with you one day! Xoxo

"Leah" and "Wendy" Thank you for taking me in when no one else would. You both have the biggest karma gift coming, if you haven't already received it! So happy to hear about your lives now. Love you both to pieces!

To my girl Marc, Rujira and all the staff at "Hollywood Cakes" Thank you to the originals who worked side by side with me for all those years and put up with my craziness. I know you guys saw the good in me and I love you like family! To the newbies: thanks for always handing the phone off to Tom with a fun spirit! I feel like I know you all already. I'll be meeting you in person one day soon!

To my family of friends at "The State Room," "The Twisted Rainbow," The Pour House, The Stonewall Inn and every other bar I called a second home: I love you all. Thank you for putting up with me and my antics for as long as you did and making me feel like we shared a special bond. I hope to see you all again one day and we can share a non-alcoholic beer over crazy stories from the past and be able to laugh at it all now.

Catherine, my French mother. I am so glad you were put into my life by the Universe in such an unexpected way. It has been a pleasure getting to know you and love you over the past few years. You never asked to be my spiritual adoptive mother, but thank you for taking the job and doing it with love.

Aziz, Michel, Cooli, Will and everyone else who has come and gone at Parigot. Thanks for being my work family and being a great support system. Aziz, you'll always be my future ex-husband! Love you guys!

Mike and Robin: Two of my original New York friends. You both have been there for me in ways that I can't express proper gratitude for. You both know what you mean to me and I thank you. Love you both!

"Ms. Gena," Mr. Darrell, Ms. Vaty and every other Case Worker, Doctor, Receptionist, Counselor, Food Pantry Volunteer and The City of New York: Thank you for everything. Through your many programs that make up "The Organization" in this book, I was blessed to survive and thrive. I owe all of you my life in different ways, and I am forever grateful. You show the world that there is help out there if people are willing to ask for it. Keep up the amazing work!

Clarke: You're the best! Proud to be your friend and your "white son." So glad we both made it out of the shelter system and still play a big role in each other's lives. Can't wait until we can have Christmas dinner in a fancy New York City penthouse that I own! Love you!

"Shane," "Tristan," Alessio and every other love interest in my crazy time on this earth. Thank you all for loving me in your own unique and magical ways. It takes a brave man to love someone like me. I will always have love for you all and wish you nothing but happiness and success in your lives. Thanks for being such great stories for my book!

Alice and everyone at Alpha NYC: Thank you for giving me my first experiences off-Broadway.

Adam, thank you for asking me to bring Britney Valentine out of hiding and put on one hell of a show. It meant the world to me.

To everyone in the cast of my very own off-Broadway show: Thank you to the moon and back! You helped me make one of my lifelong dreams come true. Maybe we will get to do it again on a big stage somewhere in the future. Love each and every one of you so much! Xoxo

To Dimitri and all the boys at Paesano's: Thank you for being the best adoptive Italian family a kid could ever have. Thank you for feeding me for free on those nights when I was too poor to pay for a warm meal. I love you guys more than you'll ever know!

Maider: My first New York best friend! What would I have done without you that first week?! You are a big part of the reason I decided to stay longer, and I am so glad I did! Never forget the froggy! Can't wait to see you again. Mucho besos para ti! Love you.

To everyone from my hometown, my high school and everyone on Facebook: Your kind words and support throughout these last few years has been the light that has helped keep me going. I love posting my daily adventures and struggles every day to get your loving, honest, and optimistic feedback. Thank you for inspiring me while I strive to inspire you. Much love to you all.

My Blacklist Girls: Andrea, Marlyn, Stephanie and Nancy. I love the four of you so much!! The season we spent together working on that show was some of the best times I've had in my life. With jokes, stories and constant encouragement we became a working family. Thank you for all the support. Love you. All my other core BG family: it's been a pleasure working with you, best of luck in your careers! Love you gang!

Amir: Thank you for treating me like a human being and inspiring me every day we worked together. I hope I get to have an exciting career like yours one day soon and maybe get to do a scene with you where I actually have speaking lines! Lol. Much love and respect.

To every director, lead actor and crew member on 'The Blacklist' thank you too! You guys have helped me grow in more ways than you will ever know. I have learned so much from all of you and that's something a college degree can't teach you. Hope to work with you all in the future. Much gratitude to you. Ryker, thank you too.

Michelle: Thank you for teaching me so much. About cigars...and life itself. You are an amazing woman and I wish you the best in your business endeavors. Much love and respect.

Annette: My German darling! So glad you are in my life. Can't wait to see you again. I've missed you so much! Xoxo love you.

Adrienne: Thanks for that lovely weekend in Jersey. Hope life is treating you well! Xoxo

Kayla: Thanks for the awesome friend date adventures! So glad you are in my life!

Sarah K: Thanks for your support over the years and with additional edits. Thank you for looking after our little boy (cat) Chauncy. Blessings to you and your family.

Aimee: Thanks for your help with the edits. We've become as close as family since we met off-Broadway. And for that I am grateful. You'll always be the Soothsayer to my Prince! Wishing you the best always. Love you.

SAG/AFTRA: Thanks for letting a kid continue to dream and for providing the tools he needs to follow them!

Britney Spears: You have been such an inspiration in my life for so many years. It's almost like we grew up together in a way. I can't tell you how much I appreciate you as a human being and the work that you do. Hopefully we will meet up again and I'll get to thank you in person. Keep rockin'! You've come such a long way, too. Proud of you. Much Love.

To my Grandma Ellen: I miss you so much. I can't imagine the pain you must have felt when you lost your daughter. Thank you for your strength. I wish you were here to read this work.

To my Mother, Ulla: You may have left me physically many years ago, but your spirit has always been with me. That tiny little voice that never let me give up was you. Thank you for everything you taught me, it allowed me to be who I am today. The other day I felt your spirit say to me "I'm so proud of you." I miss you every day. I love you.

To all the readers: Thank you for reading my work, I hope it touched you in some way. Remember: it's never too late to take a chance on yourself. Stay Strong and Dream Big.

IT ALL STARTED like this.

An innocent child who already seemed most comfortable posing for the camera.

My parents should have known right then that my life was going to be different. Maybe they did. But I had no clue.

The pictures below are from where the story in this book begins. Both sides of me naively unaware of what is to come.

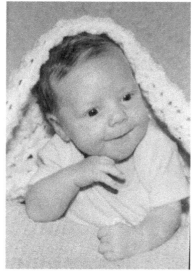

A few months old. A star already.

At "Holywood Cakes" holding an autographed photo of myself and Gena Davis.

My first Hollywood photo shoot

News&stuff
ALL THE STARS, ALL THE STORIES... THE TIME

EXCLUSIVE!

Got a showbiz story?
Call the local news team on 020 7654 4673
Or e-mail polly.hudson@mmxp.com

Details
New series!

Britney befriends drag impersonator

With Britney Spears at her restaurant NyLa. The first time I made world headline news.

(Above) On the set of Miss Congeniality 2. My first big screen debut.

(Left) With Ricki Lake after winning. And with the shirtless hunks who presented my crown.

With Tommy Lee at his bar in Hollywood

The cake that would be delivered to the first gay couple to legally wed in California. The second time I made world healine news.

Decorating cupcakes with Jessica Biel and this sweet girl at the Children's Hospital Los Angeles. A beautiful memory.

Sharing treats with Hef and the girls at the Playboy Mansion. Just another day in my Hollywood life.

Teaching Mila Kunis at the shop.

With my father figure, "Tim," at "Hollywood Cakes" before all the drama.

Me and "Cheri" on one of our girl-talk dates.

With Annette at "Hollywood Cakes."

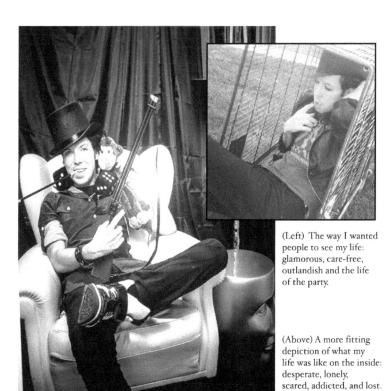

(Left) The way I wanted people to see my life: glamorous, care-free, outlandish and the life of the party.

(Above) A more fitting depiction of what my life was like on the inside: desperate, lonely, scared, addicted, and lost.

Never one to follow the rules.

"Natalie" pretending to be me at "State Room."

My first big sign from the Creator. If I can make it here, I can make it anywhere! Right?

With Maider ar Paesano's in Little Italy.

The room at "The Sunny Day" with its chicken wire roof and lack of space.

Snorting "lines" of Splenda without being nearly arrested.

With LaVonia on a girls' night away from the shelter.

Feeling a little bisexual with "Natalia."

(Above) The ring Alessio gave me before he left and the scar from yet another blackout.

(Left) Getting all dressed up at the shelter after the box of my belongings from LA arrived.

MY MOTHER

Ulla
A German born,
award-winning
nurse who taught
me how to love
unconditionally.
She always accepted
me for who I am.
Her voice is my
light and my strength.

MY GRANDMOTHER

Eleonore
She was like a second
mother to me. Nothing
beat the comfort of her
cooking. Her strong
German attitude
taught me how to live
outloud and never hold
back.

(Right) After hearing about the death of my grandmother, I was inconsolable. It was in this wig that I stopped traffic in SoHo and danced drunkenly in front of Parigot. I also wore it to Boston where I tried to grieve. In this photo you can see the pain in my eyes.

(Below) The moment I decided to shave my head, I wasn't thinking about the Britney Spears connection. It just felt like I needed to start over.

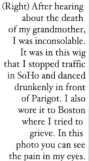

(Below) A diet of drugs and alcohol left me rail thin. In my haze I was unaware of how unhealthy I appeared.

My room at "The Melrose" was where I tried to get sober the first time, but failed.

(Right) Trying to make the best of a bad situation, I bought a star and some extra decorations for the shelter Christmas Tree.

(Below) Waking up in Tristan's apartment, naked in his bed, I took a photograph with his teddy bear and hat. I was a mess and completely unaware of what had happened the night before because of a blackout.

A bad sign: three different types of alcohol.

One of the better days in the shelter. Learning how to cook from Clarke.

Clarke calls me his "white son" and it is a nickname I am honored to have. We spent many nights drinking tiny bottles of vodka and watching sports. He told me about his days in the army and taught me that your best friend can be someone you never expect. When he left the shelter my life took a turn for the worse.

(Right) Without the support of my best friend in the shelter, I started to drink and use drugs again. This photo is from a few days after the brutal attack by a crack dealer in the Projects a block away from the shelter. In my blackout haze I tried to bandage my wounds which resulted in a large chin scar.

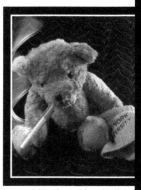

I took a photo of my NYU teddy bear after learning I was not accepted.

Becoming an official New Yorker meant the world to me.

"The light at the end of the tunnel," as they say. My first apartment outside the shelter life. I remember how grateful I felt when I woke up in my own bed, used my own restroom, and ate food from my own fridge. I take nothing for granted anymore.

(Right) Acting led me to some amazing friends who became like family. Aimee and me at my 2nd off-Broadway show.

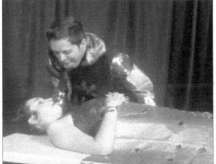

(Left) With Kayla on the set of "The Affair" where our friendship blossomed.

My acting dreams started to become real once I put on this prince costume. Thanks to my director, Alice, for believing in me and to Emily for being a great scene partner.

(Left) With Amanda on one of our friend dates. I owe a big thanks to this girl for showing me what true friendship really is. She inspired me to finish this book and for that I'll be forever grateful.

(Below) I never felt more free than when I was pretending to be in jail. If I hadn't gotten sober, there is a good chance I would have been locked up for real.

Working weekly on a hit TV show, with some very talented actors, taught me some invaluable lessons about my chosen profession and life itself. I gained an enormous amount of confidence working "The Blacklist" and I say, "Thanks."

My FBI Tech character was drawn into the "Blacklist" comic book!

Wearing a Britney shirt given to me by my friend and castmate, Rob, during rehearsals.

Celebrating with roses from my cast after successful completion of our sold-out show. One of my greatest accomplishments in sobriety.

My first promo shot for the show.

Singing "Creep" onstage with "Joshua" was an emotional moment that brought tears to the eyes of the crowd. I will cherish that moment forever.

THIS IS NOT THE END.
It is just the beginning.

I am proud to say that I am happier,
healthier and more fulfilled
than ever before. But there is
much work left to be done.
Through sobriety, and writing this
book, I have begun to live again.
I know the world will continue to
open up as long as I
STAY STRONG
and
DREAM BIG!

RESOURCES FOR
HOPE AND HELP

Here is just a short list of some helpful resources. For assistance with homeless, food pantry and other services in your area, please look online. There is NO SHAME in asking for the help that you need. Strong people know when they need help and are brave enough to ask for it. You don't have to suffer alone. I'm glad I had organizations like these when I was in need. Please reach out to someone if you or someone you know is hurting. Thank you. Stay Strong and Dream Big! -Kody

NEW YORK CITY
DEPARTMENT OF HOMELESS SERVICES

What do single adults need to bring to the intake center in order to apply for temporary housing assistance?

The following forms of ID are very helpful during the intake process (but are not required):

Any form of ID with a picture and proof of age, such as a driver's license, state-issued ID, passport or visa, welfare card or green card. Social Security card. Medicaid card, if available If working, your most recent pay stub What if I don't speak English? Interpreter assistance will be made available for individuals who do not speak English.

http://www1.nyc.gov
/site/dhs/shelter/singleadults/single-adults.page

FOOD BANK FOR NEW YORK CITY

To help New Yorkers in need access programs in their communities, our Food Program Locator, below, can be used to locate food pantries, soup kitchens and senior centers throughout New York City. To find other types of programs in our food assistance network — including low-income daycare centers, shelters, rehabilitation centers and youth programs — contact Food Bank at (212) 566-7855. Food Bank also operates a Community Kitchen, Pantry, and Senior Center in Harlem.

http://www.foodbanknyc.org

ALCOHOLICS ANONYMOUS

Alcoholics Anonymous is an international fellowship of men and women who have had a drinking problem. It is nonprofessional, self-supporting, multiracial, apolitical, and available almost everywhere. There are no age or education requirements. Membership is open to anyone who wants to do something about his or her drinking problem.

www.aa.org

TREVOR LIFELINE

Our trained counselors are here to support you 24/7. If you are a young person in crisis, feeling suicidal, or in need of a safe and judgment-free place to talk, call the Trevor Lifeline now at 866-488-7386.

http://www.thetrevorproject.org

GLBT National Help Center

The GLBT National Help Center is a non-profit, tax-exempt organization that is dedicated to meeting the needs of the gay, lesbian, bisexual and transgender (GLBT) community and those questioning their sexual orientation and gender identity. We offer two national hotlines. The first is the GLBT National Hotline for people of all ages (youth & adult). The second is the GLBT National Youth Talkline, specifically for callers age 25 and younger. We help end the isolation that many people feel, by providing a safe environment on the phone or via the internet to discuss issues that people often can't talk about anywhere else.

http://www.glbtnearme.org